Conversations with Contemporary

Chicana and Chicano Writers

Conversations with Contemporary Chicana and Chicano Writers

Hector A. Torres

University of New Mexico Press ⌒ Albuquerque

12 11 10 09 08 07   1 2 3 4 5 6

Printed in the United States of America

Library of Congress Cataloging-in-Publication Data

Torres, Hector Avalos, 1955–

  Conversations with contemporary Chicana and Chicano writers /
Hector A. Torres.

     p. cm.

Includes index.

ISBN 978-0-8263-4088-7 (pbk. : alk. paper)

1. Mexican American authors—Interviews.

2. Authors, American—20th century—Interviews.

3. American literature—Mexican American authors—History and criticism.

4. Mexican Americans in literature.

5. Mexican Americans—Ethnic identity.

I. Title.

  PS153.M4T67 2007

   810.9′86872—dc22

                    2006039088

Design and composition: Melissa Tandysh

Contents

Acknowledgments

⁓ This book was a long time coming, and it would have taken all the longer without the constant encouragement from students, friends, and colleagues to take these interviews out of electronic reserve and put them into a book. I am thankful for the generosity of each of the writers comprising this text. I am indeed lucky that they were so willing to talk about their works and days with such generosity of spirit. I wish to thank Patricia Perea for all the hard work of transcription she put into almost all of these interviews. Her bilingualism was invaluable to this project and her secondary research in its behalf cannot be discounted. *Conversations with Contemporary Chicana and Chicano Writers* would not have met the deadline without the crucial intervention of Associate Professor and UNM Regents Lecturer Teresa Márquez, Curator in the Chicano/Hispano/Latino Research Program. She and her graduate assistant Katherine E. McCully intervened during the Zimmerman Library crisis to provide me with the necessary information to complete this work. My colleague Professor Mary Power also stepped in and offered generously of her time to edit the interviews of parts one and two with a careful eye toward preserving as much as possible the rhythms of speech without the loss of content—not an easy task. I also went through all these interviews to do additional editing and the difficulty of the task reminds me that language is practical consciousness. My colleague Jesse Alemán also played a crucial role in the completion of the introductory essay; every conversation with him is an exercise in historical thinking. I am indebted to all these friends and colleagues. I am most indebted to my parents Ralph Q. Torres and Dolores A. Torres for their constant support through all the vicissitudes of my career here at the University of New Mexico. I dedicate this book to them and to Maymie and Junior—family.

Introduction

The Labor of Value in Contemporary Chicana and Chicano Literary Discourse ⁓

Opening

⁓ In this introduction to *Conversations with Chicana and Chicano Writers*, I want to give a sense of the issues that shaped these interviews. While this doesn't mean that I can provide anything like an original context, I do hope that something like their structures of feeling emerges.[1] The dates pertaining to each individual interview deliver the sense of certainty that the interviews indeed took place but perhaps the rest is fiction. It is that critical fiction that this introduction seeks to unfold. In the section "Coming to the Interviews," I give a short history of how I came to conduct these interviews and outline my position *vis à vis* the writers in this collection and the field of Chicana and Chicano cultural studies. The story of how and why I came to conduct these interviews is far less a story about a systematic approach to the study of contemporary Chicana and Chicano literary discourse than something more akin to the genre of autobiography. My friend and (now deceased) colleague, Louis Owens, was probably the first person to encourage me to conduct these interviews. Our conversations often led to comparisons between Native American and Chicana/Chicano literatures—the politics of identity to which each gives literary representation. As someone who wrote in both literary and critical genres, Louis had been on both sides of the microphone, as interviewer and interviewee. The interviews owe much to Louis as a point of departure. Inasmuch as the politics of identity go hand in hand with the social act of writing, remembering those conversations, I'm struck by the power of the politics of the social act of writing both to construct and deconstruct identity.

In the next section—"The Spacing(s) of Chicana and Chicano Literary Discourse"—I situate *Conversations with Contemporary Chicana and Chicano Writers* in relation to *Chicano Authors: Inquiry by Interview*, Juan Bruce-Novoa's landmark work in the field of Chicano and Chicana critical discourse. I turn to the critical and aesthetic theory of Bruce-Novoa because his thesis that Chicana and Chicano literary/aesthetic space is a fount of intercultural possibilities places Chicano literary discourses squarely within the heart of modernity.[2] True to the "predictive" powers of Bruce-Novoa's theory of Chicano literary space, the writers comprising this volume continue to work out (of) the intercultural possibilities that the U.S.–Mexico borderlands represent historically and culturally. What the model is less able to "predict" today is the extent to which the artists inheriting the signifier "Chicano" enact or represent discursive repetitions in a long historical chain of American imperial practices. The laissez-faire liberalism Bruce-Novoa endorsed in the formalization of his theory of literary space meant to stem the tendency in the Chicano Movement to mobilize political criteria for the definition of an authentic Chicano identity.[3] Against this essentialist practice, for his part Bruce-Novoa urged that the term "Chicano" be left undefined.[4] In this critical matter, Bruce-Novoa anticipated the anti-essentialist discourses that inform cultural studies today. In a post-Chicano Movement epoch, the name "Chicano" in literary production continues to represent more a dislocation of the term "Chicano" than a secure grasp of it. This dislocation is commensurate with a long history of contact between Spain and England, Mexico and Anglo America.[5] If his model of literary space ends in contradiction, it is because the model harbors the contradictions of the Chicano Movement itself.

Coming to the Interviews

"If history is made up of the modes of production, the subject is a *contradiction* that brings about practice because practice is

always both signifying and semiotic, a crest where meaning emerges only to disappear."
—Julia Kristeva, *Revolution in Poetic Language*, 1984

In my initial venture into the interview process, I met with Gloria Anzaldúa, Ana Castillo, Sandra Cisneros, Rolando Hinojosa, Arturo Islas, and Gary Soto for the first time, except for Rolando Hinojosa whom I had already met at the University of Texas when he arrived there in 1981 to take a position as a professor in the English Department where I was a graduate student. I had read *The Valley* and liked the narrative technique Hinojosa used to tell the story of south Texas and I ended writing my first published essay on that literary work, studying it for the way the technique evoked layers of temporality rather than linear time alone. And indeed Hinojosa's storytelling technique did remind me of William Faulkner and Flannery O'Connor also, two southern writers I liked a lot, again for technique and the critique implicit in the way the story is told. When I first read Gloria Anzaldúa's *Borderlands/La Frontera: The New Mestiza*, it was the epigraph. My first contact with the works of Castillo, Cisneros, and probably Islas came from my interactions with Teresa Márquez, Diana Rebolledo, Erlinda Gonzáles-Berry, and Maria Dolores Gonzales, who all hold academic posts at the University of New Mexico. Castillo's *The Mixquiahuala Letters* is a marvel of art and politics in story form, as is Cisneros's *The House on Mango Street*, and Islas's *The Rain God*. My colleague Antonio Márquez encouraged me to read Arturo Islas's *The Rain God* for its transformation of El Paso, Texas, into literary space. It was these experiences of dialogue and interaction with colleagues that led me to select these writers, rather than a systematic approach to Chicana and Chicano literature born of scholarly training.

Following this initial venture, I got lucky in that the following year Sandra Cisneros and Ana Castillo came to teach in the UNM Department of English, Castillo in the fall and Cisneros in the spring, facilitating the second interviews. The following year I read *Paletitas de guayaba* and recognized the deconstructive work the novel was doing of sexual stereotypes, Mexican-Chicano relations, and Chicano and Anglo patriarchy and I decided to ask my colleague Erlinda

Gonzáles-Berry for an interview, again in search of insight into her narrative technique and voices. In 1999 again I got lucky because Pat Mora came to the honors program of the University of New Mexico and assumed the Distinguished Garrey Carruthers Chair. She had won the 1997 Prémio Aztlán for *House of Houses* and I had reviewed it for *Aztlan: A Journal of Ethnic Studies*, whose editor, Chon Noriega, had given me generous space for the review. I first contemplated interviewing Rodriguez when in conversation my colleague Jesse Alemán asked me if I had interviewed him and I said I had not. Alemán had been in contact with him at the University of Kansas through a conference he had organized where Cherríe Moraga had spoken along with Rodriguez. Through Jesse Alemán I was able to get Rodriguez's e-mail and pose the question of an interview. He responded generously to my request and soon thereafter I obtained a small stipend from the Research Allocations Committee to travel to San Francisco and conduct the interview. The interview with Kathleen Alcalá was also a product of her visit to the Creative Writing Program in the Department of English as a visiting lecturer in 2003. Demetria Martínez I came across at the Border Book Festival in Mesilla, New Mexico. I caught her in flight but long enough to do a short interview.

When I started these interviews I was interested in mapping the distances these Chicana and Chicano artists had traveled to gain access to the literary modes of production. This interest mirrored my own reflections on the distance I had traveled from my native origins in the U.S.–Mexico border to the exercise of the social act of writing in the Anglo-American academy. While I was born in Tijuana, Mexico, in 1955, family circumstances brought me to live with grandparents in a small *rancho* in the Mexican state of Chihuahua, until by an act of fate in 1965 Rafael Q. Torres and Dolores A. Torres adopted me and brought me to live with their family in El Paso, Texas. My birth and adoptive mothers are first cousins. Both of my adoptive parents being native-born Americans, they took my Americanization seriously. Looking back on this personal history, I now know that my adoptive family formed part of the Mexican American generation.[6] Members of LULAC (League of United Latin American Citizens) for a time, my adoptive parents have embodied for me many of the historical traits of the Mexican American generation as the historian Mario T. García has scripted them: "Americanization for LULAC revolved around the following issues: (1) adjustment to American values and culture (2) political socialization (3) cultural pluralism (4) desegregation, and (5) education."[7] The drive for full integration into American society that traversed the homespace of my new family and that I consequently inherit from them is a reminder that English was the official language of LULAC.[8] For LULAC, English has been the official vehicle for the exercise of power in American civil society and politics.[9] For my adoptive parents, there has never been any question that English is a vehicle of power. Whether one praises or blames it, the Mexican American generation is an important step in the long history addressing asymmetrical power relations between Anglo and Mexican America.[10] If my adoptive parents took a fundamental position with respect to English as the expressive instrument of a fundamental power relation in Anglo-American culture, they did so without the benefit of a Marxist articulation of language as practical consciousness.[11] A World War II veteran, my adoptive father has an unwavering faith in the *idea* of America. The stories he has to tell about his south El Paso childhood in the 1920s are not about victimhood, but they do contain the themes of racism and linguistic prejudice. As for my adoptive mother, to this day she will exhort in her own inimitable way the unenglished to learn the language. Yet, she was also a Spanish teacher in the El Paso School District from the late 1950s to the mid 1960s. I don't know whether their work ethic comes from the Puritans, but regardless of origin, it is a work ethic that drove them to overcome the poverty of their El Paso childhoods. It was no doubt the surplus in the Torres family that made it possible for them to adopt me. The fact that today I earn my livelihood in the English language can easily be construed as an overdetermined effect of my adoptive parents' linguistic ideology. Overdetermined effects usually imply a psychic pathology in those who experience them. If these effects form a pathology, it is one that allows me to practice the social act of writing today.

The politics of the social act of writing are in fact a guiding theme in these interviews. The questions I pose these writers revolve around issues of language and of life between languages, of the creative drive that leads them to their crafts and commits them to their art. I say that the history of how I came to conduct these interviews is more autobiography than an objective academic concern precisely because the politics of language, identity, and work have been constant forces on my own writing. The politics of the social act of writing have always involved questions of discursive economy: who has access to the modes of production and under what social conditions? How many subject positions are available at any given time and who can represent whom? What is value, how is it determined, and where is it housed? According to what criteria, standard, *numéraire* or measure of power is it legitimated in discursive exchange? If I pose these questions of ideology abstractly, it is because I want to cast the social act of writing in terms of both a theory and a practice.[12] As a theoretical practice, it is the vehicle for the construction of modern knowledge and as such it is deeply embedded in relations of power. The social construction of knowledge through the act of writing is the frank concession that knowledge is power and whoever can write about the one assumes a measure of the other.[13]

With the equation of power and knowledge I have in mind Michel Foucault's theory of discourse formations, which, I believe, throws a familiar light on Chicana and Chicano discourses, literary or otherwise. In *The Archeology of Knowledge* Foucault pursues a line of inquiry that puts the emphasis in so-called humanistic research—history, philosophy, literature, cultural studies, etc.—on the "axiology" of power that governs the production of Western knowledge. A discourse formation is first of all a site of institutional authority and not the site where the free and disinterested search for truth is carried out. The branches of knowledge we call grammar, rhetoric, and dialectic—the liberal arts of the Western humanities—represent the modes of production for the study of cultural production in general. Of course, I am not implying that Foucault is endorsing the Western humanities, but what I do want to claim is that Foucault's definition of discourse formations sheds light on the axiology of power at work in the history of Anglo and Spanish contact throughout their respective imperial projects and by *modus ponens*, Mexican and Chicano contact with the Anglo-American nation. When Foucault says that discourse formations are not so much unities of statements/narratives but the dispersions of those unities, the split of the signifier "Chicano" into its feminine grammatical form "Chicana," along with the stylistic choice

récit about the U.S. economy that situates my argument that Bruce-Novoa reproduces in his literary theory the contradictions that constituted the Chicano Movement.

Since the Cold War, the U.S. economy has gone through some severe shocks or vicissitudes. Chief among these was the collapse of the Bretton Woods system, the Vietnam War being at the core of its demise.[31] The Cold War imperative to contain communism was at the same time a mandate for the continual growth of the United States economy, outpacing those of the Soviet Union and China. The Keynesian economic policies of the post–World War II economic boom however seem to have run their effective course throughout the 1970s, in a certain sense, folding in on themselves.[32] At one end of this historical stretch, Keynesian economic policies underwrote America's economic post–World War II boom. Yet, at the other end, President Richard Nixon's fiscal interventions in the economy signaled not only the collapse of the Bretton Woods system but of Keynesian liberalism as well, ironically in the name of Keynesianism. Nixon's Keynesian measures gave the economy a short-lived growth spurt only to have it open onto a long stretch of little growth in the economy, high unemployment, and inflation.[33] The uncanny correlation between economic growth and aggressive U.S. foreign policy places the Vietnam War in a transitional phase in American history—at the tail end of a growth cycle in the American economy and at the front end of a long period of recession or stagflation.[34] The conservative neoliberal policies that resurfaced under Presidents Gerald Ford and Jimmy Carter predictably favored deregulation and monetarist policies but were ultimately ineffective in dealing with the stagflation of the 1970s. Vice President Gerald Ford ascended to the American presidency, as the authors of the *American Social History Project* put it: "just weeks before the nation plunged into the deepest recession since the Great Depression itself."[35] Assessing Carter's presidency, the authors write: "Jimmy Carter's single-term presidency was a failure because he never managed to tame the double-digit inflation that frightened so many Americans."[36] The appointment of Paul Voelcker signaled a turn to monetarist policies that effectively anticipated Ronald Reagan's supply-side economics.[37] The so-called Reagan boom years saw the economy bounce back but mainly for the benefit of capital.[38] This stretch of time is also a reminder that the vicissitudes of the U.S. economy and American liberalism represent so many repetitions and contradictions.[39] The current oil crisis and the Iraqi wars surely bear an uncanny resemblance to the oil crisis of 1974 and its systemic relation to the Vietnam War.[40]

I script this short story of the U.S. economy during the years that see the emergence of Chicano literary production to underscore the fact that the Chicano Movement and its literary renaissance emerged during these times of economic vicissitudes, which, given the dynamic nature of capitalism, are endemic to modernity. If Bruce-Novoa inaugurates the space of Chicano literature in 1974 as a response to chaos, it has to be a chaos mediated by the economic crises that riddled the years of the Chicano Movement and thereafter. The spacing that the Vietnam War occupied was crossed by a decline in America's global hegemony.[41] This loss in global status reverberated upon the space of Chicano literature, the Chicano Movement, and throughout all the sectors of Hispanic-Mexican America.[42] Whatever symbols of Mexican nationalism were put to use in the movement, the symbols were taking part in the discourses of American liberalism. The alliance that César Chávez and Senator Robert Kennedy crafted for the whole world to see was a nearly perfect sign of that participation. This relation to American liberalism was of course not at all surprising from the standpoint of the modes of production. Chicano and Chicana history, if it begins in 1848, records a constant and ready supply of Mexican labor, according to the fluctuations of demand in the United States labor market.[43] The momentary spacing in America's global hegemony underscores the fact that the struggles of the Chicano Movement were for greater inclusion in the society of the United States as well as for greater recognition of the material contribution Hispanic Mexican America has made to the formation of the Anglo-American nation. As one historian puts it: "we might argue that on one fundamental level, ethnic Mexican residents of the American West have been involved in a protracted struggle to prove their importance, to prove themselves significant in American society."[44]

In this picture of the U.S. economy, the uneven spacings out of which both Chicano literary and critical production have emerged since 1965 could be called epochal in the sense Raymond Williams gives this term: an analytic strategy for enriching the Marxist analysis of the "stages" of the modes of production. Epochal analysis, states Williams, "recognizes the complex interrelations between movements and tendencies both within and beyond a specific and effective dominance. It is necessary to examine how these relate to the whole cultural process rather than only to the selected and abstracted dominant system."[45] Williams's proposal of epochal analysis should not be read as the statement of a totality, but quite the opposite, a concession of the impossibility of reigning in the whole cultural process. Williams is so emphatic on this point that he italicizes his text: "*no mode of production and therefore no dominant social order and therefore no dominant culture ever in reality includes or exhausts all human practice, human energy, and human intention.*"[46] This is a remarkable statement on a number of grounds, (not least for the counter it poses to Kant's transcendental ego), but I seize it here to shed light on Bruce-Novoa's theory of Chicano literary space and its optimism about the intercultural possibilities of that space.

Bruce-Novoa is the first in the field of Chicano and Chicana cultural studies to use the erasure mark and he deploys it precisely to formalize these possibilities. The epigraph to this section tracks the inaugural use of the erasure mark to German philosopher Martin Heidegger. This critical practice required a typographical supplement in the production of text in the form of crossed lines appearing over a term. When Heidegger says that a thoughtful glance ahead would write "Being" under the erasure mark, he performs a deadly operation over the schemata of the Western transcendental ego—the desire to totalize a field of inquiry, especially such large domains of human experience and culture as ontology, epistemology, aesthetics, history, literary studies, etc. The crossed-out term remains legible but the crossed lines over it in effect devalue or float the value of the term, rendering "Being" no longer a name signifying a masterful presence in a covalence of human ego and language. In many respects, the erasure mark respects Williams's view of the complex, dynamic, and untotalizable relations between the production of culture and the modes of production. In his usage, Bruce-Novoa deploys the erasure mark not so much to denote the unstable value of the transcendental ego but to reify it as a powerful synthesizing agent *ad infinitum.* However, if Bruce-Novoa's usage of the erasure mark did not coincide precisely with this sense and function of the erasure mark as the loss of the transcendental ego, it did in the strokes of its application signify the place that Chicano literary space occupies in modernity.

Bruce-Novoa proposed his theory of Chicano literary space in 1974, updated it in 1978, gave it a topological twist in 1988, and in *Retrospace: Collected Essays on Chicano Literature* offered an autobiographical component to it, each new instance of the theory abiding by the fundamental claim that Chicano literary production was a response to the chaos of modern life. From the inception of his theory, Bruce-Novoa counseled a *laissez faire* attitude toward Chicano artistic/literary production, detesting the evaluation of Chicano literary texts according to whether they satisfied political criteria. Bruce-Novoa put into practice his liberalism to contest the essentialist practices of the Chicano Movement—the tendency within the movement to pronounce on authentic identity, and perhaps more fundamentally, the idealist presumption that an exhaustive set of predicates existed to define the signifier "Chicano." At the "stem" of the signifier "Chicano," and thus the historical configuration it names, Bruce-Novoa placed the predicate "nothing":

> I propose that *Chicano* remain undefined; that is, and thus the literature, is *nothing* . . . a *nothing* in no way negative, one which may manifest itself in many facets, but which perversely resists final definition, maintaining the ability to reformulate its totality from within, in spite of the best—worst—efforts to ossify it for whatever reason.[47]

Based on his liberal ethic, Bruce-Novoa drew a sharp distinction between the inside and the outside of Chicano literary production. Here, for instance, Bruce-Novoa supposes an inside for the name "Chicano," a condition that far from being a simple nothingness is a totality in reserve. This inwardness opposes the extraliterary concerns of sociologists, anthropologists, politicians, *patrónes*, or high priests who would impose their sociopolitical agendas on the production and interpretation of "authentic" Chicano literary texts—"as the fact that his theory of literary space had quickly earned him the title of formal critic in the field of Chicano critical discourse. His insistence on *l'art pour l'art* ran history out of the literary text, his critics asserted in unison. Joseph Sommers, one of his most ardent critics, charged the theory with transforming literature into a "separate, non-referential, transcendental reality."[62] While the charge of formalism made sense, it did so in a context in which no critic really disavowed the need for formal analysis of a literary text. Joseph Sommers, for his part, advocated a historical dialectical criticism whose project was "to challenge both writer and reader to question the text for meaning and values, which needless to say are inseparable from its formal disposition, and to situate this meaning and these values in a broad cultural framework of social and historical analysis."[63] Despite the difference he asserts from Bruce-Novoa, Sommers concedes that literary form and ideological value are inseparable and by the same token Bruce-Novoa would not disavow that the literary critic should lead readers "outside" of it. Their difference seems to be far less between them than within them and as such it places both in a very similar relation to the dominant aesthetic ideology.

In his discussion of what he calls residual and emergent cultural processes, Raymond Williams hits the mark concerning the actual activity of canon formation and sheds light on the Chicano case study. The terms "residual" and "emergent" in Williams's critical vocabulary map out the dynamic ways that the dominant culture in the form of the state and civil society "negotiates" power relations with its constituents. The residual values of a culture living under the territorial sovereignty of the cultural dominant can provide grounds for political activism that threatens the cultural institutions and traditions of the dominant, especially if the residual offers not just opposition but an alternative. A cultural residual functions like a "reagent" such that the dominant must mobilize to neutralize the threat.[64] For instance, the Treaty of Guadalupe Hidalgo has functioned as a cultural residual throughout Chicano history, as when Reies López Tijerina deployed this historical event/document to argue land grant claims against the U.S. government.[65] But residuals need not be writ large such as the Treaty. The *corrido* paradigm functions as a residual for south Texas culture.[66] The entrance of Juan de Oñate into present-day New Mexico functions as a residual for discourses of Spanish identity aimed to counterpose Anglo domination.[67] More recently, the reworking in Chicana feminism of the figure of Malintzin functions as a residual.[68] For the politics of Chicano canon formation, the Mexican Revolution functioned as a residual for all critics involved in the process, bar none. For his part, Bruce-Novoa sought the construction of an inclusive Chicano literary canon involving the residual of the Mexican Revolution in *Pocho* on the one hand, and on the other an aristocratic criterion of formal excellence: "No, the canon of the Chicano novel from the beginning, like all canons, has been as much a result—if not more so—of implicitly and explicitly expressed needs and ideologies as of formal excellence."[69] The criterion of formal excellence he asserts here is commensurate with his laissez faire liberalism, which, inclusive and progressive, contrasts with the practices of "ethnic conservatives" who would be exclusionary and even settle for second best. Nevertheless, his critique of the politics of Chicano canon formation reaches its limits at the precise moment he endorses an aristocratic criterion of formal excellence against the revolutionary-democratic impulses of the Chicano Movement. Of course, Bruce-Novoa knew this but the politics of canon formation had to go inevitably forward: "The process of selecting and eliminating works to create a superior core of definitive texts seemed less than egalitarian in a movement professing egalitarian ideals."[70] Left undefined is what counts as formal excellence, though in practice that criterion is clearly at work in the emergent practice of Chicano canon formation. Raymond Williams's description of that political and aesthetic practice seems to reference the politics of Chicano canon formation:

> Moreover, at certain points the dominant culture cannot allow too much residual experience and practice outside itself, at least without risk. It is in the incorporation of the actively residual— by reinterpretation, dilution, projection, discriminating inclusion and exclusion—that the work of the selective tradition is especially evident. This is very notable in the case of versions of "the literary tradition," passing through selective versions of the character of literature to connecting and incorporated definitions of what literature is and should be.[71]

What Williams describes here locates the politics of Chicano canon formation at the incorporated stage. Such a scenario signifies the success of the Chicano Movement insofar as its literary renaissance opened up the possibility for a revision of the Anglo-American literary canon. However, that success neutralizes any apparent difference between Bruce-Novoa and Sommers on the grounds that the one is a formalist and the other a historical dialectical materialist. For the politics of the Chicano renaissance to pose a real opposition or alternative to the hegemony of the Anglo-American canon, its canonizers would have to formalize it following the same practices that the elitist Other used.[72] Literary critics and activists alike had to work through the compromised position they occupied vis-à-vis the dominant culture's ideology. This is not a worst-case scenario if one keeps in mind that the Chicano Movement, despite its rhetoric of separatism and nationalism, was at the level of practice operating squarely within the tenets of American liberalism.[73] The compromised position of the critic is perhaps the figure of irony that makes the Chicano Movement not so much a separatist movement under the nationalist banner of Aztlán as a *de facto* move for greater integration of Chicanos and Chicanas into American culture, politics, and civil society. The evaluation Juan Gomez Quiñones gives of the Chicano Movement is here relevant: "Chicano leaders of the sixties were impeded by contradictions between their assertive rhetoric and their conventional reformist demands and programs."[74] Quiñones points to such contradictions as the movement's advocacy of separatism while also calling for "empowerment through political elections. This stance was neither explicitly separatist nor even radical. The 'cultural nationalism' of Gonzales, the student organizations, and others amounted, in fact, to an ethnic liberalism both in its basic consistencies and its contradictions."[75] In the activity of canon formation—the politics of determining literary value—Bruce-Novoa's laissez faire liberalism also ran up against its own limits and contradictions. After the Chicano renaissance, it becomes increasingly evident that if the polemic between Bruce-Novoa and his critics lingered for a while over the space of Chicano literary and critical production, it did so to good ends, demonstrating that for Chicano literature, to date, its inside *is* its outside.

This volume belongs in this tradition of interview by inquiry that

Bruce-Novoa innovated. The writers in this collection inherit the success of the Chicano Movement and divide up that success, the first division being of the signifier "Chicano" into "Chicana." It is this division signal that the inheritance will not allow to split into inside and outside. Chicano and Chicana writers know that too much politics can spoil the story, but so can too little. Witnessing the ascent of the United States to the position of global leader, these writers cross the historical terrain of empire twice in the topology of the linguistic sign, once under the historical shadow of Manifest Destiny and again under the rapid processes of globalization perpetuating America's imperial sovereignty.[76] The writers in *Conversations with Contemporary Chicana and Chicano Writers* inherit the signifier "Chicano" as a tradition of critique and as such repeat or carry forward the issues that have concerned Mexican America since at least 1848, if not prior to this datemark. What these writers bring to this tradition that is different is the voices of Chicanas. The organization of the table of contents is my attempt to signal the significance of that shift in voice(s) without doing away with the gains of the Chicano Movement, uneven as this movement was. As the interviews themselves will make clear, Chicana literary discourse registers the ascent of the United States to the position of executive position in global politics.[77] For these writers, America's history of empire bears the persistent echoes of Manifest Destiny and practices of United States exceptionalism.[78] Alongside the founding literary value that the work of Rolando Hinojosa represents in the Chicano renaissance, I place Arturo Islas and Erlinda Gonzáles-Berry as complements to that value. Indeed, with the thematic breaks I posit in the table of contents I wish to evoke layers of literary value rather than values stretched along generational lines.[79] Because Chicana and Chicano literary value is produced out of a tradition of critique, the question of the writers' generation seems largely superfluous. *Mestiza* consciousness, as Anzaldúa proposed it, does not depart from the canonical leanings that selected the work of Rolando Hinjosa but speaks to it and thus participates in that layer of discursive exchanges. No doubt, the literary work of the Chicanas in this book addresses the need to perform a transvaluation of the value set down in the first canonical leanings of the Chicano canon. However, through the exercise of their own versions of mestiza consciousness, the Chicanas writers in this collection take what is useful for their literary projects and discard or oppose what they find oppressive. This is true as well for the writers in section three—Rodriguez, Martínez, and Alcalá. None of the sections I posit, however, is a radical break from the other. This is not to say that there is a unifying paradigm to contemporary Chicana and Chicano literary discourse. The tradition of critique these writers work out of is probably as close as Chicana and Chicano literary discourses get to a unity in this age of global republicanism.

Notes to Introduction

1. Raymond Williams, *Marxism and Literature* (Oxford: Oxford University Press, 1977). Williams's definition of this analytical term emphasizes the social nature of consciousness and its fluidity in the cultural process of living one's life: "It is that we are concerned with meanings and values as they are actively lived and felt, and the relations between these and formal or systematic beliefs are in practice variable (including historically variable), over a range from formal assent with private dissent to the more nuanced interaction between selected and interpreted beliefs and acted and justified experiences" (132).

2. Juan Bruce-Novoa, *Retrospace: Collected Essays on Chicano Literature* (Houston: Arte Público Press, 1990).

3. Juan Bruce-Novoa, *Retrospace: Collected Essays on Chicano Literature* (Houston: Arte Público Press, 1990): 13–17.

4. Ibid., 75, 94.

5. Cecil Robinson, "The Extended Presence: Mexico and Its Culture in North American Writing," *Multi-Ethnic Literature of the United States* 5, no. 3 (Autumn, 1978): 3–15.

6. Mario T. Garcia, *The Mexican American Generation: Leadership, Ideology, Identity* (New Haven: Yale University Press, 1989): 31.

7. Mario T. Garcia, *The Mexican American Generation: Leadership, Ideology, Identity* (New Haven: Yale University Press, 1989).

8. Garcia, *Mexican American*, 31.

9. See George A. Martinez, "Dispute Resolution and the Treaty of Guadalupe Hidalgo: Parallels and Possible Lessons for Resolution under NAFTA." In this work, Martinez demonstrates the role of the English language, working in tandem with the American legal system, to implement power relations. Martinez presents a forceful argument for the way NAFTA represents a repetition of the Treaty of Guadalupe Hidalgo.

10. Karl Marx and Frederick Engels, *The German Ideology* (1947; New York: International Publishers, 1970). Here, Marx sketches a picture of the long and contradictory process that the proletarian or working class must pursue in the struggle to gain access to the modes of production. Devoid of a metaphysical telos, the following passage denotes this long process: "Further, it follows that every class which is struggling for mastery, even when its domination, as is the case with the proletariat, postulates the abolition of the old form of society in its entirety and of domination itself, *must first conquer for itself political power in order to represent its interest in turn as the general interest*, which immediately it is forced to do" (54, italics mine). The conflicted scene today in America with respect to immigrant issues seems to be one case of this process through which America's immigrant population is seeking to demonstrate its interests not as peripheral but central to Anglo America's economic base.

11. Marx and Engels, 53.

12. I have in mind here the theory of the subject that Louis Althusser posits in *Lenin and Philosophy and Other Essays* (New York: Monthly Review Press,

2001), in particular the essay, "Ideology and Ideological State Apparatuses" (85–126). I cite it here for both the insight Althusser brings to the understanding of the subject of ideology and the impossible formulation he gives of what constitutes the subject of knowledge. On the one hand, Althusser posits a reciprocal relation between subjects and ideology—each mutually constitutes the other and as such ideology has no outside. On the other hand, the desire for a scientific account of ideology leads Althusser to posit one such outside, which would be a scientific account of ideology beyond ideology, even when the subject is nothing but ideology: "But to recognize that we are subjects and that we function in the practical rituals of the most elementary everyday life—this recognition only gives us the 'consciousness' of our incessant (eternal) practice of ideological recognitions—but in no sense does it give us the (scientific) *knowledge* of the mechanism of this recognition. Now it is this knowledge that we have to reach, if you will, while speaking in ideology, and from within ideology we have to outline a discourse which tries to break with ideology, in order to dare to be the beginning of a scientific (i.e. subjectless) discourse on ideology" (117). For cultural studies the implication seems to be that the cultural theorist produces compromised knowledge, or in a parallel way, that no cultural theorist can simply decide to step around his/her imagined relation to his/her real conditions of existence (109).

13. Michel Foucault, "Truth and Power," in *Power/Knowledge: Selected Interviews and other Writings, 1972–1977*, ed. Colin Gordon (New York: Pantheon Books, 1980): 114.

14. Michel Foucault, *The Archeology of Knowledge and the Discourse on Language* (New York: Pantheon Books, 1972): 37–38.

15. Ibid., 27.

16. Ibid., 128.

17. Marx and Engels, 65. Marx puts this notion succinctly and, I believe, persuasively: "For instance, in an age and in a country where royal power, aristocracy, and bourgeoisie are contending for mastery and where, therefore mastery is shared, the doctrine of the separation of powers proves to be the dominant idea and is expressed as an 'eternal law.'" The scare quotes around eternal law signify Marx's desire to avoid any mystifications about a civil society being the expenditure of an Absolute Idea.

18. Ramón A. Gutierrez, "Community, Patriarchy and Individualism: The Politics of Chicano History," *American Quarterly* 45, no. 1 (March 1993): 50–51.

19. See David J. Weber, "The Spanish Legacy in North America and the Historical Imagination," *The Western Historical Quarterly* 23, no. 1 (February 1992): 4–24. Weber documents the effect of the Black Legend on the field of historiography: "Hispanophobia lasted longer in Texas than in any other of Spain's former North American provinces. Well into the twentieth century, it retarded serious study of the state's lengthy Spanish heritage, leaving the field open to distortion and caricature" (10). Distortion of the historical record is a motif in Chicano historiography also. For a critical review, see Tomas Almaguer, "Ideological Distortion In Recent Chicano Historiography:

The Internal Model and Chicano Historical Interpretations," *Aztlán* 18, no. 1 (1987): 7–28.

20. Marx and Engels, 64–68. For a historical treatment that does not see "border" as a synonym of "borderlands," see Jeremy Adelman and Stephen Aaron, *The American Historical Review* 104, no. 3 (June 1999): 814–41. If the authors want to draw the distinction between "border" and "borderlands," it is because the distinction rests on an economic criterion with strong cultural reflexes in the realm of power relations in the periods and sites of American history their analysis is concerned with.

21. Ibid., 65.

22. See also Immanuel Wallerstein, "Three Ideologies or One? The Pseudobattle of Modernity," in *After Liberalism* (New York: The New Press, 1995): 72–92. This essay traces the common root of liberalism and communism.

23. Marx and Engels, 80.

24. Anders Stephanson, *Manifest Destiny: American Expansion and the Empire of Right*, (New York: Hill and Want, 1995). Stephanson's account of President Polk's War with Mexico demonstrates the imperial logic of American expansion: "In reality . . . as Jefferson's Louisiana Purchase showed, the President had ample room in his executive capacity for maneuver and manipulation. The trick, first and foremost, was to present Congress and the public with a fait accompli. Polk was to use this commanding power to push the country into war with Mexico and nearly with Britain as well" (35).

25. Michel Foucault, "Nietzsche, Genealogy, History," in *Language, Counter-Memory, Practice* (Ithaca: Cornell University Press, 1977): 154.

26. Juan Bruce-Novoa, *Chicano Authors: Inquiry by Interview* (Austin: University of Texas Press, 1980): ix.

27. See Foucault, *The Archeology*: "after all, 'literature' and 'politics' are recent categories, which can be applied to medieval culture, or even classical culture, only by retrospective hypothesis, and by an interplay of formal analogies or semantic resemblances; but neither literature, nor politics, nor philosophy and the sciences articulated the field of discourse, in the seventeenth or eighteenth century, as they did in the nineteenth" (22). As Foucault explains, the application of a term not only undergoes change from one historical epoch to another, but the usage also lends the term and the field it names a unity based not on some inherent unity in either the term or the field it names but on institutional practices and authority.

28. Bruce-Novoa, *Chicano Authors*, 30.

29. Juan Bruce-Novoa, "Canonical and Noncanonical Texts: A Chicano Case Study," in *Redefining American Literary History*, eds. A. LaVonne Brown and Jerry W. Ward. (New York: Modern Language Association of America, 1990): 202.

30. Ramón A. Gutierrez, *supra*, note 18 furnishes the Chicana feminist motivation for putting into practice this displacement potential.

31. Nicolas Spulber, *Managing the American Economy from Roosevelt to Reagan* (Bloomington and Indianapolis: Indiana University Press, 1989): 71.

32. Nelson Lichtenstein, et al, *Who Built America? Working People and the Nation's Economy, Politics, Culture, and Society* (New York: Worth Publishers, 2000): 570–75 and 690–95.

33. Ibid., 685.
34. Brian M. Pollins and Randall L. Schweller, "Linking the Levels: The Long Wave and Shifts in U.S. Foreign Policy, 1790–1993," *American Journal of Political Science* 43, no. 2 (April 1999): 435.
35. *Who Built America?* 691.
36. Ibid., 692.
37. Ibid. The authors claim that President Carter "abdicated economic steward-ship of the economy in favor of Volcker, who instituted a set of 'monetarist' policies that severely restricted the growth of the money supply and thereby pushed interests rates toward 20 percent—their highest levels since the Civil War" (694).
38. Ibid., 710. The authors give a stark summary of the deleterious effects of Reagan's procapital, free market stance: "Thus did Reaganomics help widen the gap between rich and poor" (712).
39. For a sustained historical account of the contradictions that accompany this epoch of the U.S. economy, see Alfred E. Eckes Jr. and Thomas W. Zeiler, *Globalization and the American Century* (Cambridge: Cambridge University Press, 2003). "The period from 1973 to 1986 was alive with paradoxes. It opened with OPEC's effort to control the international oil market and ended in a global move toward deregulation and open markets. It began with a Republican, Richard Nixon, espousing Keynesian-style government economic intervention and ended with another Republican, Ronald Reagan, proselytizing for deregulation and free markets" (184).
40. Ibid. "Although many economists and pundits thought the oil shortage signaled the onset of a worldwide drop in the production of fossil fuels, the energy crisis of the 1970s was actually a political phenomenon, reflecting in the marketplace the U.S. defeat in Vietnam and the subsequent shift in power from Western consumer countries to the Latin American and Middle Eastern states that controlled OPEC and other producer cartels" (684–85).
41. Eckes and Zeiler, 178.
42. Manuel G. Gonzalez, *Mexicanos: A History of Mexicans in the United States* (Bloomington and Indianapolis: Indiana University Press, 1999): 212.
43. JoAnne D. Spotts, "U.S. Immigration Policy on the Southwest Border from Reagan through Clinton, 1981–2001," *Georgetown Immigration Law Journal* (Spring 2002).
44. David G. Gutierrez, "Significant to Whom? Mexican Americans and the History of the American West," *The Western Historical Quarterly* 24, no. 4 (November 1993): 520. See also Foucault in *The Archeology of Knowledge* for an account of the Western subject of knowledge naming discursive fields ret-rospectively: "after all, 'literature' and 'politics' are recent categories, which can be applied to medieval culture, or even classical culture, only by retro-spective hypothesis" (22).
45. Williams, 121.
46. Williams, 125.
47. Ibid., 94.
48. Ibid., 94.
49. Ibid., 95.

50. Bruce-Novoa, *Retrospace*: "This leads me to postulate the presence of a common deep structure in the works [of the Chicano renaissance], that is a topological constant in the form of a deep structure" (152).

51. Ibid., 166.

52. Juan Gómez-Quiñones, *Chicano Politics*, 115.

53. Dorothy Ross, "Grand Narrative in American Historical Writing: From Romance to Uncertainty," *The American Historical Review* 100, no. 3 (June 1995): 651–77. Chicana and Chicano literary discourses address the history Ross analyzes in this brilliant account. Taking free-market liberal democracy and American exceptionalism as points of departure for her narrative analysis of American historiography in the nineteenth century, Ross argues that American imperial sovereignty and exceptionalism "derived fundamentally from divine favor, a favor that began with the Puritan mission to New England and was sealed in the American Revolution and Constitution" (652). For a problematic sublation of American exceptionalism, see Michael Hardt and Antonio Negri, *Empire*, (Cambridge, MA: Harvard University Press, 2000). In this mammoth work, the authors postulate a paradigm shift in the Western concept and practice of political sovereignty that gives pride of place to the U.S. Constitution.

54. Jacques Derrida, *The Structuralist Controversy: The Languages of Criticism and the Sciences of Man* (Baltimore, London, Chicago: Johns Hopkins University Press, 1972): 251.

55. For a historical treatment of this cultural nexus in modernity, see Leslie Paul Thiele, "Twilight of Modernity: Nietzsche, Heidegger, and Politics," *Political Theory* 22, no. 3 (1994): 468–90.

56. Bruce-Novoa, *Retrospace*, 153.

57. My objective here is not to collapse all these terms into a single category, but to emphasize the process of dissemination that takes place under the crisis of authority pervading Euro-American modernity. For a nuanced account of the differences among these categories, see Rafael Perez-Torres, "Nomads and Migrants: Negotiating a Multicultural Postmodernism," *Cultural Critique* no. 26 (1993–94): 161–89.

58. See note 25 *supra*, Foucault, "Nietzsche, Genealogy, History." In that essay Foucault reinscribes the effects of the modes of production on historiography, pointing to those effects as the dispersion of knowledge rather than its actual unification: "History becomes 'effective' to the degree that it introduces discontinuity into our very being—as it divides our emotions, dramatizes our instincts, multiplies our body and sets it against itself. 'Effective' history deprives the self of the reassuring stability of life and nature, and it will not permit itself to be transported by a voiceless obstinacy toward a millennial ending. It will uproot its traditional foundations and relentlessly disrupt its pretended continuity. This is because knowledge is not made for understanding; it is made for cutting" (154).

59. Raymond Williams, *Marxism and Literature*: "It can be persuasively argued that all or nearly all initiatives and contributions, even whey they take on manifestly alternative or oppositional forms, are in practice tied to the

hegemonic: that the dominant culture, so to say, at once produces and limits its own forms of counterculture" (114).

60. Juan Bruce-Novoa, "Canonical and Noncanonical Texts: A Chicano Case Study," in *Redefining American Literary History*, eds. A. LaVonne Brown and Jerry W. Ward. (New York: Modern Language Association of America, 1990): 200.

61. Bruce-Novoa, "Chicano Case Study," 201.

62. Joseph Sommers, "Critical Approaches to Chicano Literature," in *The Identification and Analysis of Chicano Literature*, ed. Francisco Jimenez. (New York: Bilingual Press/Editorial Bilingüe, 1979): 146.

63. Joseph Sommers, "Critical Approaches," 151.

64. Williams, *Marxism and Literature*: "The residual, by definition, has been effectively formed in the past, but it is still active in the cultural process, not only and often not at all as an element of the past, but as an effective element of the present. Thus certain experiences, meanings, and values which cannot be expressed or substantially verified in terms of the dominant culture, are nevertheless lived and practiced on the basis of the residue—cultural and well as social—of some previous social and cultural institution or formation" (122).

65. Eric J. Sundquist, "The Literature of Expansion and Race," in *The Cambridge History of American Literature*, eds. Sacvan Bercovitch and Cyrus K. Patell. (Cambridge: Cambridge University Press, 1995): 127–74. Sundquist's survey of nineteenth century American literary production opens with a reference to Mariano Vallejo, whose life and discourse echo much of the same issues in the Chicano Movement with reference to the Treaty of Guadalupe Hidalgo. The United States's tack of dealing with these residual "reagents" with long, drawn out court battles is well known.

66. Ramón Saldívar, *Chicano Narrative: The Dialectics of Difference* (Madison: University of Wisconsin Press, 1990).

67. Raymund Paredes, "The Evolution of Chicano Literature," *Multi-Ethnic Literature of the United States* 5, no. 2 (1978): 71–110. I interpret Raymund Paredes's landmark article as a compilation of just those cultural residuals.

68. Norma Alarcón, "Traddutora, Traditora: A Paradigmatic Figure of Chicana Feminism," *Cultural Critique* no. 13 (1989): 57–87. For more fine-grained residuals in Chicana feminism, see María Herrera-Sobek, *The Mexican Corrido: A Feminist Analysis* (Bloomington and Indianapolis: Indiana University Press, 1990).

69. Bruce-Novoa, "Chicano Case Study," 200.

70. Ibid., 199.

71. *Marxism and Literature*, 123.

72. Bruce-Novoa, "Chicano Case Study," 132.

73. Leonard Dinnerstein, Roger L. Nichols, and David Reimers, *Natives and Strangers: A Multicultural History of Americans*, 4th ed. (Oxford: Oxford University Press, 2003): 229–32. The authors recount the well-known fact that the 1960s struggle for civil rights was waged on behalf of the liberal ideal of equality on all counts: "The major problems for Mexican Americans were much the same as for African Americans, and revolved

around bread-and-butter issues: satisfying jobs, higher incomes, and good educational facilities for children" (229). Clearly, all these issues are about integration into the social fabric of American culture.

74. Juan Gómez-Quiñones, *Chicano Politics: Reality and Promise, 1940–1990* (University of New Mexico Press, 1990): 142.

75. Gomez Quiñones, *Chicano Politics*, 142.

76. Michael Hardt and Antonio Negri, *Empire* (Cambridge, MA: Harvard University Press, 2000). In this mammoth work, Hardt and Negri maintain that the United States exercises a mode of political sovereignty that marks nothing less than a paradigm shift in the legal history of Western political sovereignty. This new mode of political sovereignty allows the United States to preside over a kind of global civil society. Under the name of liberal democracy, the United States republic extends its political power into every crook and cranny of the world. Wherever there is a potential for a new market, there one can find *Pax Americana* exporting the virtues of an open market, even if it has to wage war to do so. Through this current mode of sovereignty, the United States republic sits atop this new global empire in the position of executive power over a global republic. The last two wars in the Middle East exemplify this new mode of political sovereignty in which the United States acts as a kind of executive monarch in the name of peace and right. The United States presides over the nation-states, Hardt and Negri argue, because it generates consensus on the basis of the practices of the world market itself. As they state: "In constitutional terms, the processes of globalization are no longer merely a fact but also a source of juridical definition that tends to project a single supranational figure of political power" (9).

77. Jesse, Alemán "Chicano Novelistic Discourse: Dialogizing the *Corrido* Critical Paradigm," *Multi-Ethnic Literature of the United States* 23, no. 1 (1998): 58. Following on the work of Tey Diana Rebolledo, Alemán critiques the corrido paradigm, arguing that Chicano and Chicana literary production always registers "a level of socio-discursive resistance." This is all the more true with the turn to and return of America's imperial sovereignty since the first Gulf War in 1991.

78. For a critique of the historiographical discourses of American exceptionalism, see Ian Tyrrell, "American Exceptionalism in an Age of International History," *The American Historical Review* 96, no. 4 (1991): 1031–55.

79. David I. Kertzer, "Generation as a Sociological Problem," *The Annual Review of Sociology* 9 (1983): 126. "Social scientists have traditionally looked upon the diverse popular meanings of 'generation' as an opportunity for extension of the term in social science, rather than as a source of imprecision to be avoided."

Part One

Canonical Leanings

DIVISIONS

CHAPTER ONE

Rolando Hinojosa
I Reflect the Way Valleyites Act and React

⌒ The extensive body of work that Rolando Hinojosa has produced represents a major literary achievement in the history of the Chicano and American literary canon. Hinojosa's body of work spans three decades and has generated national and international critical acclaim. The Rio Grande Valley in south Texas offers the geographical, historical, sociolinguistic, and economic materials out of which Hinojosa transforms the chronicle approach to historiography into a genre useful for literary ends. As the winner of the 1973 Premio Quinto Sol for *Estampas del valle y otras obras* and then in 1976 the prestigious Casas de las América for *Klail City y sus alrededores*, Hinojosa gives literary voices/representation to a history stretching back to the 1740s with the arrival of the Escandón colony to the Valley. Historical memory is long in Rolando Hinojosa's *gran cronicón*, the name that José David Saldívar, his leading critic, uses to describe Hinojosa's literary production. The editor of *The Rolando Hinojosa Reader*, Saldívar shows the development of Hinojosa's work from *Estampas del valle*, the narrative seed of the gran cronicón, to the 1985 *Partners in Crime*. This critical survey reminds the reader of the pivotal role of Hinojosa's work in defining literary value during the first leanings toward the construction of the Chicano literary canon: "With the publication of *Klail City und Umgebung* (Berlin, 1980), a translation of *Klail City y sus alrededores* in a new French anthology of Latin American literature entitled *Anthologie de la Nouvelle Hispano Americanine* (Paris, 1983), and the forthcoming publications of *Claros Varones de Belken* (Bilingual Press) and *Dear Rafe* and *Partners in Crime: A Rafe Buenostro Mystery* (Arte Público Press, 1985), Hinojosa's role as the leader of Chicano literature will be firmly established."[1] Hinojosa remarks on the process of canon formation in the interview, calling for an aesthetic that would go beyond the nationalism that fueled the Chicano poetry of the early 1970s. His remarks indicate the divisions operating in the practices of Chicano canon formation. The critical question that emerges is how Hinojosa creates literary value without falling into a "Johnny-One-Note" aesthetic, as he puts it here in the interview. Hinojosa's pragmatic approach to this theoretical question is to weave inextricably the creative process of writing with the imperative of reading.

Hinojosa's leading critics such as those collected in the *Reader* trace the strength and resonance of Hinojosa's work to his transformation of the chronicle from a form of writing history into a form of literary representation. Rosaura Sanchez establishes the allusions in Hinojosa's "macrotext" to "historical chronicles of fifteenth- and sixteenth-century Spanish kingdoms." Similarly, in her critical discussion of *Generaciones y semblanzes*, Sánchez takes the reader back to the 1450 text of the same name by Fernán Pérez de Guzmán. Whereas Guzmán used the genre to depict the life of the nobility, Hinojosa transforms the genre by using it to record the lives of the common folk or *raza* of the Valley of Texas.[2] Thus, the play of genres in Hinojosa's cronicón is a vehicle for the exercise of deep historical memory. Similarly, Héctor Calderón notes another source of literary value in Hinojosa's literary production, the modernist practice of displacing narrative time and space: "Although the sketches are not presented in a straightforward, linear chronicle, the reader attains a better perspective with each book [in the *Klail City Death Trip Series*]. In a most innovative way, the chronicle of Belken County and Klail City is narrated and relived from an indeterminate present which should be interpreted as that place of fiction where the writer's imagination meets the reader."[3] This is perhaps one of the strongest modernist effects in Hinojosa's macrotext. The place where writer and reader meet is indeterminate, asserts Calderón, and yet it is also a space, or *topos*, following Bruce-Novoa, that yields high-value literary effects. This topos is the linguistic sign itself, the materiality of language as practical consciousness in the production and reception of the literary text. The genealogy of literary influences that Hinojosa refers to in this interview and elsewhere certainly points to the modernist leanings in his work but something more than the aesthetic elements of the modern emerges from Hinojosa's cronicón of the Valley of south Texas. This something other emerges from the deconstructive humor Hinojosa invents in order to create art that teaches and delights. *Mi querido Rafa*, says Margarita Cota-Cardenas, "serves as an excellent example of social commentary that does not alienate the reader to make a point. It is Hinojosa's controlled humor, through the use of multiple narrators, that is the key to this achievement."[4] Hinojosa sets a standard for the production of Chicano and Chicana literary discourses that balance the Horatian ideals to teach and to delight in practicing the art of *poiesis*.

If the reader is forced to reckon with the deep historical memory of Hinojosa's literary corpus, the same reader is also invited to reflect on reflection in *The Valley*. Hinojosa embraces a mimetic theory of literary representation, a position he underlines in the interview, but not without also complicating it: "The etchings, sketches, engravings, et al that follow resemble Mencho Saldaña's hair: the damm thing's disheveled, oily, and, as one would expect, matted beyond redemption and relief." This translation of the *nota preliminar* in *Estampas del valle* reflects Hinojosa's creative practice of displacing whatever impedes the creative drive. In the nota, Saldaña's hair is not "matted beyond redemption and relief" but is rather disheveled because his greasy scalp does what it wants with it *"sin permiso de nadie"*—without anyone's permission as to how to "arrange/comb" it. While there is a gap in translation, it reflects in "microtext" Hinojosa's conviction that nothing should impede the creative drive. In the interview, he insists that the work of memory in the act of creation—the act of mimesis in writing—must labor between accuracy and its displacement when it hinders creativity.

Hinojosa's major critics converge on this point in Hinojosa's creative practice: his ability to put the instability of concepts in modernity to useful—political—ends. In the critical overview he gives in the *Reader*, José David Saldívar observes: "As it stands, *Klail City Death Trip* is both integrated and disintegrated. Each narrative participates in composing an integrative work at the same time it works out its own individual detachment from it."[5] Likewise, Ramón Saldívar in his critical analysis of *Korean Love Songs* delineates something very much akin to the instability of concepts that inhabit modernity. The difference is that for Ramón Saldívar time is what is unstable in the modernity that the Valley is moving into with the movement of its raza. The Korean War sets Chicano subjects from the Valley adrift on a world-historical stage: "In Hinojosa's *Korean Love Songs* there is no 'hero' in the traditional sense. The action represented in the poem must be read not as the story of 'individuals,' nor as the chronicle of a generation and its destiny, but as the dispersed history of impersonal forces."[6] Hinojosa's skillful calibrations of aesthetics and politics in the production of his literary texts have earned him a place in the Chicano and Anglo-American literary canons. His narrative competence in English and Spanish will no doubt earn him a place in an emerging pan-American literary tradition.

DATE: June 20, 1989
SETTING: The office of Rolando Hinojosa, Parlin Hall,
    University of Texas, Austin, Texas

Family Background: The Drive for Education

H. T. Can we begin by talking about your background?

R. H Okay, what did you have in mind as far as background?

H. T. I'm interested in the kind of environment that you grew up in, the sights and sounds of that time, early childhood memories, things like that.

R. H. All right, why don't I begin with the very first day. I was born on 21 January 1929. The Depression begins in late fall of that same year so my first ten years, from '29 to '39 were enduring the Depression which doesn't disappear until 1942 and World War II. My father was Manuel Guzmán Hinojosa. He was born in a ranch just north of the town I was born in, Mercedes, Téjas, and my mother was a Texas Anglo born not in the Valley, but she came there when she was six weeks old, part of the very first Texas Anglos to move to the Valley and to settle there. My grandfather, Grandfather Smith, became the first postmaster of a village called Progreso, Texas. Well, my parents married there and I am the fifth of six children. One of the children—I was named for him—died, born in '25, died in '26, and then I was born in '29. So I was raised in a very small town, a rural background, the town had no more than 6,000 people. The high school itself was about 300 in population, the four high school grades. In fact my graduating class of 1946 had 46 kids in it and my father was a man of the soil. He also worked as a policeman, but he was a farmer as well and he had done many other things. My mother taught school briefly, despite the fact that she didn't have a college education, but that was the status of the educational facilities in the Valley at the time. She could read and write and therefore she became a teacher. So I was raised as a rural child in a small town, but not isolated because where I was born in Mercedes, which is in the heart of the Rio Grande Valley, there must be on the three main roads that make up the Valley, some forty or fifty towns of various sizes. It's very close to the mouth of the Rio Grande, by the Gulf of Mexico right on the Mexican border and we spoke English and Spanish at home, primarily Spanish because my mother, despite the fact that she was an Anglo Texan, could read, and write Spanish very well, like a native. So we were raised in Spanish and in English as well.

H. T. So she spoke to you in Spanish, addressed you in Spanish?

R. H. Both languages, yeah. Mostly in Spanish if I remember correctly, but I also remember that when all of us got together we'd just go back and forth in one or the other language. But we'd mix them as well, which is very common along the border. So to us the river was just a jurisdictional barrier, not a cultural barrier and it was not a blood kin barrier because we had relatives on both sides of the Rio Grande. So, that was the background of my father, who had also fought in the Mexican Revolution, and my mother, who maintained the house while he was away all this time. The five of us all finished high school, and the five us all managed to go to college. This is a miracle because of the fact that there wasn't money at home for this, but there was a drive for education. The three boys of course, we all took advantage of the GI Bill during different wars and all that.

H. T. How was the value of education instilled into all of you?

R. H.   It wasn't instilled only in my family, which did instill it very strongly, but also among many of the kids that I knew in my neighborhood. I think it's because we were landless, essentially powerless as well—although we did belong to the Democratic Party. The drive for education was instilled in all of us. I'm the youngest of the remaining five, and the very first school I went to, and I went to a school, a formal school, was a Mexican school when I was aged four or five before I went to the regular public school so I knew I was destined to study as all of us were.

H. T.   So the first time you went to school was where, on the Mexican side of the line?

R. H.   No, it was on the American side, but there were men and women who were Mexican exiles living in the United States biding their time to go to Mexico when one side or the other would come back into power and in order to earn their living they taught, they were professionals, these men and these women and our parents paid the whole neighborhood something like fifty cents a month for our tuition and they kept body and soul together, but they taught school and we learned how to read and write in Spanish and we did simple arithmetic but also a socialization process, how to behave when you were in a class, but I remember very well that we opened and we closed the school day by singing the Mexican national anthem in Spanish, which I found very natural. I thought it was perfectly all right and then I went to the American school just like everybody else, but being the fifth of five, by the time I entered school when I was six, one of my brothers had already graduated from high school in 1933, which is during the Depression, and then a sister in '39, also during the Depression, a sister in '40 during the Depression and then another brother and then myself. He finished in '43; I finished in '46.

Writing: The Reading Imperative

H. T.   What kind of signposts were there for you to indicate that you in fact wanted to pursue a career in education, or more specifically in creative writing?

either so in my writing of course I really poke fun at some of the inadequacies of the Roman Catholic Church as far as the Rio Grande Valley is concerned.

Hinojosa's Valley: A Texas Mexican Experience

H. T. You have a great deal of feeling and energy for the Valley that allows you to depict it in broad, sweeping prose yet you keep such a strong sense of the local spaces that form this region of the United States.

R. H. I think it has to do not only because of the accident of birth. I was born in this small town, but there's another accident. Mercedes is right in the heart of the Valley and there are these twenty, thirty towns to the east of us and a like number to the west of us, and this is the '30s and mid-'40s and many socialization processes were going on, dances that one was invited to. We'd hitchhike up and down the Valley. So while all my brothers and sisters went to these dances, as I did and all of our friends, whether I knew it or not I was noticing more things. That's why they're not writers and I'm a writer. But I could see the differences on the extreme east in Brownsville, which is Jonesville-on-the-River, which I borrowed from Américo Paredes who is a native of Brownsville and all the way up to Edinburgh which is Edgerton in Belken County and one of my brothers married a girl from Edinburgh so I was a participant but I was also an observer, and I guess I've always been that. My wide view of the Valley was also fashioned by my travels in the army and my travels as an academician, my travels when I worked in business or when I worked as a civil servant or in these other odd jobs that I've performed. I was always and I tried to be a participant in everything I've done, but also an observer. Looking back, that may explain the breadth and length and sometimes extensiveness as well as sometimes some intensiveness, by listening to people and then remembering, making it a point to remember. It isn't just that I'll remember this and I'll write it down later. No, I would remember it even without writing it down and I found that later on accuracy works one way and the other. Sometimes accuracy can be a terrible thing for creativity, but at other times accuracy is absolutely essential for creativity in some respects.

H. T. Do you recall when you began to get a sense of design for your work?

R. H. Oh, that wasn't until much later. I'm jumping some thirty-five years from fifteen 'til I was forty. I think I was forty. I know at forty I was awarded my PhD and I think it was '69. So in '70 or '71 Quinto Sol published a short story of mine, which later became a chapter of the novel called *Estampas del valle y otras obras*. When I finished *Estampas* and as I was writing it as well I was already thinking of perhaps having these characters reappear, recur. When I wrote the second novel within a year or two after *Estampas del valle*'s publication in '73 and then *Klail City* was awarded Casa de las Américas in '76.

H. T. The second novel?

R. H. Right, the second novel. By then I already knew that I wanted, in the very first chapter, to be writing some sort of series. I already had great masters: Balzac wrote a series. Benito Pérez Galdos as well, and of course a few years after that I had read Anthony Powell so I knew that I wanted to write a series such as these French, Spanish, and British writers had written and I knew that Faulkner himself had also had recurring or reappearing characters, but it wasn't until the third work *Korean Love Songs* that I realized the name for it—that I came up with the name that I called *The Klail City Death Trip* so when *Korean Love Songs* came out, I asked the editor to please call it *Korean Love Songs*, but that underneath that to call it the *Klail City Death Trip* series. After the third novel I fashioned the title for the series, but it was at the beginning of the second novel and during the writing of the first novel that I envisioned, not clearly, but at least envisioned that there was going to be a series. I knew that *Estampas* was not going to be the only work that I would ever write and it turned out to be true.

H. T. What aesthetic motivations did you perceive in yourself that drove you to depict this form of life, the Valley?

R. H. I think it was during my first or second year as chairman of Modern Languages at Texas A&M University in Kingsville, a student came up and showed me some *El Grito* copies of which I was ignorant and in that a man named Tomás Rivera had been awarded a prize for writing a novel in Spanish and being published in Spanish in the United States. Although the language factor was very important to me then as it is now, it was the subject matter that caught my attention. He was treating a particular class of Texas Mexican in Tomás's background—the migrant farm laborer. And I said, well, why don't I then write about the Rio Grande Valley, which may not be necessarily 100 percent migrant labor, but it is essentially a Texas Mexican experience. As far as the aesthetics, worldwide reading and decades of reading and reflection produced it. That was essentially the one thing by Tomás that I read and then I met him happily enough within a few months and then, of course, we prodded and urged each other to produce more and more.

H. T. Does the question of two languages in your work pose a special problem in any way at all?

R. H. I think it's more of a pleasure than a problem as far as creativity is concerned. It gives me a wider latitude.

H. T. Do those two languages, Spanish and English, interact for you when you are in the act of creating a text?

R. H. I think they do, but when I write something in Spanish I'll stay with that—the language. When I need to incorporate some English word for emphasis or for whatever use I may have for it at the time—some aesthetic thing that I may say—I think I should put something there because it fits. I'm just doing what other writers in the world have done. Thomas Mann, writing in German, writes something in French. Tolstoy writes something in Russian and he'll introduce French into it, you know that type of thing. But there is no problem. That is, do I have to make a decision which one to choose? No, I don't. Sometimes a novel will appear or the rudiments will appear in one language or the other and I just follow that particular flow at the time.

H. T. So do you think that for certain things Spanish represents that aesthetic reality better than English and vice versa?

R. H. At times Spanish, if I'm going to be writing about childhood, not necessarily my childhood, although mine is incorporated into it. Spanish also is a big help if I have to go back some fifty, sixty, one, two hundred years, the population of the Valley way before, you know during the Spanish Crown. English of course also has to appear because it would be unrealistic to exclude English from that particular environment, particularly in the latter part of the nineteenth and then in the twentieth century. I use them both and I think it is not only realistic but essential. I keep abreast of what it is that's happening linguistically in my work so if Spanish fulfills that mission, then it's used. English, if it fulfills that particular mission, then it's used.

H. T. Besides relying on your own experience, is there any other kind of research that you do when you sit down to write about the Valley?

R. H. I think that the research really is one's life experiences. In my case my life experience is in and out of the Valley. In the Valley at many different levels of my life. Out of the Valley at many different levels in my life. Age levels are what I'm referring to, so that's the type of research. Being a good listener is a help, but it's not the only thing. Being a very close, careful reader is also a help although it is not the only thing. It is a combination of those two and many other variables that one comes up with. But you have to work with what is there. That's the main point.

Identities, Literary Canon(s), Nation(s)

H. T. Let me ask you a question that relates back to your own work and concerns the general relationship you see between Chicano literature and Latin American literature on the one side, and Anglo-American literature on the other side. Where do you see your work situated between these two sides?

R. H. Let me begin linguistically because of the Spanish language usage that we do in our literature. At the very onset of contemporary Chicano literature, of course Tomás Rivera's novel was so instrumental and so forceful in this regard, people didn't know where to situate it and by "people" I mean academics. But our reality is the United States. That some may wish to place us with Mexico because it's part of our patrimony, we can't deny that, or that some wish to place us with Latin America or even with Spain because of the language usage is perfectly all right with me as it is perfectly all right with—I would imagine—men and women Chicano writers. It is an undeniable part of our lives, but the reality of it is that our culture—Chicano culture, etc.— is really an American culture. It is not the American culture as much as there is no one American culture, but it's part of it and therefore our literature, our reality, our lives, our deaths and joys, disappointments, successes and failures are all American so therefore the academic question that arose in the very early '70s that was finally settled by the late '70s, early '80s—where does this literature fit? Well, first of all it is an American litera- ture just as Faulkner's and O'Connor's Southern literature, or as is Philip Roth's, Joe Heller's, Bernard Malamud's, or Saul Bellow's American Jewish literature. It's just one more rem- nant, one more part of it, but it was the dual language aspect that bothered a lot of people when it shouldn't have both- ered them. At least it had to be answered, I guess. And it was answered by the writers themselves and it also in great part by the critics themselves. We too have those Spanish peninsular roots and the Latin American Spanish roots, but the reality of which we write is always our native land, the United States.

H. T. What kind of identity do you think Chicano literature in gen- eral, and your own creative work in particular, is forging? That identity—what can we see emerging as an identity for this literature?

R. H. I'm assuming then that you already know of the great cultural nationalism that was embodied by many of the early Chicano poets, particularly the poets in the early '70s and some may still continue that Johnny-One-Note type of play.

H. T. I think that's a recurring question . . .

R. H. But that was due to other cultural nationalism. It was very difficult to be carried through because, say, many Californians liked that idea of going to Mexico, but many Californians were absolutely urbanized and spoke no Spanish whatsoever while we Texans are more conservative as far as tradition and language and culture. But I think that the aesthetics—the idea of the identity of the aesthetics is solid enough. It is such a wide society, the Chicano society, because we have to incorporate the Midwest, Chicago, Minnesota, Iowa, the Pacific Northwest and of course the great Southwest, but the aesthetics are as varied as the Chicano people themselves are varied in their language usage, in their makings of traditions, in their makings of whatever it is that they deem worthy of retaining. Whatever you don't like in your culture, you drop. Whatever you deem worthy of retaining you maintain and it is the variance of aesthetics within Chicano literature that enriches overall American literature, whether they recognize it at first or not. Now they're beginning to see and some have seen for years that it is something that is aesthetic and based on a wide variance of that aesthetic.

H. T.   So when your characters in your novels and in your poetry talk about themselves, what identity are they forging for themselves and for the Valley?

R. H.   First, they are forging an established identity. They don't question who they are or what they are. They don't have to come up with what some were tearing their heads over, like lost identity. Valley Chicanos have always known exactly who they were and who they are. It was settled in 1749; it was free from any outside influences as far as English was concerned for a hundred years. So by the time the Mexican American War was over and the treaty was ratified on July 4, 1848, we'd been there for a hundred years and then we of course have inherited all of that. The question of identity has never applied to my characters. I think you can read it as you've read very closely my work. They know exactly who they are and that's why they behave the way they do. And what I do—I reflect the way Valleyites act and react and serve as agents and reagents for their own culture.

H. T.   I think that's one of the amazing things in your work—that identity, this question of identity is something you treat as a presupposition to great aesthetic ends.

R. H.   This may be due to the rural aspect as well as to the longevity and to being in one place for a long time. This really gives you a sense of place and I've written about this sense of place.

The Sense of Place and the Drive to Create

H. T. Can you say a few words on this whole notion of the sense of place and how it relates to your fiction?

R. H. Sure. I think that if you're an urbanite—to continue that and to tie it in with a sense of place—an urbanite has to drop off a lot of the tradition and culture and particularly the language in order to survive in an urban area. And it's very difficult to come up with a philosophy of a sense of place in an urban area as well. In the rural area where I was raised and where all my friends were raised and characters and everything else, one develops a sense of place without even knowing it. One belongs to a culture, but one also forges part of that culture. One contributes to the culture. You invent jokes and names. Whatever you do, you are forming part of that particular culture and then all of a sudden you realize that you've been living that, and you are forming part of it, and then you're stepping aside because there is someone else coming after you as far as a new generation is concerned. And a sense of place is not a mannered thing. It's not something that you learn formally, but it is something that you learn informally. You were born in a place, you develop in a place a certain love or a certain understanding for it and it's helped immeasurably in my writing as it should help immeasurably in any writer who has a sense of place.

H. T. What kinds of projects do you have at hand right now?

R. H. All right, about two and a half years ago, I started writing a novel in Spanish called *Los Amigos de Becky*. I think that's what I called it then. So I wrote the first draft and that took a few months and then I did the second rewrite and then the third rewrite and then I stopped. And then instead of waiting ten years as I did—I waited ten years between *Estampas del valle* and ten years between *Klail City* in Spanish and *Klail City* in English—and although I only waited three years between *Mi querido Rafa* and *Dear Rafe*, I decided to stop doing *Los Amigos de Becky* in Spanish and then after the third rewrite to go into the English. Well, I did the English and that took a few months again, and then I did the second, third, and perhaps the fourth rewrite. I think that's how long it took. And then I put it into typing and then I submitted the manuscript. This must be number eight or number nine, ten perhaps in the *Klail City Death Trip* and it's been accepted by Arte Público Press and it should be out according to the publisher Nicolás Kanellos, in January of 1990. Well, this is now—you and I are talking here on the twentieth of June, 1989, and I'm now deep again into the fourth rewrite of *Becky* or *Los Amigos de Becky* in Spanish and I would like to finish it by the latter part of August and then submit it to Kanellos. At the very same time, Gary Keller out at Arizona State University with Bilingual Press/Bilingual Review wants to include now in his Clasicos Castellanos series—he wants to include *Estampas* in Spanish and it's been out of print now after three printings and he wants to reissue *Klail City y sus alrrededores* again. Those are the projects. *Becky and Her Friends* which should be out in January and then the two by Clasicos Castellanos that Gary Keller is doing and after that *Los Amigos de Becky* in Spanish so I've got my hands full as well as some obligatory essays coming up because I have some ideas so I have to stop what I'm doing and write something that I feel like writing, which is different from the fiction that I'm doing.

H. T. It seems like you've always been very close to this whole issue of translation between languages in some form or another whether as an abstract or concrete project and it's interesting that your work has been translated into German . . .

R. H. And French.

H. T. French too?

R. H. Yes.

H. T. How does that make you feel?

R. H. Well, first of all I'm very proud that someone would want to translate that stuff. It was published first in German on the East Side then it was published by Zolkop on the West Side. Now it's being translated by someone else into English back again from the Spanish, and it's going to be a part of an anthology by Faber and Faber, which is a big house, as you well know. And I've been closely related as you so well put it with translation because I was raised biculturally and bilingually. My first schooling was a Mexican school for two years and then the eventual schooling of course was the American public school system going on with higher education. But in between when I was a teenager and attending high school every summer I would go into Mexico, not Mexico City, but to a village called Arteaga in the northern part of Mexico, about fifteen kilometers from Saltillo. I would spend three months there, 25 percent of a year for three years straight, in a northern Mexican, Spanish-speaking and living environment. Language has always been very important to me, as it should be to any writer. In my case because of the facility and my background, both languages just bubble up naturally.

H. T. Let me come back to the "canonical" question about the relationship of Chicano literature to the Anglo-American literary canon. What is that relationship for you?

R. H. I think it's already part of the canon. It may harm it and it may also help it at the same time.

H. T. That's a very interesting dialectical statement.

R. H. It may harm it, I think, because you would become so mannered that you can only write about mettlesome topics, but it will help it in that younger people than I who did not go through what I went through will be writing about their own experiences so that would be an aid to them. I think that Raymund Paredes's fine article that appeared in the *Columbia Literary History of the United States* just about canonizes this literature anyway. It's about time, as you well know. *The Columbia Literary History of the United States* is about American literature. Once Asian American, Native American, Black literatures are in there, as they should be, then Chicano literature too will be ultimately canonized. I would like to veer off now and go back briefly to a statement that I made years ago that has not come back to haunt me because it wasn't a statement I made off the hip. I said Spanish would never disappear from Chicano literature, but it would never be the dominant language. That might have been a few years ago, when Rivera and I wrote in Spanish, and Alejandro Morales, who continues to write in Spanish.

H. T. Have you changed your mind since then?

R. H. No. I see it because although Spanish will never disappear, we have a two-thousand-mile border; we have a two-hundred-and-some-odd-year history with the U.S. and Mexico. Our people came from there, and there are more coming every day.

H. T. So what will be the role of Spanish?

R. H. I think the role of Spanish will be secondary, but it will never disappear. Spanish will continue to be published, it will continue to be a force, it will continue to be a very good force for the beginning writer or even for the established writer, but English will prevail because this is essentially an English-speaking and an English-reading nation.

H. T. Rolando, thanks very much for this interview.

R. H. Well, it's been my pleasure.

Awards

1982 Southwestern Conference Latin American Studies Prize for Best Writing in the Humanities

1976 Casas de las Américas Literary Prize for *Klail City y sus alrededores*

1972 Premio Quinto Sol for *Estampas del valle y otras obras*

Primary Works

Becky and Her Friends. Houston: Arte Público Press, 1990.

Claros Varones de Belken/Fair Gentlemen of Belken County. Tempe, AZ: Bilingual Press/Editorial Bilingüe, 1986.

Estampas del valle y otras obras. Berkeley: Quinto Sol Publications, 1973.

Generaciones y semblanzas. Berkeley: Justa Publications, 1979.

Klail City: A Novel. Houston: Arte Público Press, 1987.

Klail City und Umgebung. Trans. and epilogue by Yolanda Julia Broyles. Berlin, Germany: Volk and Welt, 1980.

Klail City y sus alrededores. Havana: Casa de las Américas, 1976.

Korean Love Songs. Berkeley: Justa Publications, 1979.

Mi querido Rafa. Houston: Arte Público Press, 1981.

Rites and Witnesses. Houston: Arte Público Press, 1982.

This Migrant Earth. Houston: Arte Público Press, 1987.

The Valley. Tempe, AZ: Bilingual Press/Editorial Bilingüe, 1983.

Selected Secondary Sources

Busby, Mark. "Faulknerian Elements in Rolando Hinojosa's *The Valley.*" *Multi-Ethnic Literature of the United States* 11, no. 4 (1984): 103–9.

De Dwyer, Carlota Cardenas. "Cultural Nationalism and Chicano Literature in the Eighties." *Multi-Ethnic Literature of the United States* 8, no. 2 (1981): 40–47.

Martín-Rodriguez, Manuel M. "Rolando Hinojosa y su *Klail City Death Trip Series:* Una novela del lector." *The Americas Review* 21, no. 2 (1993): 89–101.

Paredes, Raymund. "The Evolution of Chicano Literature." *Multi-Ethnic Literature of the United States* 5, no. 2, (1978): 17–110.

———. "Mexican American Authors and the American Dream." *Multi-Ethnic Literature of the United States* 8, no. 4 (1981): 71–80.

Saldívar, José David, ed. *The Rolando Hinojosa Reader.* Houston: Arte Público Press, 1985.

Saldívar, J. D. "The Limits of Cultural Studies." *American Literary History* 2, no. 2 (1990): 252–66.

Stanton, Helena Villacres. "Death in Rolando Hinojosa's Belken County." *Multi-Ethnic Literature of the United States* 13, no. 3/4 (1986): 67–83.

Torres, Hector A. "Discourse and Plot in Rolando Hinojosa's *The Valley:* Narrativity and the Recovery of Chicano Heritage." *Confluencia: Revista Hispánica de Cultura y Literatura* 2, no. 1 (1986): 84–93.

Zilles, Klaus. *Rolando Hinojosa: A Reader's Guide.* Albuquerque: University of New Mexico Press, 2001.

Notes to Chapter One

1. José David Saldívar, "Rolando Hinojosa's *Klail City Death Trip*: A Critical Introduction," in *The Rolando Hinojosa Reader: Essays Historical and Critical*, ed. José David Saldívar (Houston: Arte Público Press, 1985), 47.
2. Rosaura Sánchez uses the term "macrotext" to characterize Hinojosa's oeuvre from *Estampas del valle* to *Rites and Witnesses* in "From Heterogeneity to Contradiction: Hinojosa's Novel," in *The Rolando Hinojosa Reader: Essays Historical and Critical*, ed. José David Saldívar (Houston: Arte Público Press, 1985), 76–100.
3. Hector Calderón, "On the Uses of Chronicle, Biography and Sketch in Rolando Hinojosa's *Generaciones y semblanzas*," in *The Rolando Hinojosa Reader: Essays Historical and Critical*, ed. José David Saldívar (Houston: Arte Público Press, 1985), 136.
4. Margarita Cota-Cárdenas, *Mi quierido Rafa* and "Irony: A Structural Study," in *The Rolando Hinojosa Reader*, 158.
5. José David Saldívar, "Critical Introduction," 48.
6. Ramón Saldívar, "*Korean Love Songs:* A Border Ballad and its Heroes," in *The Rolando Hinojosa Reader*, 148.

CHAPTER TWO

Arturo Islas
I Don't Like Labels and Categories ⌐

⌐ The emergence of the work of Arturo Islas into the canon of Chicano literary discourse was delayed by the vicissitude of a near-death experience in 1969. The near-death experience Islas suffered figures prominently in the birth of *The Rain God*, making this work appear as a gift from death. The Chicano canon had to wait over a decade before Islas's work could enrich it with its fine-grained literary representation of the instability inhabiting the domestic space of the Chicano Mexican American family in the process of decay and trans-formation—a process attributable to the "creative destruction" that fits hand-in-glove with the development of international capital in the bor-derlands. That the Chicano Mexican family is undergoing this process during the decades Islas's oeuvre spans—roughly from the 1940s into the late 1960s—signals the gradual but uneven ascent of the Mexican American family to middle-class consciousness in Anglo-American society. Frederick Luis Aldama, Islas's most thorough critic to date, analyzes the traversal of capital over the domestic space of Islas's fam-ily: "As Islas grew up on the El Paso/Juárez border, he experienced the contradictory tensions of capital first hand: the huge prosperity of an Anglo elite along with the simultaneous impoverishment of what was growing into a Mexican majority. While racial and class geopoliti-cal rifts were felt by Islas, because of his family's bilingual privilege and position north of the Mexican border, in the forties Islas's craft also experienced the contradictions of capitalism at home."[1] Aldama traces the development of Islas's craft to his need to deal with these contradictory tensions stemming from the division of labor at the El Paso/Juárez border.[2] From his early experiments with the short story genre to *The Rain God* and *Migrant Souls*, Islas has developed his craft to critique patriarchal paradigms governing issues of masculinity, sexuality, race, and class, at the U.S.–Mexico border, but also in the Anglo-American nation. These acts of writing began early and matured at Stanford: "When he began to study and write fiction formally at Stanford, he gave thematic presence and complex narrative texture to the contradictions felt at home and to those racial and economic tensions that were ripping bodies apart within a very real borderland space."[3] Marta Sánchez describes these contradictions at work in the social act of writing *The Rain God*, arguing that the production of the text comes through the displacements of the literary conventions and techniques of modernism. The production of *The Rain God*, she maintains, shows the reader that "literary conventions associated with the dominant tradition are neither 'fixed' nor 'natural.' On the contrary, they are subject to movement, alteration, and displacement. In the long run, both Chicano and dominant traditions are shaped by each other, as each tradition helps to transform the destructive forces of the other tradition into creative weapons for the writing of the story."[4]

In addressing the politics of trying to publish *The Rain God* with a New York publishing house, Islas links linguistic prejudice to the contingency of literary taste. The linguistic prejudice as it operates in a local space such as El Paso that Islas describes in the interview can be read as a microcosm of the politics of publishing through a mainstream New York publishing house. The narrow view of Chicano/Chicana cultures and linguistic codes that these agents of literary value hold also leads them to reduce *The Rain God* to the bearer of an ethnic cultural message. José David Saldívar points out that the delay to publication with a mainstream New York press is traceable to the fact that the literary value Islas constructs out of the fundamental unit called the family fails to satisfy the expectations of these agents and brokers of literary value: "The rejection of *The Rain God* by New York publishers can best be explained, first, by acknowledging that the novel does not stereotype Islas's Chicano and Chicana characters. More significantly, it did not conform to the editors' ideas about ethnic American literature."[5] Saldívar castigates the Eastern establishment for failing to notice the hemispheric and ultimately global sources Islas relies upon in crafting his work: "The value of Islas's *The Rain God* lies not in the author's depiction of traditions alien to American readers but in the specific way he bridges the gap between North American and Latin American cultures and unites...literary and transnational traditions."[6] Islas constructs not just local value but hemispheric American literary value, as much from the unstable unit called the Chicano family as from the unstable value of the transcendental ego in modernity. Marta Sánchez points to the precarious and paradoxical conditions under which Islas constructs literary value: "Thus, *The Rain God* is about the formation of the protagonist's 'I' with no 'I' overly present at any time."[7] The double logic Sánchez proposes here to describe the narrator of *The Rain God*, Miguel Chico, affirms the effectiveness of the novel's narrative subject but also its instability. If these conditions poise Miguel Chico somewhere between being and nothingness, they also point to the genealogy of literary influences he mentions in the interview. The world stage of writers Islas names as literary influences teaches him to put premium value on the displacement of nationalisms, and is no doubt the reason he leaves Chicano literature undefined. This value is definitively performative in the way that Islas doesn't refuse Chicano literature an identity, but he also doesn't provide necessary and sufficient predicates to define it. Rather, he puts the emphasis on the practice of writing itself and the processes of history.[8] Ironically, the emphasis on the historical process over conceptual definitions does not turn into a call for a new realism, but represents a break from it and a foray into the play of magical realism.[9]

When Islas discusses contemporary Chicano and Chicana writers of the emerging canon, his discussions include the stalwarts of the early canon—Tomás Rivera, Rolando Hinojosa—as well as writers born a good twenty-plus years later—Ana Castillo and Sandra Cisneros. This can be adduced as a sign that the process of canon formation doesn't proceed easily by generations. The discussion also signals that Islas does not fit easily into a generation of Chicano writers, or perhaps more fundamentally that the category of "generation" is categorically unstable. His passing away due to complications of

AIDS on February 15, 1991, when only fifty-three seems to denote the uneven passage of time, at any rate.

DATE: June, 1990

SETTING: The office of Arturo Islas, Stanford University, Palo Alto, California

A Stanford Education and More

H. T. Can we begin with when and where you were you born and go from there?

A. I. Sure. I was born and brought up in El Paso in 1938. I was the first of three sons. My father is the last of ten children, so I have on that side of the family a lot of relatives and three of my aunts—his older sisters—are still living. His brothers have died. I have lots of first cousins and we all went to public schools in El Paso. In fact, a lot of us went to the same high school where my parents went—where my parents met at El Paso High. I was the first in my generation to go away to college straight out of high school. I mention that not as bragging, but to show you what education is like for people from my background in those years—the '40s and '50s. It was very rare that anybody in my generation went away to school on scholarships. You had to do really, really well to even be noticed.

H. T. Where did you go for your undergraduate?

A. I. Here. Stanford. All my education has been here—my BA, my MA, and my PhD. And in my graduating class here in 1960 I was the only Spanish surname and there was one black woman in the class. That will show you what it was like.

H. T. Even as late as 1960?

A. I. Even as late as 1960 because, you know, it was the end of the Eisenhower era. Kennedy was elected in the fall of 1960 and that was the beginning of the '60s revolution and the civil rights. The changes here were very dramatic toward the late '60s.

H. T. What was that like for you being on the Stanford campus?

A. I. Well, the first two years were very alienating and very lonely until I got used to the place and after that it was okay. I started out as a premed because I always had said I wanted to be a doctor, but at El Paso High I hadn't really had the kind of chemistry, biology, and math courses I needed, even though I had very good teachers there. It's not their fault. I'm not blaming them, but I hadn't had calculus. I hadn't had all the things that the students *now* are getting—the Chicano students and Chicana students—and so I switched. I had to maintain a very high grade point average in order to keep my scholarship, so I switched to literature where I could maintain that high grade point average and stay. Then I got another scholarship to stay for graduate school. Then I left for five years. I left Stanford for five years and then they hired me back in the late '60s, early '70s.

H. T. Where did you go for those five years?

A. I. Well, I'd been a student all my life. And I wanted to see the world, you know. I wanted to *live*. And I wanted to get out of the academy. I didn't want to read a book, take exams, or anything. I had five part-time jobs, one of which was a teaching job at the VA hospital in Menlo Park where they sent the hopeless cases. They were all zonked out on Thorazine and I was supposed to teach them public speaking. Actually, they taught me how to speak. They taught *me* how to communicate to people. They were wonderful, and pathetic—sad, sad men and women— because their lives were essentially on medication. Once you're on Thorazine for *that long* you become an institutionalized personality. Anyway, I learned a lot from their courage and from them. And, you know, if I could get some of them to put two sentences together and understand what they were saying, that kind of thing was a triumph. I learned a lot. And then I had a cashier's job and a delivery job. I held down little jobs like that. And I saved enough money to go to Europe for the first time. I wanted to go. I wanted to see. I went to Mexico a lot. I moved to San Francisco during the Haight-Ashbury time. Though I never partook of that, it was going on when I was there.

H. T. So that's part of your education too?

A. I. You bet it is. And I learned to see myself as somebody in the world and not just as somebody in an academic setting or academic community and that was very good and that was an education. And I think my own education is all the richer for me having done that. Anyway, then in 1969 I accepted a job at San Jose State. They wanted me. But then I almost died. I had cancer. I almost died and I couldn't take the job in the fall. So Stanford kept me on just teaching Freshman English so that I'd draw a check while I was recovering. And then the following year they hired me as a regular faculty member.

H. T.   What was the date on that near-death experience?

A. I.   June of 1969. I draw from that experience in my portrayal of Miguel Chico in *The Rain God*. He himself goes through a life-threatening series of operations and I use my own experience in order to draw his character. And then in 1976 I was given tenure and I've been here ever since.

El Paso, So Close to Mexico

H. T.   What about your home life? What was it like growing up in El Paso?

A. I.   Well, we were from a lower-middle-class Mexican family. Where I grew up in the Five Points Area were mostly lower-middle-class Mexican families who could afford to buy a house. I think you could buy a house in those years for three thousand dollars. But that was the hardship of my parents. Both my parents worked all their lives. My mother was a secretary for various companies in El Paso and my father was a policeman, one of the first Mexican policemen on the force. There were three of them when he started out as a rookie in the late '30s, early '40s. My brothers—who are quite a bit younger than I, one is six years younger, one is ten years younger—we grew up in the same *barrio*, the Five Points area. It wasn't considered a barrio, but I think it was. It wasn't the projects, but it was pretty much. In fact, two blocks away, there was a black neighborhood. There were about twenty black families in that same area. And we all went to the same public schools. The prejudice against Mexicans was still very, very strong in that period. Even though El Paso was at that point 40 percent people from a Mexican background, they weren't allowed to hold high-level jobs. In fact, my father, when it became his turn to become chief of police, they wouldn't let him be chief of police.

H. T. Really?

A. I. Yes, and the clear reason was that he was a *mexicano*.

H. T. Were there signs that you could read that showed there was a systematic exclusion?

A. I. Well, I always occupied a kind of privileged position because I was a very good student. I think that surprised a lot of my teachers. Maybe it did. Maybe it didn't. I'm not really sure. So I was treated in a special way. But I always had the feeling that I was unusual, or thought to be unusual in some way. And I could see, even in grade school, the division between the Anglo and the Mexican kids. It was always there. And I always walked the line in between partly because I was a good student. And I remember when a friend of mine—I was around eight years or nine years old—he wanted me to join the Cub Scouts with him.

H. T. Anglo friend?

A. I. He was an Anglo friend and I went to one meeting with him, and then I never heard again why I wasn't invited back. He quit the Cub Scouts because they wouldn't let me, a Mexican, be a Cub Scout. A lot of prejudice. It was insidious. It was never up front—you know it never is. People are awfully nice to you but Mexican people were kept in their place. They didn't know what to do with people who did well in school because we weren't supposed to do well in school. We weren't supposed to know how to read. I had been taught to read by my grandmother who had been a teacher. I had been taught Spanish by her. And so had my cousins. They did very well in school, too. In fact, my first cousin, who is the oldest in my generation, is also the first PhD in my family. He went away after he went to Texas Western, now UT–El Paso. He then went away to school in the Midwest and got his PhD in physics. He was brilliant, and his brothers, *también*. They were, too.

Life with/in Two Languages: *Realpolitik*

H. T. What was your experience with language?

A. I. My experience with language . . . I am so glad that I was brought up speaking Spanish.

H. T.   You said your grandmother taught you Spanish?

A. I.   Yes! That was no big deal for us. I don't understand all this to-do about bilingual education. I think it's *great*. I think any-body and everybody should know more than one language flu-ently. It can only make you a richer person. And so I was really happy, later. Not at the time. It didn't occur to me. It just seemed so natural to speak Spanish and to speak English as well as we could. We knew we weren't supposed to speak Spanish on the school grounds, you know. We followed the rules. Some of us did. Some of us didn't.

H. T.   How did you know that?

A. I.   We were told.

H. T.   Direct signs?

A. I.   You will be punished if you speak Spanish on the school grounds. Like at recess and so on.

H. T.   Were you ever punished for doing so?

A. I.   Not in any overt way. For instance, I would get Bs in PE, which always distressed me because I wanted to get straight As in everything. But the reason I was getting Bs in PE was that I was speaking Spanish on the school ground during recess. And even though we were told that this was not the thing to do, I would just slip and do it. And the teacher would overhear and knock me down for that, *in that way* never directly. So there were subtle forms of racism operating, and there still are. El Paso is a big military town and a lot of those people come from outside of the city and they treat Mexicans like dirt, and that has always upset me. A lot. All of us. Not all the military people do that, but some of them have that tendency. They come from elsewhere and they've been taught the bigotry against any peo-ple of color. But anyway, I grew up in a bilingual, bicultural atmosphere, which to me was natural. In fact, I go back to El Paso a lot for that.

H. T.   So, for instance, how did you and your parents communicate?

A. I.   We communicated in Spanish and English, screaming and yell-ing just like a normal family. I guess we used the Chicano lingo, or what we would call the slang. My father talks like that. My father doesn't speak English or Spanish perfectly. He has this wonderful mixture of both languages. You know the barrio was the same and it's still like that in El Paso. I mean the Mexican people who are American citizens communicate with each other in both languages and in a mixture of both. I wish I could give you a tape of my mother on the phone. It's just a language all its own and I like it. I think it's wonderfully alive and vibrant and I'm just sorry not everybody can understand it.

H. T. Do you draw on that linguistic code for your creative work?

A. I. Yes I do. I do. The only problem with doing that, though, is you won't get published doing both languages like that because people simply will not publish you unless you write completely in English—at least the northeastern established presses won't. The smaller California presses and some of the Chicano presses will do it, but you're not going to get the same kind of distribution or backing that you get out of New York. So you know that presents its problems. Take my books for example, *The Rain God*, and then for this new novel, *Migrant Souls*, one of the challenges was to give the flavor of the language in translation because all the members of the older generation in my book, all those older characters speak Spanish; they don't speak English. And so the trick was to get them to speak in English and make it sound as if it had a Spanish flavor to it, and sometimes I just go right out and say "Don't talk to me like that," said Mama Chona *in Spanish*. But I couldn't use the Spanish because nobody would publish it that way.

H. T. What kind of other strategies do you find yourself using to connote the flavor of the Spanish language?

A. I. When there were words that you can't really translate completely, I just went ahead and used them, like *sinvergüenza*, *malcriado*, or words for foods. So the trick became how to explain them in English without seeming to be explaining it. And that was fun. It was fun to figure out ways to do that and I'm still doing it in this particular book. Because the main thing is to communicate the atmosphere of that culture any way you can do it. Sometimes you're successful and sometimes you're not, but the thing is to try it. The *ideal* way to publish the kind of work that I do and that a lot of writers from my background do would be to do it in Spanish and in English and a mixture of the two, but who's going to publish it? And so we end up then talking and reading to each other. That's okay. That's fine. But we need to get out there in the imaginations of the rest of the country. That's my feeling about this generation. It may be different in another generation. I hope so. And a lot of us have this problem. Denise Chávez, I know, has this problem because we talk about it, and Ben Saenz, another writer, a younger writer. Ana, I'm sure. Sandra. All the writers you're working on. Rolando, Tomás. They all had this problem of how to do it. Tomás, for example, resolved it by having Spanish and English facing page to page so that you could read either. You know there are various ways to go about it.

H. T. Any other strategies that you can think of?

A. I. I've written another novel that I'm having a hard time getting published because it's in barrio dialect. And there are small presses—Cinco Puntos Press in El Paso wants to do it—but we keep holding out, hoping that a larger press will do it because the imagination of this character needs to be out there. And he speaks in this Spanglish dialect that I'm talking about. And you know it's interesting to more and more people, at least to the people who attend my readings. I give readings to large audiences like the California State Teachers of English, for example. I'm going to do that for a literacy project that they're doing this summer and I mean these are like three hundred to five hundred people—most of them Anglo. But in California, anyway, they all have a familiarity with Spanish terms and Spanish. They're not like the Northeast. The Northeast constantly surprises me. They should have some familiarity, given the large Puerto Rican population in New York, for example, and now the Cuban population from Miami coming up north along the Atlantic seaboard, but apparently they don't. Anyway, the linguistic problems will continue for a while. And here at Stanford, I urge all of my students, minority and nonminority, to learn more than one language. And it seems to me perfectly natural that the language they ought to learn is Spanish because that's the language that's spoken *most* in the Western Hemisphere, not English. Spanish, so they could get jobs. It seems a practical suggestion. But the minute you say that, all of a sudden it turns into this big political issue and I'm labeled a revolutionary radical and a this and a that, which to me is perfectly ridiculous, because to me it's perfectly natural to me to speak and think in two languages, not just one.

Chicano Literature: On the Disruption of Categories

H. T. Changing the topic, just a little bit. What in your mind is the relationship between Chicano literature and American literature?

A. I. Well, I think there's a big relationship. Let's look at Tomás Rivera's book, for example, *y no se tragó la tierra*: the format, the organization of that book is modeled after Hemingway's *In Our Time*, and Hemingway, as we all know, was enamored of the Latin and Spanish spirit/soul. So there are all these connections that are at work. Rolando Hinojosa, the same. We all were educated in English in institutions—well-educated in institutions like Stanford and so on, or the UT system—all the writers that you've mentioned to me have had good educations and so naturally they've read the literature of Britain and this country, especially if they're interested in writing and novels and poetry and so on and now they want to do their own thing. They want to speak in their own voice, but everything they've learned is sort of, whether you acknowledge it or not, whether you want to admit to it or not, it all gets incorporated into your imagination, and the exciting thing about writers like Denise and Ben is that they are now giving voice to a group in North America that's been here and contributed to North American life for *years*, decades, centuries even. And they're writing in that voice and eventually people are going to listen. It's already starting, I think. It's a lot more than it was twenty years ago.

H. T. What is the history of Chicano literature?

A. I. Well, some people date it back to the Treaty of Guadalupe Hidalgo. I never like to argue about that or talk about when. Constantly now students are uncovering, mostly in Spanish-language newspapers, that period in the late nineteenth century and early twentieth century and writers are beginning to sur-face and all of that is interesting. I mean that's what scholars do. They uncover all that material and then make it available to us. You know some people will say that's too far back to go to date the beginning of Chicano literature. That it really starts in the '60s with the Chicano political movement—the people who look at literature through political and historical perspectives will date that. That's fine too. I don't care, so long as people keep writing it. Just keep doing it.

H. T. Is that tantamount to saying that Chicano literature doesn't have an identity?

A. I. No, I don't think so at all. I mean to *me* it has very much its own identity, its own flavor.

H. T. What is that identity?

A. I. Well, it's multiple, you know. It's not just *one* identity. It isn't fair to get a writer to speak for an entire concept or mythical concept. It doesn't work that way. Some guy or woman writing in the barrio of East L.A. is going to have her or his own voice. Some guy or woman writing from the migrant experience in Téjas is going to have his or her own voice. And yet they both come from the same history, you know. They're Mexican. To me, that's all part of the same thing. It's just like a cut crys-tal with lots of different facets. It's the same crystal, but you get lots of different lights shining on it, and that's how it is. A culture that is static is dead. So no, I think there's a definite, distinct, and unique voice there and it's part of what we call American literature. I define American broadly. Not just the United States is American—Canada, the United States, Mexico, Latin America, South America. That's all America. *All of it.* And so maybe that's why I'm having a little bit of a problem with the definition of American literature. I mean, as we teach American literature here at Stanford, what we mean is United States literature and I always say that at the beginning of my Masterpieces of American Literature class. I say, "We are taking only a narrow part of a larger literature."

H. T. Isn't that the case with, I would say, practically all American literature classes? Wouldn't you say so?

A. I. Yes. That they only do U.S. literature?

H. T. And take a very narrow view . . . ?

A. I. I do. That's right. That's exactly right. But you know how people are—very jealous of their turf. And they don't want anyone to be intruding on their turf. But the plain fact of the matter is that a lot of the most exciting writing that's being done in the United States is being done by so-called minority groups—people from those groups who have systematically been excluded from the canon. The Afro-Americans, or blacks, or however they want to be called, have made great strides in American literature. Now they are taught in the canon. And that's going to happen with Chicano writers—it's bound to—or Hispanic writers, whatever we're going to be called in that process. It's bound to happen because the voices are exciting. They're interesting. They're new. They're keeping the tradition going and alive. If you stay within one little tradition, it's going to remain static and die. No matter how good the writing is.

H. T. Does Chicano literature have a relationship to Latin American literature?

A. I. I think it does, too—some—depending on the writers. There are some Chicano writers who draw from the Latin American or the Mexican tradition of writing. As a writer myself I don't even like to think in terms of nationalisms or traditions because all of that seems ridiculous to me.

H. T. What kind of categories do you feel comfortable with?

A. I. None. I don't like the labels and the categories. You know I use them. In my role as a professor, I use them to say these are labels and categories and they're arbitrary. They were chosen by a committee deciding what we were going to teach in an American literature course, or in a French literature course, or in a whatever-the-literature course.

H. T. Are your students distressed when they find out that these categories are social constructions?

A. I. No, I don't think so.

H. T. What kind of reactions do you get?

A. I. At least in my classes, they're usually very openminded. There are some narrow-minded students, students who want to have those demarcations—those boundaries—because they feel more secure having them. But there are pedagogical ways to deal with that and to talk about that.

H. T.   What are some of the ways that you use to begin to dismantle some of those arbitrary categories?

A. I.   Well, I always start my introductory lectures in every big class that I teach by saying that I'm looking at these works from a writer's point of view, not a critic, not a sociologist, not an anthropologist, not a linguist, not a professor of American and English literature, but as a writer. What have I learned from these fellow writers about writing? Fiction is my interest. And so *that's* my entry into it, if it's an American literature course— a so-called American literature course—and I have to get that notion across. That's easy to do. You know in everything's that's written by the writers that we read or talk about there is something that we can say, "What is distinctively American about this?" And why do we say that? Why do we call it that? Why isn't it European, Eurocentric? Why isn't it Mexican? Why isn't it Latin American? And so in that way you bring the distinctive, the uniqueness of these different voices. But I don't like to do it as a nationalistic thing. That to me is wrong. The best writers from any country are usually pretty critical of the countries that they're writing in, you know. It's one reason that makes them good writers because most of them see what a sham nationalism is, I think. That doesn't mean they don't have pride in their countries, or have visions about their countries like the Russians—for example, Tolstoy and Dostoyevsky in the nineteenth century—but it means that they're also critical. They're not nationalistic. They're not the pseudopatriots.

The Production of Literary Value

H. T.   Can you talk about your own work? When did you first begin to realize that you wanted to be a writer, for instance?

A. I.   Well, I think people are writers when they're writing. You can't want to be a writer. You're either writing or you're not writing and when you're not writing you're not a writer. I tell my students this because I always have students coming in and saying, "I want to be a writer." And I'll say, "Well, what have you written? Show me what you've written." And they'll say, "Oh, I haven't done anything yet, but I *want* to be a writer." I say, "Well, go write. Then you're a writer while you're writing. Then we can talk about what you've done." I've been writing all my life, as a student, in one way or another. I never thought I would write a novel. I never thought I would be a novelist.

H. T. So what happened?

A. I. Well, what happened was that I got a year off when I was a junior professor, and instead of writing literary criticism, which is what I was supposed to do, I took a chance. And also I had some material to work with. I knew there was this story I had to tell—several stories and so I just started writing them.

H. T. And out of that . . .

A. I. . . . came *The Rain God*.

H. T. What was the design behind *The Rain God*? What did you have in mind?

A. I. Well, I didn't have anything in mind at first. To answer that question I can tell you how the structure changed over time.

H. T. Okay.

A. I. Right from the beginning. Well, at the beginning it was called *Día de los Muertos* slash *Day of the Dead*. It had a bilingual title. And it was only three long chapters, and then gradually as I kept looking at it again and revising it, it turned into six chapters with different titles, but I knew that the organizing principle was the family—the Ángel family. I didn't want there to be a central character or a central voice. I wanted the family to be the hero of the novel, or the idea of that family, and I think I succeeded. But it was also the reason why it wasn't published for a very long time. Because when I would send it off to New York, or my agent would send it off to New York, they didn't find characters they could identify with so they didn't find a central intelligence. That's the way they're used to reading, you know, so they wouldn't publish it.

H. T. How did that make you feel?

A. I. *Horrible*. I didn't like rejection. Nobody likes rejection. And so finally I just gave up. They're not going to do it. They'll do it after I die. But then a small California press published it. You know they did it. And we changed the title to *The Rain God*, which was okay with me. And changed the organization of the book. So it grew over time. It took about three years to write it and it took about ten years to publish it.

H. T.   And *Migrant Souls*?

A. I.   Well, *Migrant Souls* took about two and a half years, but I was lucky with that one. It's getting published right away. And it's getting published out of New York, which is a first.

H. T.   And what was the design behind *Migrant Souls*?

A. I.   Well, already I had established the Ángel family as a group of characters and *Migrant Souls* grew out of that because I'm still with the Ángel family and we're still in a border town, but the two characters who are the major characters in this new book— one of them I hadn't mentioned at all in *The Rain God* and the other one I had mentioned, but I was very unfair to her because in *The Rain God* she just comes off as a religious fanatic. And there's a lot more to her than that. And I wanted to do that. So that's how that book grew out of that desire. And a lot of sur- prises, a lot of good surprises, come along the way. Characters you never dreamed would show up all of a sudden there on the page. *Migrant Souls* is in two books that are interrelated and that weave together.

H. T.   Would you say that the spiritual/religious dimension plays an important role in those two works?

A. I.   Yes, because this family is Catholic and the minute you bring the Church as a force into the lives of the characters it's bound to determine character. I have my own quarrels with the Church and what I see the Church to be doing in real life, but in my fiction I can really use it. I can use all of these dimensions and watch people, and have fun with the way people are, given their religious leanings away or toward the Church.

H. T.   Can you talk about those quarrels?

A. I.   Oh, I do. I portray them. I constantly have characters arguing with each other about religion—mainly the Catholic Church. I grew up with those discussions. All of it is very rich, rich material for fiction. In this new book, one of the supporting characters, a strong supporting character, is a priest. He's Miguel Chico's brother. Gabriel is his name and the novel ends with his meditation, but before we get to that, there are definitely key scenes where the Church figures as a point of departure for the characters to argue.

Genealogy of Literary Influences

H. T.   Are there any writers that have influenced you especially?

A. I.   Everybody I've ever read has influenced me—everybody—even the bad writers because they teach me what not to do. I have my favorites, and they're my favorites for various reasons, but I couldn't tell you from this person I learned this and from that person I learned that. It's sort of a mixture of things. They opened doors for me. That's what good writers and good writing can do: open doors to your imagination so then your imagination is larger. I love the Russian writers—Dostoevsky and Tolstoy and Turgenev and Chekov. Great writers. I don't care so much for the twentieth century Russian writers, but I sure like the nineteenth century Russian writers. In the twentieth century my favorite writers are French: Colette and Proust. The Latin Americans I love—Gabriel García Márquez and Juan Rulfo in Mexico, now dead, alas. Mario Vargas Llosa in Peru; Jorge Luis Borges, though his kind of writing doesn't appeal to me as much because it's too abstract—too intellectualized—and that's not my cup of tea, but I enjoy reading it, and I learn from it. I recognize that there's a genius at work and by that I don't mean he's a genius; I mean there's a genius inside of him that's working and that's exciting to look at.

H. T.   What kind of doors has Márquez opened for you?

A. I.   García Márquez? I like his way of dealing with everyday reality and turning it into a miracle every time. That's terrific. And he does it better than anybody. I also like the way they incorporate historical or social or political movements into their fictions without giving up the beauty of the writing. They don't become ideologues. They don't start writing propaganda. Propaganda's okay. I'm not saying it's not. But if you're talking about writing a novel, at the same time you still get the feeling that there's some kind of commitment going on here. Have I answered your question?

H. T. Yes. What about from the standpoint of the reader? What kind of things would you like your readers to read out of your works, or into them? What kind of reading dialectic would you like to establish with your readers?

A. I. I'd like to think that my characters are so alive and interesting that the reader, after finishing the book, will be thinking about them, and wondering about them as if they were real people. And if I can bring them to life, or if they can be brought to life like that on the page, then I've succeeded as a writer. I also draw and discuss controversial things in my books, and I'd like people to look at these things with compassion rather than having to take sides. It's more complex than that. It's much more complex than that—life is and that's what I would like. I'd also like my readers to enjoy reading my work. To laugh and to cry and to think, "Oh, that character is acting so stupid and why doesn't she do this?" Or "Why doesn't he do that?" And yet still feel sympathy because they would understand from their own experience in life that that's the way it is sometimes.

H. T. After *Migrant Souls*, are there other projects?

A. I. Oh, yeah. There are two. Well, there's that novel that's already done that I told you about that has nothing to do with the Ángel family. It's completely different characters.

H. T. Do you have a name for that?

A. I. It's called *La Mollie and the King of Tears* and you have to read the book to find out who La Mollie and the King of Tears are and it's a first person narrator. His name is Louie Mendoza and he's from the barrio in El Paso and he's a musician and now lives in San Francisco. It takes place in the early '70s. So that's already done. I read from that to a lot to people, teachers especially, because of the character Louis—his buddies in the gang that he belongs to call him Shakespeare Louie because he knows Shakespeare and so that's a lot of fun. And it's a tragic life. I mean he's had quite a life, this guy.

H. T. Drawn from someone you knew?

A. I. Well, various people, you know. All my characters are composites. I never draw from one single person to characterize. I do composites. And then there's one more book about the Ángel family that's in my head. I have several scenes. I think I know what direction I want to go in, but we'll see. We'll see if it goes in the direction I want it to go in.

H. T. So do you think you're going to be producing regular installments on the Angél family?

A. I. Well, I know there's one more. If there's another, that's great, but I know there's at least one more.

H. T. So you write mainly in the genre of the novel. Do you have any possibilities for writing in poetry?

A. I. Well, I have written some poetry. And I've had some of it published. But poetry's always a surprise for me because I never think of myself as a poet. To me, poetry is the hardest of all of the genres. It requires the most self-discipline so you don't get self-indulgent and wacky, you know, which several poets do. In any country. So I don't think of myself as a poet, but I have written some poems, and they have been published, and that's nice. I like that, but whether there's enough for a book, I don't know. I have a book of poems that I've never had published. That's in a drawer somewhere. I don't know if I'd be embarrassed reading them.

Issues of Gender in Chicano Literature

H. T. Let me ask you one more question concerning the notion of gender in Chicano/Chicana literature. What's your point of view?

A. I. Well, we were talking about this in an interdisciplinary seminar that Tomás Ybarra and I offer this quarter on Chicano culture and we were talking about gender, and there were quite a number of women in that seminar, some of whom are feminist, some of whom are lesbian and last night there was a gay student, a man who gave a presentation on John Rechy's novel *City of Night*, on *The Rain God*, and on a Mexican novel called *Adonis García*. He's from Mexico City, that particular writer [Luis Zapata]. It was very interesting how that opened up the whole question of gender. If you look at the Chicano literature that's available for us right now—the novels—you see the different gender roles that characters play because that's the context in which they are. The example that I give from my own work, in this new novel, there is a woman character who some people will think is a lesbian and she may or may not be, but that's not important to me in her characterization or the way that people read her. I like leaving it a mystery because within the culture, that's how it's done, that's how it's looked at, at least in the culture that I'm writing about. There are several members of the Angél family that are now going to be out either as divorced women, or as gay men or as the various roles that are available in that spectrum of gender. All the roles of men and women in that culture, I think, are called into question as I portray them, or at least I hope they are. But also what should a woman be in this culture, what should a man be in this culture? There are some things that we can see that are continuous, good and bad. It's a mixture. It's complex, but I call all of those myths about masculinity and femininity into question in my work. At least I hope I do.

H. T.   What kind of productive effects do you think can be had in raising the questions of gender?

A. I   I think it opens up other possibilities. That's a good question. At least I hope in the way I'm doing it . . . I can't speak for other writers, but I hope that in the way that I'm doing it, what it will evoke is compassion in the reader for all of them, for all the characters, no matter what gender role they are assigned in my work.

Awards

1985 Regional Border Library Association Award
1976 Dinkelspiel Award for Outstanding Service to Undergraduate Education
    at Stanford University
1974 Carnegie Mellon Faculty Award
1973 Howard Foundation Fellow
1963 Woodrow Wilson Fellow

Primary Literary Works

Arturo Islas: The Uncollected Works. Houston: Arte Público Press, 2003.
"Can There Be Chicano Fiction?" *Miquiztli* 3 (1975): 22–24.
Migrant Souls. New York: William Morrow and Company, Inc., 1990.
La Mollie and the King of Tears. Albuquerque: University of New Mexico Press,
    1996.
On the Bridge, at the Border: Migrants and Immigrants. Stanford: Stanford Center
    for Chicano Research, 1990.
The Rain God: a Desert Tale. Palo Alto: Alexandrian Press, 1984.
"Writing from a Dual Perspective." *Miquiztli* 2 (1974): 1–2.

Selected Secondary Sources

Aldama, Frederick Luis. *Arturo Islas: The Uncollected Works*. Houston: Arte
    Público Press, 2003.
———. *Dancing With Ghosts: A Critical Biography of Arturo Islas*. Berkeley:
    University of California Press, 2004.
Marquez, Antonio C. "The Historical Imagination in Arturo Islas's *The Rain God*
    and *Migrant Souls*," *Multi-Ethnic Literature of the United States* 19, no. 2 (1994):
    3–16.
Saldívar, José David. *The Dialectics of Our America: Genealogy, Cultural Critique,
    and Literary History*. Durham: Duke University Press, 1991.
Sánchez, Marta. "Arturo Islas's *The Rain God*: An Alternative Tradition,"
    American Literature 62, no. 2 (June, 1990): 284–304.
Sanchez, Rosaura. "Ideological Discourses in Arturo Islas's *The Rain God*," in
    Criticism in the Borderlands, ed. Héctor Calderón and José David Saldívar.
    (Durham: Duke University Press, 1991): 114–26.

Notes to Chapter Two

1. Frederick Luis Aldama, "Bending Chicano Identity and Experience in Arturo
   Islas's Early Borderland Short Stories," *Journal of American Studies of Turkey*
   12 (2000): 51–58.
2. Ibid.
3. Ibid.

4. Marta Sánchez, "Artuo Islas's *The Rain God*: An Alternative Tradition," *American Literature* 62, no. 2 (June, 1990): 295.

5. José David Saldívar, *The Dialectics of Our America: Genealogy, Cultural Critique, and Literary History* (Durham: Duke University Press, 1991), 111–12.

6. José David Saldívar, *The Dialectics of Our America*, 107.

7. Marta Sánchez, "Artuo Islas's *The Rain God*," 287.

8. For an account of the play of history in *The Rain God* and *Migrant Souls*, see Antonio C. Márquez, "The Historical Imaginations in Arturo Islas's *The Rain God* and *Migrant Souls*," *Multi-Ethnic Literature of the United States* 19, no. 2 (Summer 1994): 3–16.

9. Ibid., 5.

CHAPTER THREE

Erlinda Gonzáles-Berry
On the New Mexican Borderlands ~

⌒ The critical work of Erlinda Gonzáles-Berry makes her a pioneer in the field of Chicano and Chicana literary and cultural studies. Her scholarly discussions of Chicano sociolinguistics reverberate inside and outside the entire canon of Chicana and Chicano literature, probably regardless of what date of origin one assigns it—1519, 1848, or 1965. Her experiences at the University of New Mexico, as both an undergraduate and graduate student, take her through the constitution of the Chicano Movement on the UNM campus and result in her becoming an accomplished critical theorist, and with the publication of *Paletitas de guayaba* in 1991, a creative writer. Her discussion of the paths her career has taken demonstrates her ability to withstand some of the strongest reverberations of the sociocultural politics of the Chicano and post-Chicano epochs of social activism and literary production. Some of this fortitude can certainly be traced to her New Mexican childhood on the *llano*. The year she and her family lived in Guadalajara, Mexico, put her on a cross-cultural course that also contributed to her drive for further education, and, as she says in the interview, boosted her linguistic confidence in Spanish.

Paletitas de guayaba takes the year in Mexico as a source for her creative drive. This text is a marvel of postmodern narrative technique, weaving distinct narrative trajectories and multiple perspectives to tell a story of a young Chicana on her way to becoming a sociolinguist/academic and an artist. Issues of language, identity, and sexuality are made the motive forces for the novel's plot. The plot compresses in one slim volume the history of New Mexico and offers it for a critical reading through the grid of sociolinguistics. Marina, the protagonist, is from New Mexico, while Mexico teaches her she is a Chicana. The text in many ways also shows that Gonzáles-Berry constructs a sort of protofeminist in Marina. Gonzales-Berry began writing a dissertation in 1974 in Chicano/Chicana literature at the University of New Mexico, Department of Modern Languages, as the Department of Spanish and Portuguese did not yet exist in the College of Arts and Sciences. The decision to study Chicano and Chicana literature meant in practical terms that she had to virtually invent the field at the university. Her struggles to gain fair and equitable treatment throughout her program parallel those processes of self-discovery that Marina experiences in her struggle for liberation from oppressive gender roles present as much in Chicano/Mexican culture as in Anglo-Saxon. Elizabeth C. Martínez rightly argues that Gonzáles-Berry reaches for practices that deconstruct oppressive gender roles with the very instrument of power that oppresses her to begin with: "In Gonzáles-Berry's novel, the woman/subject takes control of the sexual act by describing sexual organs, sexual pleasure, and articulating sexual desire—all symbols of the artist's power and control over her craft. The principal character owns her subjectivity and the object learns from her observations and initiative. Not gender, but subject and object are the players in the sexual tryst. The author attempts a genderless consciousness, thus reaching a new consciousness for the artist."[1] The intimate connection between language and libido that Gonzáles-Berry establishes in *Paletitas* is done with great deconstructive humor. Tey Diana Rebolledo points out the effectiveness of this humor to deflate the transcendental phallus of orthodox pyschoanalysis.[2] These narrative triumphs of *Paletitas* have as their background the history of anger that Gonzáles-Berry recounts in the interview. The literary transformation that *Paletitas* represents means that this petit récit is a sort of cultural "reagent," dissolving anger with humor, practicing a creativity engaged in a struggle for liberation. The protofeminism that both Gonzáles-Berry and Marina practice takes place in the decades of the '60s and '70s, the heyday of the National Organization of Women, whose movement barely touches the lives of Chicanas and in fact does little to reach out to them—a theme that pervades Chicana feminism.

For this reason, Marina/Gonzáles-Berry has to invent her own liberation. On this issue, *Paletitas* has much in common with Ana Castillo's first novel, *The Mixquiahuala Letters*, and not only because they both employ the epistolary genre to represent their respective protagonists' emerging Chicana critical consciousness. Both protagonists, Marina and Teresa, respectively, travel to Guadalajara, Mexico, during roughly the same time period in terms of a chronotope. Clearly the texts of an emerging Chicana feminism have been looking at and laboring over a South-North chronotope, dialoguing with Mexico.[3]

Written in Spanish, *Paletitas* participates in a real alternative tradition of literary production in the United States. It forms part of a literary production that would include Estevan Arellano and Eusebio Chacón in New Mexico, Miguel Méndez in Arizona, Alejandro Morales in California and, of course, Rolando Hinojosa in Texas. This literary production probably holds the key to understanding the aesthetico-politico problem of producing writing in English that connotes Spanish, much in the way Arturo Islas discusses in chapter two. Gonzáles-Berry's critical and creative work, because it mines the field of sociolinguistics, also deserves to be placed in dialogue with such classics as Fernando Peñalosa's *Chicano Sociolinguistics* (1980) as well as recent work such as Otto Santa Ana's *Brown Tide Rising: Metaphors of Latinos in Contemporary American Public Discourse* (2002).

In 1997 Gonzáles-Berry left the University of New Mexico to chair the Department of Ethnic Studies at Oregon State University. At the time of the interview, she was the chair of the UNM Spanish and Portuguese Department.

DATE OF INTERVIEW: May 25, 1993
SETTING: Chair's office of the Spanish and Portuguese Department, University of New Mexico, Albuquerque, New Mexico

Culture, Conflict, Borders

H. T. Let's begin by talking about the region in northern New Mexico where you were born and raised. Can you tell us when and where you were born and why that time and place is important to you?

E. G. B. When we think of northern New Mexico I guess we tend to think of the heart of the north, you know, Santa Fe and north. I was actually born in northeastern New Mexico, which is very close to Texas and to Oklahoma so that will have a very important influence on cultural development there in terms of our own culture—how it will be tremendously influenced in both positive and negative ways. I was born in 1942 in northeastern New Mexico. My family had a ranch. My dad came from a ranching family. I was born in Roy and of course we came to town. My grandmother lived in town and she was a *curandera*, a *partera*, and so she assisted at my birth. I spent the first four years living out on the ranch. You know one can never really examine the historical context in which one was born. I was just happy to live in what I thought were ideal conditions. My memories of childhood on the ranch—it was paradise and my parents very often talked about it as paradise. That was when my family could produce their own livelihood, produce their own food. Eventually, we had to move to town and they always recalled that time with nostalgia; that was paradise for them. My mother used that very language. Moving to the small town of Roy I always viewed as a fall from grace, a real kind of purgatory. But I guess I was born at the height of World War II, 1942, right after Pearl Harbor. One's time doesn't really begin to become very important until the adolescent years, the teenage years, of course. Growing up in the '50s, learning to jitterbug in the '50s, music from that period was so important to us and made it a wonderful time to grow up. It was a time when life was on many levels simpler for us because of the kind of cultural isolation I had in the early years of my life. Life was simple. We didn't have to deal with a lot of the issues that children growing up in cities would have to deal with. We were very aware of the conflicts and the problems that arose when we were exposed to the dominant culture, but for the most part I lived within my own cultural milieu, and very was secure in my sense of self and identity and language because of this idyllic childhood. When I became aware of differences, there were conflicts.

H. T.   You speak about conflicts—I don't want to make too much of that but what kinds of conflicts were you aware of?

E. G. B. Well, we moved when I was about ten years old. My mother got a teaching job in a one-room schoolhouse out in a place called Rosebud and this was really out in the plains, the llano. The community was composed of ranching families, many large ranches, large landowners, and cattle ranchers. Many of them had come there from Texas, primarily from Texas. The world I grew up with then was *antimexicano*. We didn't have a word that was equivalent to that kind of racism. When we went to Rosebud we were the only mexicano family there. The rest were all Anglos. My mother was the teacher, which saved us in effect. She had a very important position, a kind of privileged position so that rubbed off on us. We were the center of that community through the school, but we were accepted there because of that privileged position of my mother. That place was sheer hell. I remember my sister and I as adolescents would go to these meetings at the 4-H Club and they would have dances and of course it was a very fundamentalist community, primarily Baptists, and you couldn't do any of what I considered dancing. They could only do round dances and square dances and no couple dancing. My sister and I would go with these other young kids from the ranching community and we would stand or sit against the wall and no one would ever, ever, ever ask us to dance. That's the only place in my childhood that I ever remember being called a dirty Mexican. If we ventured out of Rosebud where we had a place in the community, there was conflict there that created this whole sense of self-consciousness. That is part of my psyche that will be exacerbated later when I come to the university.

Mexico-mexicano: Crossings

H. T.   What comes after that period of time?

E. G. B. Well, as I look back at my life I have spent it crossing borders, many, many times over. First growing up on the ranch with family. At the age of eight we went to Mexico and lived there for a year. That was a tremendous shock and a tremendous crossing—crossing into a space that for me was just wonderful at that age because it's probably an optimal age for adapting to new cultures. I felt a part of it in terms of language but it was a new culture.

H. T.   What part of Mexico?

E. G. B. In Guadalajara. I wanted to stay there the rest of my life. I really liked it. I was able to adapt very, very readily to that environment and to the language there. That's when I became literate in Spanish, which I felt was going to become very important to me down the road. I went to an American school—Spanish in the morning, English in the afternoon, or vice versa. Children of well-to-do Mexicans went there because of the English school. I felt I was so bright. I was just sharp. I knew more than the teacher. In the Spanish portion, I was the dunce, but I learned some literacy skills. I learned to read and write in Spanish when I was eight years old, something that would never have happened had I not had that experience.

H. T.   So you think that event was crucial in your life and motivated the fact that you are now a university professor in Spanish.

E. G. B. [Living in Mexico] facilitated it for me because once I started studying Spanish formally, it just really came very easily for me. I didn't have to overcome a lot of the handicaps that some of our students who grow up speaking our dialect of Spanish have to overcome in order to mainstream their language, or in order to learn a more standard and formal variety, so that was very easy for me. It facilitated it. Although I'm not sure it motivated it and you know we can talk about that.

H. T.   What brought your family—or took your family—to Mexico?

E. G. B. My dad went to work. The U.S. government went to help Mexico help to stamp out their hoof-and-mouth disease that had attacked all the animals. Of course they wanted to protect the United States so they sent down armies of men—not a formal army—workers to vaccinate the cattle. The government came into the Southwest and they rounded up cowboys, mexicano cowboys, who knew Spanish and who had skills in ranching and they formed the core of the workers down there, the rank and file who went out into the communities and did the vaccinating. So that's how my dad got involved and for him it was a great experience, an adventure of a lifetime. He went off to an exotic land and was paid very well by Mexican standards, certainly for our class in Mexico. We got to Mexico and immediately we lived in a neighborhood in which we were forced to get a maid. Initially my mother said, "Maid? What the hell? I'm a maid." Given the total environment, we would have been totally ostracized. There was money to get a maid and so we had a maid, which was really interesting because in Mexican circles all the maids in the neighborhood would come knocking on our door wanting to work for us because ours was the best paid and in a sense the best treated because we didn't have those notions of class and hierarchies. We would invite the maid to eat with us at our table. Of course she never would. When we left we wanted to bring the maid to live with us because she had become family and she was more a nanny than a maid. I mean she became a surrogate mother.

H. T.   *¿Cuánto tiempo dúraron en México?*

E. G. B. *Estuvimos un año, mi papá estuvo dos años pero la familia solo un año.*

H. T.   Yeah?

E. G. B. It was one of the highlights of my life because the novel *Paletitas de guayaba* eventually started with that experience. I wanted to recall that experience and then it grew into something else so that part of the novel is autobiographical—the year I spent in Mexico as a child. I've always felt very special, very blessed to have had that experience. Coming back into the old cultural milieu with family, familia, *'buelitos*, my relationship with them was totally enhanced because I spoke Spanish before, no doubt, but I came back from Mexico speaking a very sophisticated Spanish, which gave me a real "in" with the grandparents. They're saying, "Oh my gosh, this child is so developed." I started to be treated like an adult by my own family and by my grandparents and that was also a kind of privileging that was important. So then that was a comfortable experience, but shortly thereafter we went out to Rosebud, crossing completely into the dominant culture when I was about ten years old, spending four years there. From there I went to a boarding school in El Rito, the heart of the north. In El Rito, the boarding school that I went to was 99.9 percent Chicano kids, although we didn't call ourselves that then, but mexicanos. I was back in a kind of cultural womb of sorts. It was very protective.

H. T.   What was that experience like?

E. G. B. It was wonderful. The school used to be a normal training school until Highlands took over that role. El Rito was founded in 1911 as a teacher training school for Spanish Americans. It was called the Spanish American Normal—for Spanish American teachers to train to go out into the little villages to teach the children.

H. T.   At that time, did you have a sense that you wanted to devote your life to teaching?

E. G. B. Well, my mother was a teacher, so I had a built-in role model. I always admired her not only as a mother, but also as a woman in the public sphere and as a teacher. And then I got to high school and teachers took a tremendous interest in me. I had wonderful teachers. At one time I toyed around with the idea that I would do medical technology because I loved science. Nevermind a doctor. I mean that was not within the realm of imagination, but medical technology was. I'd be a lab worker. When I came to UNM and found out I was not prepared to do science courses, there was no way I could do it. I couldn't even pass a math class here, which had to do with the kind of education that we got. So after that, it would be teaching. The question was what area and what field. So that was crossing another border, spending time in this kind of secure cultural space then from there coming to the big university, to UNM—another crossing of borders and another tremendous cultural shock. So my growing up was kind of conditioned by these crossings into foreign spaces, crossing back into secure spaces, and back out into foreign spaces. I think that really molds one's psyche. When I left El Rito I was a scholarship girl. I was valedictorian of my class. I was poised to go out there and conquer the world. I had felt so good about myself. I thought I was the brightest thing that had ever happened and I came to UNM and went to work. After the first semester, I started to develop a social life, to develop a space for myself. I ended up doing what a lot of Chicano students did at the university—the handful of us that were here—sitting in the back of the class, feeling totally stigmatized, feeling totally inferior and not very intelligent.

H. T.   Do you have any idea what the percentage of enrollment was back then when you came to UNM—just a rough idea?

E. G. B.   We were like Afro-American students are on campus right now, just a handful of us. Maybe 5 percent. Maybe. That's in the sixties, early sixties. I've never figured it out, but we were visible and we hung together. There were no Hispanic Student Services. There was no place for us here. The rallying point or space for us was the Newman Center because we were basically Catholics.

Spanish and English: Familiar Performances

H. T.   I'm still curious about your homelife, the religious background, and the linguistic environment that you grew up in. I know you mentioned already that you felt very secure except for the outer edges in which you encountered some conflicts. Say a little bit more about your linguistic and religious homelife.

E. G. B.   I was just in Juárez last week and some woman came up to me and asked me, "Where are you from?" And I said, "From New Mexico." She said, "Really?" and I said, "Yes." She said, "But your parents must have spoken only Spanish in the home" and I said, "You know, I don't really remember or know." My mother became a teacher when she was seventeen years old and she claimed always that she taught us both languages as children and that she made every effort to teach us English in the home, so I assume that by the time I got to school I was probably bilingual. My abuelitos didn't speak any English so I know that Spanish was used a great deal around the extended family. My father had a high school education, my mother a college degree, and they were quite bilingual—literate in English, more so than in Spanish. At home together Spanish was always their language. It was their language of intimacy. And even as we grew older and began to bring more and more English into the home and English really began to establish itself as more important in the home, my parents' intimate language has been always Spanish, but they never made it one of those situations where it was their language but not ours. It was their language and ours anytime we wanted it to be.

H. T. Do you think that the fact that there wasn't this kind of antagonism of linguistic codes was unique with your family? Witness, for instance, the case of Richard Rodriguez, who talks of English and Spanish antagonistic codes.

E. G. B. I'll tell you what did happen to me after the Rosebud experience where we were away from extended family. We were exposed only to Anglos. I started to squelch Spanish with my peers. I began to feel it. When I went to El Rito where a lot of those kids were Spanish dominant, their English was very marked, although the city kids were pretty bilingual. Those kids we would call the *serreños*—from little villages—their English was incredibly marked and they were dominant in Spanish and struggled with English. So in that setting Spanish was very much a part of the social life amongst us teenagers, but I remember speaking it very little. I understood it perfectly, but I remember generally speaking English. Recently I ran into friends from high school and they were really amazed at how much Spanish I speak now. They said, "You know, back in high school we were never sure." Plus I didn't speak accented English—well, I do. My English is still marked, but in comparison, my English was pretty slick because I'd grown up around Anglos. But they said, "We were never really sure that you spoke it." So I guess that I was not that comfortable with Spanish or among peers for whom English was dominant.

H. T. Do you now or did you then feel a special kinship toward either language?

E. G. B. For me, generation and place really makes a difference. If I'm

rote memorization. I was great at that, but then I started taking literature classes, culture classes, and whoa!

H. T.   Something clicked?

E. G. B. I had been cheating myself. It was like discovering the world all over again. At that point, I thought, "Okay, I'll do a Master's." In the meantime I had had a baby, but since my husband was working, we decided I would take another year or two to come to school and do a Master's. That's when it was really tremendous. After the first year in the MA, everyone had assistantships. I didn't even know what they were but I applied for one, but didn't get it. I went to the chair and said, "I want to know why I didn't get an assistantship. I have about a 3.9. I've got very good grades. I look around and I'm doing as well as anyone in this department who got assistantships. Can you tell me why?" He goes, "Well, I don't know, everything's in order and blah, blah, blah." I then went to a professor that I just had a class with. I was doing A-plus work in his literature class and I said, "I've come to ask for your help. I applied for an assistantship and didn't get one and I don't know what to do. I'm not usually the kind of person that asks for favors but maybe you could enlighten me about how I can get one." I was one of two Chicanos in the entire graduate program. Sometime later, the next year, I was waiting to get advisement. They gave me my folder and said, "Stand in line and see Professor Cobos." I stood there and thought, "It's my folder; they gave it to me. I'll read it." I knew this was confidential and I wasn't supposed to read it but I opened it up anyway. There was a note from that one professor to the chair, saying this young woman, Mrs. Berry deserves—I was Mrs. Berry then—deserves an assistantship. She's an excellent student. Despite the fact that she's a New Mexican, her language is excellent, her Spanish is excellent. It became very clear to me why I didn't get the assistantship in the first place. So I got an assistantship. At the end of the MA, they sent this note around that said, "If you want to be considered for an assistantship for the PhD, fill this out." I looked at that and I thought, "PhD! Wow! A doctor? No way!" It wasn't even in my realm of possibilities. I went home and said to my husband, "What do you think?" I wasn't sure that this husband was going to put up with me going to school anymore when I had a kid and he was home taking care of the kid a lot of the times while I was studying. I said, "What do you think? I can't do a PhD, can I? I'm not really smart enough to be doing a PhD. I don't have what it takes." He just looked at me like I was crazy and said, "If you want to do it, do it. You're probably much smarter than those around you. All it takes is for you to get in there, figure out how the system works, and do it. Do it." I thought, "What a different attitude." How come I didn't grow up just thinking, "You want to do it, so do it"? Instead I grew up thinking, "Oh my god, I'd like to do it, but I can't and that's that. That's been the story of my life. I'd really like to do that, but I'm not capable." So I applied, signed the form, and a few weeks later, they let us know. My letter said, "Dear Mrs. Berry, we are sorry to inform you that you have not been guaranteed your TA for next year. You will have to apply along with all the new candidates." In the meantime all my peers had been moved on to the PhD with a teaching assistantship. Some of them quite frankly couldn't even speak the language very well. I thought, "This is really unfair. What is going on here?" The beginnings of Chicano stuff, a word I had heard and read a little bit about. I went to two professors in the department and said, "You're Chicano professors, aren't you?" and they said, "Yes, yes," and I said, "Well, let me tell you what just happened to me. What are you going to do about it? I'm the only Chicana left in this department; the other one dropped out of the MA program. What are you going to do for me?" They went to bat for me and I got into the PhD program.

H. T.   Is there a layer of antimexicano sentiment in our society that, while sometimes hard to pinpoint, to identify, somehow is always at work against the Chicana and the Chicano?

E. G. B.   It certainly was true for me. Sometimes we don't see it and don't understand what's going on. What's interesting is that I had started to see it. But I think it had to do with everything that was going on, which gave me the framework within which to analyze my own personal experience. After that I started to be aware of it. Before that we grew up in a time when we didn't understand those things and we internalized it all—"Oh gosh, it must be our fault. Oh gosh, we must have a propensity for being drunks. Oh gosh, we must have a propensity for being stupid"—never understanding that experience in the larger picture. It took for me the Chicano Movement and the whole re-education to understand that. At the time I didn't. Later on, a friend of mine, who had been a student with me but then graduated, came back for a visiting stint here as a professor, but his allegiances were still down with the ranks. He had been at that meeting where they considered my case and he told me what one of the erstwhile professors of mine who is still around had said: "Well Mrs. Berry is married, she has a child, she has already taught in high school. The best thing for her is to go back and teach in high school for the rest of her life. She's got an MA now; she can go back and make a wonderful high school teacher and take care of her kid." That's when I first became aware of the other stigma.

H. T. So you got into the PhD program and here you are, the chair of the department now. What's that like?

E. G. B. Well, I'm not a humble person, and sometimes I really like to rub people's noses in it. I consider myself very lucky on some levels. I also feel I've fought hard to get where I am and it hasn't been easy. During the first years of teaching in the job, I was not politicized—not until I started the PhD. I just did everything. I was a good girl. I did everything by the books and I wanted everyone to love me. And I knew that if I did my job right and everyone loved me that I would have an okay career. At some point I couldn't do that anymore. I really started to push issues and to push for Chicano and Chicana students. But once I did that, life really became difficult. Down the road what I saw was attacks, some veiled and personal, but others were out-and-out open attacks—attacks against me and Diana as Chicana feminists. "The raving Chicana feminists are sending this department to hell." There's a memo in my files that says exactly that. "The Spanish Department is being destroyed by the triumvirate of Chicana feminists. They're taking control." Diana did a presentation at the MLA in which she talked about this and how the institution really militates against our progress. She told all these stories and she ended it by saying, "Now my colleague is chair of the department." She said there was a standing ovation. I wasn't at this session.

H. T.   Wonderful.

E. G. B.   As I became politicized, I came through a very angry period. I was a very, very, angry person and I fought out of anger and sometimes hate. The one thing that this position gives me is I don't need to be angry anymore and I can be much more rational and I can get things done without being violent about it in my language and in my approach to people, and that's a good feeling. I haven't given up on my worldview and what needs to be done, but I can do it differently because I'm in this position. But when I think back, I'm surprised my husband survived me through the angry years because that's been a strain on a cross-cultural marriage and I have been a very, very, very angry person. My novel is a very angry novel. People have said that about it but I think justifiably so.

Trail-blazing America

H. T.   Let's talk a little bit about your scholarly work beginning with your dissertation.

E. G. B.   I did my dissertation on Chicano literature. It was one of the very early ones. I started in '74 and didn't finish it until '78. I was going to work on male Mexican writers. I had a very male-oriented graduate education. I even internalized a great deal of the sexism in my education because I didn't think there were any women that were worth reading, that were worth belonging to the canon. I just adored male writers. Octavio Paz, I loved him. Carlos Fuentes, the big Boom writers. I had decided I was going to do my dissertation on La Nueva Onda, mexicano writers. I loved them, too. And then my director said to me in '73, "There's some real stuff going on out there." I started to teach *la mujer Chicana* here quite by accident.

H. T.   Who directed your dissertation?

E. G. B.   Tamara Holzapfel. She said, "There's something happening and it's really going to impact the profession. You know what you need to do. You need to write your dissertation on Chicano literature, those writers who write in Spanish. That's what's going to get you a job." She was a good literature professor but she didn't know anything about Chicano literature. I didn't know anything about Chicano literature. No one knew anything about Chicano literature. There weren't any classes. So I did it all on my own and she stood behind me.

H. T.   Beginning in '74.

E. G. B.   And she directed it and I educated myself. I started out by reading Rudy Acuña. I was never the same. *Occupied America* changed me. It was like going to college all over again. I had to read the sociology, the history, the political science. I had to get this broad grounding before I could even begin to understand the writing and then look at it as literature. So I went off. My first job was at a Quaker college in Richmond, Indiana.

H. T.   Let me backtrack a little bit to the point you're making about having to get this broad base in order to study and understand Chicano literature. Do you think that's a point that the institution, the university institution, rarely understands?

E. G. B.   Yes, and I think it handicaps those of us who had to do that. Imagine I had stayed in my field where I was grounded—Latin American literature. The years I spent re-educating myself, I could have been doing theory and moving at a much more rapid rate. I had to backtrack and do the PhD all over again on my own just to get the grounding to then begin to do the work. It was a setback for those of us who wanted to work in that period.

H. T.   You had to start somewhere.

E. G. B.   We had to start and it took me four years to do the PhD dissertation because I was teaching and reading and reading and reading and trying to educate myself and scared to death because I knew I couldn't do it. I knew I could never do the last obstacle, the dissertation. Tamara Holzapfel was great and she really did mentor me and help me through and finally

I wrote it. But after that I was in a marginalized field. Finally, a couple of years later, I ended up in this department teaching undergraduate courses and always being made to feel that what I did was not valid, that what I did had no place in this department. A lot of people were resenting the fact that the Southwest component of this department had been built at the expense of the real program and the real program suffered because we made bad hires and we put our eggs in the wrong baskets. If it hadn't been for Diana Rebolledo coming into this department I would have never made it.

H. T. You had a friend and an ally. So your first job was where?

E. G. B. At Earlham College, a small Quaker, liberal arts college in the Midwest. It was truly a wonderful experience. I left New Mexico. I had left before, but that was before. I was leaving now after a Chicano birth. Before it didn't matter if you left because wherever you went you assumed you had to assimilate. But I now had a different mindset. I went there and I was out of occupied territory and leaving the occupied territory allowed me to decolonize my own mind. I was treated very well. None of the assumptions were made about me—in fact I was a very special person there and was considered a resource. I taught Chicano literature to these students who didn't even know what the hell a Chicano was but were just fascinated by the literature. It helped me to grow, my teaching, my knowledge of self because they were so interested and made me feel that I was giving them something that they could never have access to if it weren't for me. So I spent four years there after having gone on a one-year visiting appointment. The market was bad that year.

H. T. Do you remember the year?

E. G. B. 1973. Those were gloomy times for our profession. I remember some of my friends that I went to school with couldn't even get an interview. I was asked to go to Irvine for an interview and Earlham. Do you know that I was so scared to go to Irvine that I didn't go to the interview because I still did not have the sense of self and the confidence that would have gotten me through a big school like that? I called them and I said, "I'm not going

to accept your job and so I'm not going to waste your money."
I didn't even go to the interview. Alejandro Morales got hired
that year for what maybe could have been my position. I don't
know. Anyway, I went to Earlham, a small college where I felt
comfortable. I needed to be in an environment that nourished
me. I needed that desperately. Earlham nourished me. It was a
good place for family. It really promoted the notion of family
so it was a good place to bring up a child. I thrived there. I went
for one year at first, then they renewed me the second year,
then the third year. The end of the third year things started to
get really tight. They were going through a recession. We were
all going through a recession. They were having problems and
they started to panic about how they were going to fit me in.
They tried to get one of the older fellows—who had come to
UNM to get his degree here and was instrumental in taking
me there—to retire earlier or move him out into administration
so I could get the slot and I said, "No way." I wouldn't hear of
it and wouldn't displace him because he had been very good
to me. The end of the third year there they gave me money
to come here to write my dissertation. When I came here, I
locked myself up and I wrote it that summer. I went back and
started looking for a job just in case. At that point they told
me, "We are going to make a decision at the end of this year.
We are going to do everything we can to create a tenure-track
position for you." I knew that meant displacing this man so I
went out on the job market and I remember I had an on-site
interview at Middlebury, which for language teachers was it. I
didn't get the job. I hadn't finished the dissertation. I applied at
New Mexico State because I had realized at that point if I got a
tenure-track position there I would never go home again and
I couldn't face life with that thought. I could not live with the
thought of not coming back to my place. My roots. So I applied
at New Mexico State. I got the job at State and I came there
thinking, "I'm home." Las Cruces was going to be home. I was
willing to stay there the rest of my life. I taught there for a year,
but then a position opened up here and I got it. I walked in
through the back door. It was a kind of second-class position.

The position was to direct the native track. The person who had held the position never had a PhD and had always been an instructor. They decided to convert it into a tenure-track position with a PhD. They all had their favorite candidates and there were some internal candidates that they were trying to work in. In the process I got the job because the vote was so split. So I always say I came in the back door. I came to UNM to take my position in '79, knowing of the dangerous, really dangerous waters. I was now going to be a colleague to my ex-professors and Earlham had really strengthened me. With all my readings and my work in the field of Chicano studies, I would never be a lackey to anyone again.

H. T.   So what kind of scholarly projects are you involved in or have you been involved in for the last ten years?

E. G. B.   What I've worked on primarily is Chicano narrative. I prefer working there. I've never done any major projects. I like doing textual analysis and I like working on small projects, getting a good article out on a specific text. If you look at my record, you will see a lot of scattered articles on specific works and that's the way I work. I've done a little bit on language also—more broadly defined sociolinguistics—but mostly on Chicano literature. I don't work real well in broad areas; they scare me to death probably because one is creating a canon and that's a dangerous thing to undertake. I've always felt more comfortable with the close textual analysis, probably reflecting my own training in New Criticism.

H. T.   I think we've all been trained as New Critics.

Tradition and Canon in New Mexico

E. G. B.   I'm still trying to play catch-up in terms of theory, doing as much reading in that field as I can. I've been recently influenced by the work on postcolonial studies. I just recently finished a paper in which I look at a nineteenth century text—a short novella written in the nineteenth century by a New Mexican. The first time I read it I thought, "Where was this man in the late nineteenth century?"

H. T. What's the name of the text and the writer?

E. G. B. His name is Eusebio Chacón and the text is called *Detrás de la Tormenta, la Calma*. It appears to be a little narrative based on the honor code. You know, the love triangle.

H. T. I heard your talk on that. It was very interesting.

E. G. B. The postcolonial work that's being done on Latin America and the formation of nationhood gave me a new opening into that. I'm still working on that. It takes me a long time to get it out. I don't crank out the stuff. I'm really becoming interested in the whole nineteenth century and especially how Nuevo Méxicanos had to begin to construct their own identity and how they were positioning themselves vis-à-vis this loss of identity. It was a very precarious position—how they were handling the discourses they were creating to position themselves and maintain a foothold in order to create a strong sense of identity.

H. T. Discourses of resistance?

E. G. B. Resistance and survival. There's a lot of resistance, but also some accommodation going on to survive. But what was important to these writers was to preserve a sense of cultural identity. There were so many new things happening around them and they were taking what was coming in and reissuing it to construct their identity. I don't think we've worked on that positionality enough. We've always talked a lot about resistance, but I'm real interested in the transculturation of that position—how they take it and rework it to create something new, this sense of identity, which is what makes the history of New Mexico and the development of us as Chicanos here a little bit different.

H. T. As you know, Ramón Saldívar talks a lot about the corrido as an oral form and the corrido as a form of resistance. Of course you know he invests a lot of theoretical weight in that notion. What do you think was going on in New Mexico with respect to art forms being forms of resistance?

E. G. B. Sure, the oral genres were there and were important but they don't seem to have progressed as much as the tremendous amount of written production in the nineteenth century. We don't have a terribly rich corrido tradition here, although there is some evidence of corridos. The oral traditions almost stay stagnant. Eusebio Chacón wrote two novellas in '93. I have the manuscript from '83 or '86 that Arellano found, and he has loaned me the manuscript. It's probably the first novel written—a New Mexico pastoral novel that has never been published. We've got to get that out. These were people who were educated and who were making the transition, being influenced by the American presence and the fact that there were presses and also by Mexican and Latin American traditions. So they were taking all of that and they were out there—they were writing.

H. T.   In Spanish?

E. G. B. In Spanish and they were making the move from the oral genres into the written in a very self-conscious but veiled way. That's the point. We haven't read those texts correctly. When I started redoing the reading of these texts I was shocked, amazed, and flabbergasted at what I was reading because in my first readings I was just seeing it as kind of a gratuitous writing. I had done a paper on Eusebio Chacón in my book *Pasó Por Aquí*. Someone who had studied him before me had said something like, "Well, this was just kind of cute, occasional poetry." I don't think that's true. Now I think we need to see that text in terms of the transculturation and construction of identity.

H. T.   Is there a closeness between the Spanish you see in those manuscripts—those texts—and the Spanish that survives in New Mexico today?

E. G. B. These men were—and it was mainly men; we have yet to find if there were women writing, though Diana is busy on that—very conscious about trying to write very standard, polished Spanish. They were studying at Colegio de San Miguel. They were obviously studying Spanish literature. Their allusions to *Don Quixote* are there. Many of them were being educated at Notre Dame, in St. Louis, and some of them in Mexico. They were quite consciously trying to develop a formal register of Spanish in their writing. Sometimes the local dialect seeps through and there are what one would call errors. I asked one of my colleagues to read this one text because he's done work on the *comedia del siglo de oro*. I wanted him to give me his reactions to it, mainly to look for the traces to the Spanish tradition, allusions I wasn't seeing and he started correcting all the errors.

H. T.   Right. So-called errors.

E. G. B.   Some of them we might have to say were truly errors because they were trying to write in formal style.

H. T.   Was there hypercorrection?

E. G. B.   Yes, there's an incredible amount of hypercorrection. Every now and then you get dialect forms that would just seep through.

H. T.   That's phenomenal. What kinds of distinctive features of New Mexican Spanish do you see? What identifies New Mexican Spanish for you?

E. G. B.   For so long people have said that New Mexican Spanish is identified exclusively by its archaic forms, that it's an archaic dialect. And it certainly is still part of the colonial dialect and that's true, but on the other hand we've never really explored the extent to which it's really just part of the greater northern Mexican dialect and the links to Chihuahua. There was a great deal of trade and interaction. Gabriel Meléndez was telling me that one of the newspapermen that he was studying here had gone to Chihuahua and spent a year there working on newspapers. So there was an intellectual exchange also. After New Mexico becomes a state, I think that is what characterizes it. The people here that were immigrants downplayed it and tried to fit into the Spanish fantasy heritage so that they would not be marked and stigmatized. I've had occasion to talk to people and I've said, "My grandfather was from Mexico," and they'll go, "Oh really! My God, I never knew that!" It's like this great revelation because they downplayed it as they tried to blend in and then it was a frozen dialect. So that would be what characterizes it.

H. T.   What do you think fosters the maintenance of Spanish nowadays in New Mexico?

E. G. B. Well, it's this incredible sense that New Mexicans have of being a people, a distinct people and a place, a sense of place. And the truth is, Hector, perhaps I'm agreeing more and more with Eduardo Hernández-Chávez that there's less maintenance going on than we all claim there is, especially if we look at the very young generation. However, the people themselves refuse to admit that they're losing it and insist that they see Spanish as part of their identity. I was doing some work and I looked at the census and it was something like maybe eighty to 85 percent of those who identified themselves as Hispanic also identified themselves as bilingual or as having some control over Spanish because Spanish was used in the home. Those figures can't be, but what it tells me is that if people can say *órale, ése,* they consider themselves Spanish-speaking because Spanish is so locked in with identity here. Historically, the writings in the nineteenth century also made that an issue: "We've got to learn English, but we cannot give up Spanish." The struggle was always so tremendous to maintain it, but what our people did wrong was they simply did not protect themselves legally. I don't understand how that happened, given the fact that we had such a foothold in the political arena, that we had so much participation in the political arena, that we did not protect our language rights more than we did, even if the protections are minimal in the state constitution. What it tells me is that the people here never believed that they could lose it. They just could not imagine themselves without it.

H. T. Good point.

E. G. B. And as long as they couldn't imagine that, they didn't build in the protections.

H. T. So do you tend to think that there is a danger of losing Spanish?

E. G. B. Oh, yeah, unless there is a lot of political language engineering.

H. T. What about the role of writers like yourself who are writing in Spanish?

E. G. B. Estevan Arellano just won the prize in Mexico. He won a five-thousand-dollar prize. Estevan Arellano is from northern New Mexico. He wrote a novel in this local Spanish about ten years ago. It's a very sophisticated handling of dialect. He sat on this manuscript for years until Gustavo Saenz saw it and said, "This has got to be published; this is so tremendous in terms of language." Gustavo finally got it published for him in Mexico this year. It just came out. In the meantime he sends it to a *concurso* that is held in Juárez every year and sponsored by the Universidad Autonóma. They give a prize for the best Mexican work in one year and the best Chicano work the next. The work has to be in Spanish. Estevan won the prize, which is so important, because as a New Mexican writer, he has written in our language in an exceedingly sophisticated way. It's in a totally authentic way that he's done it and he won the prize and I am so happy.

H. T. What's the title of the work?

E. G. B. *Inocencio* and then it has *el que no escarda pero siempre se comen mejor elote*. It's a riot and it just won *refran* after the other. It's language in its broadest sense, the entire cultural baggage of the languages. It's so fantastic.

H. T. So New Mexican writers are really taking part in the maintenance of Spanish.

E. G. B. Who's going to read this stuff, though? The professors?

H. T. Those are good questions.

E. G. B. We legitimate that language and that's important. We say, this is our language and it can be used for our writing and our literature. Ulibarrí started this a long time ago in 1964.

H. T. He writes in Spanish, too.

E. G. B. But I don't know who else is going to keep doing it after my generation. The young people? That's a part of our role here in this department.

The Creative Drive: Crossing Genres

H. T. Let's talk a little bit about your novel *Paletitas de guayaba*. I'm curious about how the narrative design was born and how long it took to write it.

E. G. B. Gustavo Saenz was here in the department doing a writing class and everybody was taking this class and everybody was writing, and about every other week, they would have an open forum and everyone would come and read from their works. It was this disease that had afflicted our department and everyone was catching it from these creative writers and everyone else was starting to write. So one day I sat down and I wrote the first twenty pages, which were the part about the train ride going back to Mexico because I had always sensed something there. So I wrote about that, and I thought, "Well, this is something that will appeal to him since he's a great Mexican writer." I gave him those twenty pages and he said, "Whoa, write! Keep doing it." So he really encouraged me.

H. T.   This was around . . . ?

E. G. B. I think it must have been in '84 or '85. I wrote it in that one academic year. I was very excited about writing it. I'd sit in fits and starts and then all these things that were really weighing heavy on my mind about my political rabidness, all that started to come through. These were issues that I was going crazy over—going back and forth to Mexico now as an academic and the culture shock that we suffer in the crossing. The battles that I was having in academia all began to find their way into that text until I finished it. I got tired of it in the first-person voice. I had never written creative literature before. So first-person voice got real tedious and so I tied it up at the end and put it away. I just let it sit there. In the meantime Diana came to UNM and at first we were kind of standoffish when we would talk to each other. Then one day I gave her the manuscript and I think she put it aside. I just sat there waiting and waiting for some feedback and finally I asked, "Have you had a chance to read it?" And she said, "Oh, you know, I've been so busy," and that tells you a lot. If someone isn't excited about reading your work, the person who wrote it really interprets it as, "Well, this must not be important." One night, she called me and said, "Erlinda, I have been reading your work. It is the funniest thing I have ever read." With that she really encouraged me. I hadn't finished it yet so at that point I had some verification of what I had done. So then I started sending it out and getting devastating rejection letters: "too political, too much political harangue, sounds like a Chicano Studies 101, do this, do that," and so I put it away and every now and then I would do public readings and the response was so fantastic that I'd say, "Well, what's wrong?" Then finally a couple of years ago Diana said, "Let's get it out." At that point I had totally lost interest. I didn't care about it, but she pushed me so we did it.

H. T.   There was a review of the novel in *The Albuquerque Journal* that was completely unfavorable.

E. G. B.   Yes.

H. T.   Can you talk about that?

E. G. B.   God, I remember the first review. Teresa Márquez was very involved in this. She was part of El Norte and has her connections, so she worked up *The Journal* people to review it. Diana and Teresa sent them photos. They were so excited because we were going to get full-page coverage. The woman in charge at *The Journal* called Teresa two days before and said, "The review is in and it is really bad." Teresa called Diana and Diana said, "Don't run it" and the woman in charge said, "It's too late." I was really angry at her for running that review because it was a really naïve review. They had turned it over to someone who didn't have the baggage necessary to read it. Some people will say, "Well, if it's universal and good, anybody can read it." I don't think that's necessarily accurate because she really could not understand a feminist way of looking at the world. She couldn't understand any of the things that I was saying. She said that I code-switched to prove that I was bilingual. I mean right offhand that just tells you something about the naiveté of the reviewer.

H. T.   But isn't that typical in a certain sense of the state of Chicana and Chicano literature in search of a wide readership that can understand the aesthetics of a Chicana or a Chicano text?

E. G. B.   Yes, but what killed me about this review is that it was my hometown review and many of the people that I know will never read that text. The only thing that they can do is take this woman's word. That's what was bad, but I think you're right. Then I get responses from Chicanos and Chicanas, especially critics like Angie Chabram who called me in December from UC–Davis and said, "Hello, this is Angie Chabram, I want you to know I just read your novel. We're using it in my Chicano literature class. I've got to get you out here to Davis. Will you come?" She interviewed me for three hours. Her students all showed up. Some of the Chicano students drove to the airport to meet me. They wanted to meet me personally and pick my brain apart and get to know me because this novel just spoke to them. It was incredible.

H. T. That's validating.

E. G. B. It was so validating and meant so much. Those students would say, "What did you mean on page so and so when you said this?" I did a reading and a talk and we had so much fun. Afterward one young woman—a very shy, reserved mexicanita—asked me a question: "Would you talk a little bit about religion? In order for us to free ourselves, do we have to do that to religion? Are there no other ways out of this conundrum? Do we just have to go for the juggler?" So I said, "Well, this is very difficult because of where we come from and because of what religion means to us as a people, to us, our parents. In my case I can only tell you what I had to do and that is go for the juggler because I to this day have not gotten over my resentment over what I believe the people in charge of the Catholic Church did to me as a human being. That's how I have to deal with it." Afterward she came to me and talked to me privately and said, "When I read your work I could not believe it because of where I stand with my parents and religion. I could never take it on like that. Afterward, when I started writing, I felt as if I were completing your text. I'm writing where you left off and I'm dealing with such issues." So who knows what this young woman was doing with it. I'm starting to get some very positive feedback from Chicanos and Chicanas, especially critics and teachers who are using it in their classes. On the other hand, a lot of my Chicano writer friends have never said one word, either way.

H. T. That's a mystery.

E. G. B. I know they've read it, but it's as if that text does not exist. One writer in Texas whom I admire very much and with whom I've always had a very good relationship, I sent him the copy right off and he wrote back and said, "I read the first part and I'm just really excited about this." That's the last word I ever heard from him. I saw him since then and he never said a word.

H. T.   What do you think is going on?

E. G. B.   Well, on the one hand, some of the really polished writers believe that there's no place in literature for political harangue. I respect that. On the other hand, a few Chicano males have said to me, "God, this is so funny." The people who can't see the humor are the ones who can't stand this literary text because if you take it real seriously, which it is, there are some real vicious attacks. But if you understand the irony, the narrative voice constantly undermines her own position of authority. It makes it a little bit easier to understand, don't you think?

H. T.   Yeah, oh yeah.

E. G. B.   If it weren't for that, there would be no saving grace to that book.

H. T.   I've found that I've had to read the text three times to really appreciate it and for me that's a good sign. That's not a bad sign. Every good text . . .

E. G. B.   . . . merits another reading.

H. T.   At least another reading. I've had to read it three times to begin to see the narrative techniques that are at work in the text and I for one will be using it in a seminar in the English Department as well putting it as part of the reading list for those students who can read in Spanish because I think it's an important work, especially for the fact that it's in Spanish and for the question we've already raised somewhat about the role of the writer in the maintenance of a literary Spanish. Can you say a little bit about your decision to write in Spanish?

E. G. B.   I hate that question more than any other question I get asked.

H. T.   But it's an important sociolinguistic question, don't you think?

E. G. B.   Training—my experience with literature is not in English; it's in Spanish. You know I don't have a comp lit degree. My exposure to American literature was minimal. I'm sorry to say that, ashamed to say that. I don't have enough time to read everything that I need to read in just North American literature. My experience with literature is in Spanish so I've tried very self-consciously to make it a part of that literary tradition—allusions to Latin American writers are in there that I was very self-consciously working at. There may also be a mask there. Spanish may be a persona, so that I'm talking about things that I don't want some people to ever know about me or know—people who can't read Spanish—sometimes I wonder about that. What I know about narration I've learned in Spanish. It's important for a Chicana to tackle it and to be able to say, "Hey, I can handle this language; it's mine, too." I guess I wanted to do that. I'm very aware of the fact that it limits the readership. My older sister went to one of my public readings and when it was over she said, "Wow, I really enjoyed it, I really understood it." Of course she called me up and asked me to give her a dictionary so she could read it. And I like to do oral readings for Chicanos because they can really pick it up, no problem.

H. T.   Maybe that's the role of the New Mexican writer in the maintenance of Spanish.

E. G. B. That's a really good point. Because when I read for public audiences, even just raza, they really get into it. But the reading's too much. It's like my mother. I took her a copy of *Y no se lo tragó la tierra*. I thought, "Easy, right?" But she just looked at it. Then one day I was over visiting and I said, "Would you all like me to read to you?" So I started reading Rivera. God, they loved it! But she had not read it; it was too challenging.

H. T.   The oral aspect is different?

E. G. B. The oral, they get into it, yeah and we grew up in a storytelling environment. We are storytellers. I told my first story when I was four years old. My mother was called to the Catholic school to substitute because one of the nuns was ill and she didn't have anyone to leave me with so she took me along and I guess I was getting a little unruly and she said, "Okay, would you like to tell the class the story of the three bears?" and I

CHAPTER FOUR

Gloria Anzaldúa
The Author Never Existed ⌐

⌐ May 15, 2004, saw the passing of Gloria Anzaldúa, still at her scene of writing, working on a manuscript. Students and scholars who were affected by her work know the loss her death represents. In the postmodern condition Anzaldúa saw an opportunity to pen a body of work that would critique the hegemony of American empire, contesting its elision of a Mexican contribution to the formation of the American nation, challenging the exclusionary practices of the Anglo-American academy, foregrounding the politics of the social act of writing. *This Bridge Called My Back: Writings by Radical Women of Color* (1981), which she coedited with Cherríe Moraga, contains contributions from Anzaldúa that anticipate the generic play that will generate her literary masterpiece *Borderlands/La Frontera: The New Mestiza* (1987). Similarly, Anzaldúa edited and contributed to both *Making Face, Making Soul/Haciendo Caras: Creative and Critical Perspectives by Feminists of Color* (1990) and *This Bridge We Call Home: Radical Visions for Transformation* (2002). Through these acts of writing, Anzaldúa addresses Anglo and Mexican America at practically all levels of discourse and domains of practice: for example, the blindness of white feminism vis-à-vis women of color in the United States, the systematic exclusion of Chicana writers from the literary canon of Chicano and American literature, and the racism and homophobia at work in both Anglo and Latino cultures. Keenly aware of the demise of epistemological foundations for the logic of identity, Anzaldúa seizes the postmodern day when she decides to write in the genre of autobiography. As the interview here shows, she will not use the genre without transforming it for her own aesthetic and political ends.[1]

In autobiography as she decides to conceive it, Anzaldúa turns into an advantage the disunities of culture and self that begin spelling out a shift in aesthetic sensibility in the 1970s under the name of postmodernism. Biddy Martin, in her critical work on women's autobiography, describes this historical moment moving through American culture and institutions as it impinges on the social act of writing for Chicanas and other women of color: "The autobiographical contributions to *This Bridge Called My Back* . . . serve as a concrete example of how the politics of identity has been challenged on its very grounds. For the writings of Moraga, Anzaldúa, and others participate in attempts to attend to the irreducibly complex intersections of race, gender, and sexuality, attempts that both directly and indirectly work against assumptions that there are no differences within the 'lesbian self' and that lesbian authors, autobiographical subjects, readers, and critics can be conflated and marginalized as self-identical and separable questions of race, class, sexuality and ethnicity."[2] In Martin's account and many others, the variables of race, class, ethnicity, sexuality, and gender negotiate a field of tension in which aesthetics and politics cannot be separated. These variables intersect in such complex ways that attempts to disengage them serve in fact to "falsify" straightaway their empirical irreducibility. Anzaldúa takes the challenge to the politics of identity at this historical juncture in multicultural America as a condition of possibility for her own theoretical vision of life. *Mestizaje*, or mestiza consciousness, is the name Anzaldúa gives to her mode of critical thinking in order to negotiate a world being made increasingly complex by *movimientos* after movimientos, simultaneous doubles, and lack of epistemological and ontological foundations.

Through this ideological practice she calls mestiza consciousness, Anzaldúa pens a body of work that negotiates the question mark punctuating the politics of identity in multicultural America at least since the political activism of the 1960s. Anzaldúa's work began to see the light of publication during the late Reagan years, when the economic policies of his administration had generated staggering deficits, not only widening the gap between rich and poor in the United States, but also enlarging the scope of the international division of labor. In many ways, *Borderlands/La Frontera,* with its discussion of NAFTA in chapter 1, anticipated the processes of globalization that came with the end of the Cold War. Anzaldúa's social act of writing is situated in this maelstrom of social, cultural, and economic forces, in the midst of the irony called the death of the author. Anzaldúa makes explicit reference to this figure of the demise of the Western author in the interview. Anzaldúa puts together a critical vision of life she calls low theory out of both the breadth of her reading and her lived experience not to reassert one more form of fixed or reified subjectivity, but to radicalize the epistemological and ontological exhaustion of the subject of knowledge in modernity. The "I" that writes recognizes the folly of taking anything for one's own, in a way that plays with private property in the realm of capital. Just as death deprives the capitalist subject of any private property, so the nonexistence of any self-sustaining author/ identity in the first place deprives the death of the author of the cultural capital it holds in Western critical theory. In a sense, mestiza consciousness writes without foundations inasmuch as the new mestiza puts no faith even in a dead author—a mestiza must write because she must write. Hence, through her oeuvre, Gloria Anzaldúa is neither dead and nor alive but exists somewhere in between, *en los intersticios.* Through the exercise of mestiza consciousness, Anzaldúa affirms and displaces metaphysical opposites, pinpoints cultural contradiction and tensions, all without the benefit of foundations.

DATE OF INTERVIEW: June 1990
SETTING: Gloria Anzaldúa's apartment home in Santa Cruz, California

Mestiza Consciousness in the Making

H. T. Can we begin by talking about your background in terms of home, family, and religious background?

G. A. *Sí.* I was born in the ranch settlements Jesús María. They weren't exactly towns. They were plots of land where two or three or four families would live together and then a few miles further down there would be two or three other ranches and then fifteen miles away there would be two or three ranches and they would get together and sometimes hire a teacher. I lived in the ranch settlements, which have now disappeared. It's history now. My father met my mother because they lived in two adjoining ranches, Los Vergeles and Jesús María. When my mother was eight my father fell in love with her and started courting her pretty early. I was born when my mother was sixteen. And so I spent a few years in the ranch settlements and then we moved to a series of tenant farms called Río Farms. Our father would farm and ranch and 60 percent would go to him and 40 percent would go to the corporation. So I grew up in a ranch/farming environment until I guess maybe around the age of ten or eleven. My father had a house built in this little *pueblito* called Hargill, which has only a highway that crisscrosses and one signal light and thirteen bars and thirteen churches and a Minute Mart for you stop and get something quick.

H. T. You talk about that in *Borderlands*.

G. A. Yes, I talk about that in *Borderlands*. And then my father died when I was about thirteen or fourteen. I took it pretty hard and we had to virtually support ourselves from then on so I've been supporting myself from that age on. My mother and I and my brothers and sisters had to go back into the fields and work. All along I'd been a fieldworker on Saturdays and Sundays and after school. But after my father died, we really had to work and it was like I say in *Borderlands*, it's backbreaking animal work. You start feeling like an animal, like a beast of burden. It does something to your self-image. I really have a lot of love and respect for *campesinos* because it's a really hard life.

H. T. You did a lot of that work yourself?

G. A. Sí, I had to pick a lot of cotton, all kinds of vegetables from cabbages to broccoli to picking oranges, strawberries, even irrigating, working in packing sheds, where you get to pack the food, wash and pack the food.

H. T. Who were the bosses/*quién eran los bosses*?

G. A. Los bosses were always these white people and the mediators would be the Chicanos who would be the contractors. They would come and pick you up at five o' clock in the morning and you'd get in the back of a pickup and be taken to the field where you worked. So those were Chicanos. They were the middle people, the middlemen. But the bosses were mostly *gringos* because they were the ones that could afford . . .

H. T. You were saying the Chicanos were the mediators.

G. A. Yes, they were always the bosses that gathered us up, the ones that had the contracts for clearing this field, picking this field, irrigating this field, or whatever and so they would go and find people to work. What would happen is that a large percentage of the valley would evacuate because of migration into other states to do the crops, so there would be some of us left and we would do the farm labor around there. I migrated when I was little one year, and then later as a teacher I migrated with my students. I was teaching in high school, teaching migrants. The state of Texas would select two teachers from the whole state who had taught and worked with migrants to go to the Midwest. You got to pick your state so I picked Indiana, but the rest of the time the fieldwork I did was stationary.

H. T. What was your homelife like?

G. A. Well, I think I had a very dysfunctional family, in psychological terms, because I think Chicano families are really hard on women. Maybe they're very hard on men, too. Very early you start being taught how to be a man and how to be a little woman and the divisions are pretty rigid. My father had a very strong personality. My mother had a very strong personality. And I was very rebellious. They tried to mold me into what a good Chicanita should be, which for them meant good Chicanitas didn't go to school. They drop out in the sixth or seventh or eighth grade. Good Chicanitas cook and clean and sew. I come from a very old-fashioned community in which those roles are very defined. The fact that I wanted to study and read and draw was being lazy. Instead of being encouraged to go to school it was the other way around. I think my father wanted his children to get an education and that was fine with my mother, except not for the girls. My family was actually different from the other families in that I got to high school, my sister got to high school, my one brother almost graduated, the other dropped out as a sophomore and was drafted to go to Vietnam where he was almost killed. So while my family was unusual in some respects it was also typical. I started reading very early on and my sister and one brother became readers too, sort of through imitation. And they're still readers even though my sister reads stuff like romances and my brother reads Westerns, popular culture stuff. My other brother reads farming magazines, magazines about horses and agriculture and that's the extent of their reading, but they do read, which is not true of the other people, the peer groups that we grew up with. They didn't read. They dropped out of school.

H. T. So, in that sense, you mean your family was typical, but you were also different?

G. A. Right. Sí. The difference comes from the fact that I starting to read early on and used reading both as an educational tool and also a way to escape from the oppression of our culture. My sister and one of my brothers took that on also as a way of coping. I don't know what their motivation was. And then I went to college and I was the only woman, not just the only woman, but also the only person from that area that had ever gone to college.

H. T. What college is that?

G. A. Well, the first year I went to Texas Women's University in Denton. And then I went to Pan American, which is in the Valley. But now I look at my brothers' kids and my cousins' kids and they're all going to college. One of my cousin's kids is going to Yale. So there's been this complete change.

H. T. Do you feel like you participated in that?

G. A. I feel like I was one of the early models for that and people will tell their kids, "Oh yeah, *yo quiero que mi hijita vaya al colegio así como Gloria.* I was one of the models. In the beginning though it was like, "What is this woman doing going away from home? God knows what she's doing. She's probably out there fucking men and stuff." If you left the house, you were a prostitute. Only men were allowed to walk in the streets and congregate and travel.

H. T. What was your source of strength, your fortitude for going against those currents?

G. A. I think it was the reading. It gave me an entry into a different way of being.

H. T. And what kinds of things did you read?

G. A. *Pues*, I mostly read the usual junk. I started out reading Westerns, which really upset me because the Mexicans were always the slimy characters. But I also read Jack London's *The Call of the Wild*. Charlotte Brontë's *Jane Eyre*. And I think that Jane Eyre, even though she's feminine instead of feminist, she was very rebellious and lived under oppressive conditions but she was strong and survived. I think that was a model for me until I got to reading Chicano stuff and Mexican literature and Latin American literature. I read mostly American literature, mostly animal things—*Black Beauty, The Stallion, The Mustang, The Call of the Wild*—where the dogs and the horses had that strong instinct for freedom that I really like. And especially the horses. One of the stories that I have been working on the last couple of days called "She Ate Horses" is about the relationship between two women, one of them repressing her sexuality and her instincts. She doesn't trust her instincts. So the animals were the ones that were my models for freedom, for movement, because it was very constraining for me to be this little *huerquita*. I walked around with boots and jeans and a Western shirt. I had a BB gun and a .22. I had a pistol. The whole works. And then after a while you're supposed to outgrow that so I think that nature and animals were my models for wanting more freedom. But I suffered a lot of guilt because if I was reading or writing or drawing I felt like I was in some way being a bad girl because I wasn't helping my mother and I wasn't ironing my brothers' shirts.

H. T. Did your mother let you know?

G. A. To this day, to this day she lets me know, although she's kind of ambivalent about it now because she used to think it was all laziness. If I was reading in bed instead of washing the dishes or scrubbing the walls, it was not a useful activity. But when I graduated with my Master's and then I went to Indiana I started sending her money.

H. T. Your Master's from the University of Texas?

G. A. Sí, in art and literature and education. And then I studied comparative literature but I never advanced to candidacy because I had three focuses—Spanish literature, feminist theory, and Chicano literature. But at Texas, my advisors discouraged me because they didn't recognize Chicano literature. For them it didn't exist as part of American literature, so I could not focus on Chicano literature because these white guys didn't know anything other than English literature and Anglo-American.

H. T. So, the reception you received from your advisors when you were doing your Master's—would you say they saw your diverse interests and tried to suppress them?

G. A. Well, they wanted me to write papers in comparative literature based on the masters—Sterne or Lawrence or Steinbeck. I could even write about Spanish authors but Chicano literature was not okay; it was not an official literature, and neither were Feminist Studies legitimated. Those were not things that I could focus on for my dissertation. So I left and waited a few years and then I went back. I went over my transcript and found that I had gone over the allotted time and would have to repeat classes. The classes that I had taken for my language requirement for some reason or another didn't get listed as fulfilling my language requirement. So I thought that it wasn't of any use for me to go back and repeat classes that I wasn't interested in. If I did pursue a PhD in the future, I thought I would take my areas of interest and plug them into courses. For example, on woman, the Chicana in space, the mestiza in space and identities, of ethnicity, of the author's subjectivity, of working class, gender, feminism, feminist and lesbian identity. But I wanted to do it in the kind of way that I did in *Borderlands*. That's one of the reasons I'm back in school because school gives me the opportunity to be near libraries. I can plug into classes, books, and theories I need to learn and be supported by a fellowship or whatever, so that's really nice.

H. T. You came to UCSC as a professor, right?

G. A. Yes, as a distinguished visiting professor for one term. I have taught a course on women of color in the U.S. and a writing class.

H. T. And then how did you move into the History of Consciousness program?

G. A. I'm not in the History of Consciousness Program. No, they rejected me. They felt that I was too established and that I didn't need to learn anymore. That was one opinion. Another opinion was that I didn't know any theory and was too far behind and wouldn't be able to catch up. And what was the other one? Oh, the final blow was the fact that I was a creative writer and they already had too many creative writers.

H. T. How do those categories . . . ?

G. A. Well, I was judged on the performance of other Chicanas. One Chicana was suing the department for sexual harassment and I don't know what else. Another Chicana has been here twelve years and has not finished her dissertation. Another Chicana was late with her papers. Several other Chicanas were late with their papers. So I came in being judged on their abilities. White people tend to see Chicanas and people of color generically as a collectivity rather than as individuals. The white students that applied were not judged on the performance of other white students. The day I was rejected by the History of Consciousness program, the literature program grabbed me. They put me on the top of their list. They had like two hundred and fifty applicants and they felt that it was an honor for me to be in their program. It was the complete opposite. Donna Haraway, one of the History of Consciousness professors, was on leave then but when she came back she started yelling and screaming at them "Are you crazy?" because they didn't accept me into the program. The History of Consciousness program here advocates high theory and my writing, because it incorporates lived experience, is considered low theory so there's that split here between high and low critical theory. And when I came into the literature program I made it very clear to them that I came with very specific goals and that if their guidelines for orals and PhD dissertation were things that were not in line with what I was trying to do I wasn't going to stay for the degree, I was just going to be here taking classes.

H. T. What kind of goals?

G. A. Well, my goal was to put together this book on the mestiza and how she deals with space and identity. I wanted to continue reading Lacan, which I had started in Texas, and read some of the feminist psychoanalysts also. I wanted to read some of the French feminists. I wanted to read the current important theoretical writings. And I felt that being in a school, I could catch the latest stuff. The good teachers are usually aware of who's writing what and in which journals, like *Cultural Critique*. I don't know if you're familiar with it.

H. T. Yes, I am.

G. A. *Feminist Issues* and *Signs*—these are different kinds of journals where the latest stuff is being done. I also needed a rest from being too exposed to the world—the tons of phone calls and mail, people inviting me to do this or that. I needed a refuge and to me the university has always been a refuge because I can say, "Okay, now I'm a student—*me retiro, poquito.*" That's been a struggle because I can't seem to disappear. You know I thought it usually takes people about three months to catch up with me. So I end up moving every two or three years. And this time people found me. So it's my own discipline. I need to have the ability to say no. And I don't seem to have that ability.

The Spirit of *La Facultad*

H. T. Speaking of the idea of a refuge. This might seem like a leap, but can that lead us into the idea of spirit? Is there a tie between your need for solitary space, solitude, and the spiritual dimensions of your life?

G. A. Sí, I think that I sought school and spirituality as a coping mechanism to deal with a very oppressive reality. I was mugged once, a man tried to kill me. I was knifed once. I've had four near-death experiences. The last one I was declared dead on the operating table about nine years ago. I had a near drowning. I fell off a cliff and broke most of my body. But it's really about all women. When they're in the street, they're prey. Men prey on them. One out of every three women gets raped. The statistics show that there's a real war going on. I was attacked in Austin in 1974 by this guy who had just gotten out of Huntsville while I was walking along Waller Creek on the UT campus. After he tried to kill me, bueno, he tried to throw me off a little bridge into that creek and that was when I could no longer trust the woods or the water.

H. T. Sure.

G. A. Nature became associated with violence for me so that I became afraid to go out in the woods, whereas before I loved to be out alone in the woods. I wasn't afraid. And I would walk in the streets at night. I wasn't afraid. All of a sudden I became afraid. The universe was no longer a safe place. I couldn't control the external environment. The environment of men, the environment of the streets, the environment of what the neighbors were doing. So then I had to create a kind of imaginary inner space and I started doing it through meditation. I started doing it through using incense and candles and meditative music. I took classes in psychic development. I studied under a Basque teacher. I studied tarot, numerology, and symbology. I studied palmistry. I studied all these occult ways of knowing, of knowledge, *pero* illegitimate in the university, not acceptable modes of knowledge. By going into myself, I could at least control my inner space, at least my apartment. The little space that I could control allowed me to expand that space into the community. When I would lecture during '81 and '82 I would start by having everybody put their hands like this, their feet on the floor, doing their breathing and I would guide them through their meditations. Every reading I did I would start this way and the audience would freak out. I'd be in New York, in Boston, Harvard, Yale, and I'd be doing this, and the audiences weren't used to this, but they would do it. And I did that for years but about two years ago I stopped because it wasn't necessary anymore. Other people were doing it now; those spiritual modes were okay now. I would take just a few seconds and do these spiritual rituals by myself. I would travel with my little candle and my tape recorder so I could play my meditative music.

H. T. Is this related to the idea of *la facultad* that you talk about in *Borderlands*?

G. A. Sí, I think that when you are a person that is powerless, as a Chicano, as a gay man, as a short person, as a person in a wheelchair, as a woman, you develop; you heighten your senses because you need to be aware of danger, sort of like the rabbits in the woods. They have these big ears and because they're afraid of predators, they compensate with hearing or smelling. I think humans do the same thing. And people of color have always tried to see through their patrónes, their oppressors, to see what they are up to so that they can be ready or defend themselves. The campesino, the Chicano, the black, the Asian they will have a finely developed way of reading or seeing through their oppressor. They see through them, they take them apart and critique them. This is now called a deconstruction of these systems of oppression, but even if along comes somebody from France and says, "Well, I invented deconstruction," it's the black maid that had to do that with her mistress and her master. The Chicano campesino can also deconstruct. So that's part of the facultad.

The Codes of Chicana/Chicano Literary Discourses

H. T. I'm interested in getting your perspective on Chicana/ Chicano literature as phenomenon, historical and spiritual, or whatever.

G. A. Bueno, I first read John Rechy in the middle and late '60s. He is a Chicano from El Paso whose mother was Mexican and father was Scottish. He wrote *City of Night* and was published by the mainstream presses, but did not write as a Chicano, but I consider him a Chicano because to me, Chicano literature is literature written by a Chicano or a Chicana and it doesn't have to be about Texas or about growing up Chicano. If I write science fiction—which I am doing—and not mention any Chicanos, or anything that has to do with being Mexican I would still be a Chicana writing, but my Chicanoness would come through the writing anyway.

H. T. Is there any historical texture to Chicano writing?

G. A. There is a historical texture to Chicano writing and sometimes we get it via the oral, listening to our uncles and aunts and grandparents and listening to the Chicano radio and reading the Chicano papers in Spanish so that's one avenue. Another avenue is actually reading things in Spanish whether they be Mexican or things written in Spanish by Chicanos. There's a kind of osmosis—the word order of our sentences is a mixture of the Spanish and the English. It's not quite either. And I find myself when I try to translate my own things that the gap between Spanish and English gets closer—whereas with Mexican and English it's like this, or with French and English it's like this. There's a kind of a borrowing from both the Spanish and English to create this Chicano way of talking and writing.

H. T.   You seem very sensitive to the syntax of Chicano writing. What makes you so sensitive to that syntax? I know you write about it in *Borderlands*. You have a whole chapter devoted to the sociolinguistic dimension.

G. A.   I think it's because I grew up speaking in half and half. I grew up, my schoolmates, my brothers and sisters, all speaking in Spanglish, half and half. With my mother and my grandmothers I would speak entirely in Spanish. And with my white friends I would talk entirely in English. So that's my native, my home language. So when I'm writing "She Ate Horses," for instance, I go back and forth because there're certain things that only the Spanish will do, but then there are other things that I cannot say in Spanish because I did not acquire Spanish via school or books. It was an oral acquisition. So then I need the English to explain certain things if they're scientific. The more lyrical things and the more philosophical things I can say in Spanish, but the everyday world of dealing with businesses or certain kinds of realities, the English language is what I use because that's how I learned my math, that's how I learned my geography, that's how I learned my science. So, I don't think I'm particularly sensitive to the syntax. Most Chicano writers are sensitive to it.

H. T.   Do you feel that writers have to do something to awaken the awareness that you're at an intersection of what the two languages can do?

G. A. I think that there's two ways to plug into that. One way is by having grown up in that kind of crossroads, in that kind of borderland where you're hearing working-class language, Mexican Spanish, Anglo, redneck English, the more formal school English. You're born into that. That's one way. The second way is if you, your parents, have become Anglicized or been ripped off of their language and they are monolingual English speakers. There's a way that Chicanas and Chicanos that are born or raised in this kind of environment can go back to reclaim their Spanish. And sometimes the person going back to reclaim the language is the better speaker because they— well, maybe not the better speaker—but they can understand the Castilian Spanish, whereas somebody like me, I know the working-class Chicano Spanish, which is not acceptable. The people who have problems with my book *Borderlands* were the ones in the Spanish and Portuguese Departments because they do not recognize vernacular Spanish as legitimate. To them, the language is to be kept pure. They can tolerate Mexican Spanish, but Chicano Spanish, no. So those are the people who criticize it the most.

H. T. Do you think that Chicano and Chicana writing has something to say to the mainstream, purist attitudes in literary English and literary Spanish?

G. A. Sí, I think that the first thing that it shows to them is their ethnocentrism because most other peoples in the world know two or three other languages. If you live in Europe, you learn Swiss German. You learn German. You learn French. I think the same thing in Indian countries, in Asian countries. You learn different dialects. Pakistani. There are nine different languages. Most people know four of them. So here's this very ethnocentric nation of Anglo Americans and all they've ever known is their mode of talking, their mode of thinking, their mode of writing, their mode of culture. The Chicanas and Chicanos who are using a combination of languages and switching codes are very good for the Anglo Americans to learn, to know, because it shows that identity is not fixed, that you can code-switch from one reality to another just like you can with language. So I think it opens up their minds a little bit. They complain. I have people say, "Oh, you know, I have to read you with a dictionary." Or they'll say, "I really feel like I'm missing something because I don't understand Spanish." And they get angry. It's frustrating for them. And I think, I say to myself, "That's good because here were all these little Chicanito kids that were being frustrated most of their lives because they were being taught a language that was not their native tongue and they were not allowed, bilingualism was not allowed. So finally here's this Anglo person who's being frustrated but they can cope with the frustration better because they have the privilege."

H. T.   Do Chicano writers use the codes differently than Chicana writers, do you think?

G. A.   You mean the women from the men? No, I don't think the women use the codes differently as distinct from the men. One of the things that I think I'm getting to—and I don't know if other people have done it—is that I'm doing it in a theory. Most of the Chicanos that I know do it in their stories or in their poems or their speeches, but when they sit down to write criticism, even José Limón and José Saldívar will employ a word now and then, but they pretty much stick to English so I think that I'm one of the few that in writing my papers, my critical and theoretical papers, will have whole sections in Spanish. So I don't know if there are other women that are doing that. I don't think there are because I read Norma Alarcón who does not do that. Alvina Quintana does not do that. Angie Chabram and other critics stick to English in their critical pieces.

H. T.   To the normative code, would you say?

G. A.   Sí, but I don't do that.

Genre and Author(ity)

H. T.   What is it that allows you to work that way?

G. A.   It was a hard struggle for me to go against the dictates. There were these two forces. My instinct said, "Gloria, you have to write in your own way, however it comes out from your heart." And there will be these professors, both Chicanos and Anglos and Spanish who will be saying—even today I had a class where I was being told how to write—what approach to use. I was told that I had to write critical stuff, and I said, "No, I don't." But it took me a long time to believe in my own voice, that it was okay for me to write in a creative way, that I didn't see a division between theory and fiction or theory and poetry, that poetry derives theory and you can derive theory from poetry. It was a false dichotomy that Anglo-American feminism and European male discourse have advocated that there's a split between theory and fiction or theory and practice.

H. T.   Would you go as far as to say that that's true even for genres?

G. A.   Yes, they want to keep the lines very distinct. They don't want any of the blurring of the lines. I get attacked constantly for blurring the lines, especially for blurring the lines between theory and lived experience. I'm not supposed to be autobiographical in my theory. Somewhere along the line I think there were a few people who liked my writing. I can remember an English teacher at Texas Women's University. I can remember Dr. James Sledd in Austin. I don't know if you know him.

H. T.   Yes, I know him.

G. A.   He liked what I was doing. So there have been a few people who say, "Yes, just keep going the way you do" against the hundreds who have said, "You can't write a paper like that. You can't write criticism like that. You can't do this. You can't do that." Up 'til now. This woman in my class was still arguing against my mode, and my response to her was, "What gives you the right to think that there's only one way of doing this? Why is the university in the U.S., the academy, so insistent in there being only one way—one way of knowing, one way of approaching that knowledge and writing about it?" It's very racist.

H. T.   It sounds like you see that blurring the lines, the social act of writing itself, is a way of knowing. The graphic signified is a way of knowing, and the graphic signifier, because it is free floating, allows us to blur those distinctions.

G. A.   Exactly. In my lectures, I always insist on having a blackboard because I like to make what I call my hieroglyphics or these little pictures out of which I can explicate my theory. For *Borderlands*,

I had the figure of a woman with all these little squares that were the plots that she was standing on. One plot was being a lesbian. Another plot was being in the academy. Another was being a working campesina, working-class. Another was feminist. Another one was the writing profession. As many worlds as there are and the mestiza has to operate in all these little plots, in all these little worlds. So, in crossing from one to the other, in this constant traveling back and forth, her subjectivity, her identity becomes multiple, moving, movable subjectivity or identity. That's threatening to people because their lives are so insecure that they want one stable identity that they can anchor to. Take you as an example.

H. T. Use me, my name as an example?

G. A. Sí. Héctor Torres. There's the Héctor Torres that the friends you grew up with know. Then you probably went away from home and you acquired other identities, your academic identity for one. When you go back home, your friends tend to see only the identity you had before you left. Or, if you are in a political meeting with Chicanos and they happen to be male and it happens to be a fraternal *compadrazgo* kind of thing, that particular "you" is different from still another "you" if you were a corporate executive or worker in the corporate world—identities tied to your job. If you had risen from the working class, which you probably did, to whatever class you happen to be now. If you go from New Mexico to Montreal, Canada, and you give a talk on bilingualism—in Quebec there's this dialogue about English and French and the bilingualism there is very similar to what's going on in the Southwest—in Quebec you would be a different identity. Some parts of that identity would be highlighted and others would be repressed, depending on which plots or roles you're in. Right now what's being highlighted is the academic, this person that's writing a book dealing with literature. If you were talking to an old school friend from grammar school or your mother or your sister or your brother, another part of you would be highlighted and the academic part of you would not come to the forefront. So this is what we do when we have access to so many worlds—a white world, the academic world, our

Chicano world, a working-class world. This kind of mobility and flexibility enriches a person. Your survival has depended on your ability to adapt and this threatens white people. They would like to do that. Then along comes poststructuralism and it privileges a lot of what happens in the minor literatures, the literatures from the margin such as my book and these theorists are saying, "Well, this book proves our theory right," as when their theories say that subjectivity is not a single, fixed, core identity, that it is multiple and plural. All they have to do is look at *our* lives and *our* books and say, "Oh yeah, the margin is verifying us, the dominant people." Now that marginal people are finally getting to a space where we can say, "I am creating my subjectivity. I am taking center stage," all of a sudden they say, "The subject—there is no such thing." For example, they'll refer to Barthes who has an essay on how the author is dead—just at the time when the marginal writers are becoming authorial. They're taking that authority to be a voice, to be a subject, and what it seems to me is that the white European, male author is dead. The white, male European subject is dead. And we, the minor, are not ready to relinquish the space that we have just won in our struggles. But I also feel that the author never existed because when I write, I write from the raw material that I read, from the people that I come into contact with, from the experiences that other people tell me about. And I am sort of like this pipeline that gathers up material and synthesizes it and puts it out so that it's not me, a single author, but I belong to a collectivity that is invisible, but it's in my head when I'm writing. So I don't believe that the author ever existed, so how can the author be dead? ¿*Tú sábes?*

H. T. *Sí, creo que entiendo.*

G. A. The stuff about subjectivity—who says you have to be fixed, anchored, and solid to have subjectivity? Switching positions—a subjectivity that moves from one position to the other—to me is just as real as the old one where you had an autonomous, core self that was coherent. To me, there's a coherency in a multiplicity of positions despite the chaotic, schizophrenic, traveling back and forth from one position to the other, from one identity to another. There's a cohesion to it and I feel very whole when I talk. All of me is there except maybe the campesina is in the background, or the spiritual person switches to the background. Sometimes the lesbianism comes out very much to the forefront, and sometimes other identities, but they're all there, just not taking center stage. They're letting some of the other facets of my personality take center stage.

The Chicano Movement: Inheritance

H. T. Is it possible to generalize that experience and what does it say about the subject of Chicano literature, its identity?

G. A. Well, for me, it's not identity and it's not subject. It's identities and subjects.

H. T. Yes. In the past, what has been foregrounded, what has been backgrounded? Currently, what is foregrounded? What is backgrounded? And, if you can project, what will be foregrounded and what will be backgrounded in the future?

G. A. For Chicanas, I think there's going to be a privileging of different Chicanas, of differences among Chicanas, instead of an emphasis on one Chicana, or a universal kind of Chicana, a typical Chicana. There can be Chicanas who speak in broken English, Chicanas who don't know any Spanish, Chicanas who were raised away from a Chicano community and raised in an all-white environment. I think there's going to be a privileging of diversity in the Chicano community away from a nationalist trend—"Let's all have a united image of ourselves that's a standard image." That's in the future, but not before the struggle. Because to survive, which a lot of times means a minor group and literature has to go nationalist, it has to come together in a highly nationalist away, and even in a separatist way until its identity as ethnic people is validated. Afterward you can pretty much uphold a diverse image of subjectivity and identities.

H. T. Do you think that there have been certain historical antecedents that allowed for that nationalistic cohesion so that now there can be the dispersal you're talking about?

G. A. *Pues*, yes, there have been several movements, mostly political movements, the last one being the Chicano Movement, which I think is still going on in a different kind of form. The Chicano Movement, instead of being a movement headed by men in an external kind of way, it's also the women, the Chicana feminists who are heading their own kind of movement, their own separate kinds of movements. We are carrying on the work instead of staying in the same ground with our own literary movement. The literature was very important to Chicanos as a movement because it gave us *I am Joaquín* and even gave us the term Chicano. Before that, I can remember when I was growing up I called myself a mexicana and there was not that much of a distinction between *los mexicanos de este lado* in Téjas and *los mexicanos del otro lado*. The term Chicana to me was a special kind of identity that meant that you were a person of Spanish and Mexican descent who was comfortable living in the white world. *Y un mexicano del otro lado* is not comfortable unless they've lived here for many years. The Chicano Movement coalesced identity and I have a lot of respect for it despite its sexist attitudes. For that reason it started diminishing. It's not dead, but the male aspect of it is diminishing because the men would not confront anything but racial issues. The movement to me is now like a mosaic with all these little pieces. The little pieces are the ones that are now being activated so that a poet like Lorna Dee Cervantes is her own little miniature movement. Francisco Alarcón, Norma Alarcón, José Limón, all the people who are writing are carrying out the struggle against domination and subordination in the kinds of things they focus on—language, folklore, just anything. So the movement has gone in two directions, in a kind of grassroots way where women are setting up *centros de familia* and rape crisis centers, things to help la raza—all these little grassroots things that don't seem to be very revolutionary but they focus on the preservation of some form of the Chicano culture. So that's one way. The other road is like my road—the social act of the writing, of recreating, representing, translating these experiences of the Chicano people into writing. Right now the writers are probably the ones that are documenting all these changes and historical trends and history.

H. T. Do you feel like your work has gone through certain phases, certain stages that make you feel like in local contexts, through your writing, you are participating in a larger movement although it doesn't have to speak about the whole thing all at once?

G. A. Sí, what you've seen thus far. I started writing in '74 and some of the stories that are in the book I'm working on now called *Entre Guerras, Entre Mundos* are about these topics that I've been talking about except that when I was writing these first drafts of these stories there was a lot of Spanish, a lot of stuff about the different aspects of the Chicano culture, a lot of stuff around sexuality and lesbianism. All of the stuff that's in *Borderlands* had its genesis in these earlier things that I did in '74, '75, '76, which I'm now putting into this book.

H. T. In *Borderlands*?

G. A. No. *Tengo dos libros—tres libros.*

H. T. Talk about these . . .

G. A. All right. Well, the stories that I'm talking about and that I wrote first drafts of in '74, '75, and '76 are called *Entre Guerras, Entre Mundos* and the concept of the switching worlds is in there but I'm presenting it in the fact that I believe different worlds exist, different realities. So there's a lot of supernatural stuff.

H. T. *Y antes*, before those stories?

G. A. Antes, what I have in *This Bridge*; that was the first book. Between *This Bridge* and *Borderlands*, I did an autobiography which I'm not going to publish called *La Serpiente que se come su cola*. And a lot of those things from that manuscript went into *Borderlands* and some are going into *Entre Guerras, Entre Mundos*. And some of them are going into this Chicana space identity book.

H. T. So that text sounds like it's disseminated into different, other texts.

G. A. Yes. I think what's happening is that up to *Borderlands* there was this preoccupation with certain topics and a certain style, and now I'm trying to find a new mode, a new approach, and I'm banging my head against the wall because I end up doing what I did with *Borderlands*. I keep thinking I want to do something different—reach another level—but I haven't gone beyond the first level.

H. T. I see what you mean. It sounds to me like you're refurbishing and drawing from the margins what you hadn't been able to integrate into other writing. I don't know if that's a fair characterization exactly.

G. A. My writing hasn't gone through several stages. The first thing that I ever wrote was the beginning of a novel and I started writing it in Spanish and it had all Chicana characters, so what I notice is that all these preoccupations were true back then; the only difference is that I didn't publish them. I sat on this stuff. I like to sit on my stuff for ten years. So I'm still in that first stage. I feel like I'm now cranking up to go to the second stage. Growing up in this country, most of our literary influence is Anglo-American and English and in the past few years I have read more of the marginal literature. I try to get in a lot of the Mexican literature so it's not just Spanish and Anglo American. Another thing that I'm trying to do is read more of the top guns in theory—Foucault, Lacan, Derrida, Kristeva, Hélène Cixous—all these big, top gun writers. And I'm now looking to see what can I appropriate from the major literature where in the past it had been forced on me. I had been fed these Anglo-American and English writers. I didn't have any choice. I mean that was the only thing that was offered in school. We had to take those requirements. I backed away from them because I wanted more of the Chicano literature, the black, the Asian, the Mexican. Now I want in this third stage to see what I can appropriate from the major because the major has always appropriated from me. *Borderlands* is one of the books that is being appropriated in classes. Instructors take only that which is, *como te digo*, a highly tokenized appropriation. So I figured if they appropriate from me, it's okay for me to appropriate from them. So I think this is what the theories of the minor are in the process of doing. They're looking at the theories of the major and seeing what they can learn and can use without being subverted or assimilated by the major, without being swallowed.

H. T. I see what you mean. It sounds so interesting; I don't know exactly the word for it. I keep groping for the proper characterization. Maybe "proper" is not the word for it, but at least something that is faithful to the experience you're going through in order to push your talents and abilities.

G. A. And I think this is where the new mestiza comes in. You know, the category of the new mestiza that signals in these postmodern times that we do not have to adhere to a "closed windows and doors" identity that remains in the Chicano community. That we can be transcultural, that the very concept of mestizaje is this mixture of cultures and that we can do that intellectually so that the mestiza is quite open to reading theories of the major, theories of the minor, world literature, and world feminism. Not everybody is at that stage. There are some feminists who still need this enclosed Chicano community to give them a foundation, to give them a sense of security as a Chicana. All these doubles are operating simultaneously: the Chicana that is just becoming aware that she's oppressed as a Chicana and coming into her feminism, and the Chicana who's already gone through all this—movimientos after movimientos and all this struggle and these two worlds—the world of the airplane and the world of the horse-drawn buggy simultaneously exist so that you have a succession of historical periods existing now. It's like bringing south Texas to the middle of San Francisco, *tu sabes*? They both exist.

H. T. That's a nice image. I think that really does clarify what you mean by the fact that there are two worlds simultaneously operating. Is that what you're talking about?

G. A. It's probably more than two worlds. It's probably the world of my mother where everything is very rural and traditional from not being exposed to the Anglo world, the cities and all that. Then there are the intermediate small towns, the bigger cities, and then finally you get to a megametropolis like New York. There are all these stages or levels and each of them represents a historical period and they're all legitimate. And even though I can say, "Well, south Texas is twenty years behind the times," and I can try to be funny, it's not that San Francisco and New York are that much more ahead because they're not. It's just that in terms of mass media it does seem like south Texas is backward.

H. T. Is it fair to say that you're trying to articulate what is essentially a nonlinear concept even though it's thoroughly historical?

G. A. Right, sí. South Texas is so full of illegal Mexicans, of *mojaditos/mojaditas* coming from central Mexico or wherever into this modern republic, the United States, living in south Texas, mixing with sixth- and seventh-generation Chicanos. There are all these different worlds. So then you take this Chicano to China or you take this Chicano to New York, and you will see all these worlds that have a historical period attached to them and that coexist at the same time. Another visual would be to see a campesino, a mojadito from Mexico, newly arrived, in the middle of New York, a rural campesino, mostly Indian with the tall buildings and the subways. The concept of new mestiza/new mestizo can say that these worlds exist at the same time and that these cultures coexist and that if you have the skills and you survive it, which you and I have, then we can go from one world to the other without too much of a culture shock, *tu sabes*?

For a Chicana Literary Difference/Renaissance

H. T. What do you think is needed to read Chicana literature sensitively, with all these worlds in mind? What can I do, for instance?

G. A. Well, I think you're doing it already. I mean, you're reading my book and evidently you are reading other women, right?

H. T. Yes.

G. A. Lorna Dee Cervantes . . . I don't know if you're familiar with her.

H. T. *Emplumada.*

G. A. I think that it's already there. Like I was telling you, in people like José Limón, José Saldívar, yourself. You're not like the old guard that would write women off and say they don't have anything interesting to write about. They're writing about babies and gossip, illness, *tu sabes*? So I think you're already doing it. You're reading us. You're talking with us.

H. T. And in teaching? In the classroom?

G. A. Pues, in teaching if I were you and I had a class full of people, I would ask the women what they wanted and I would say here's some texts by women, you know. There's Lorna Dee Cervantes, there's Denise Chávez, there's Gloria Anzaldúa, Carmen Tafolla, whoever you're reading. Ask about what makes their literature different from the literature of the males. What experiences do they have that are analogous to the experiences that these women writers are writing about? Have them start doing the reading, send them out, and say, "Find texts by Chicanas and do exploratory reading of them and then come back to class and tell us what you found." Don't put the women writers on your syllabus as token women; balance the syllabus.

H. T. Balancing the syllabus is step one.

G. A. Sí. The other thing that's exciting is that I think the women are writing the exciting things. I remember when I was reading Cortázar and Borges, there was a renaissance in Latin American literature. Then I remember the Anglo women in the latter part of the '60s and '70s and their Anglo feminism was exciting for me to read and then it got flat and now I think it's the women of color that are having a renaissance. They're the ones that are reading, that are writing exciting things and among them are the Chicanas. So we're having our renaissance. I don't know how long it's going to last. Then the writers, the other writers who are more understanding, the less macho writers, Chicano writers that are less invested in a macho identity, they'll admit to having fears or to having identity or their identity as male is blurred because they may feel there's more of a woman in them and they're taking that risk by proclaiming that. Those are the people to read. That's why I didn't want to read Hinojosa. What should I read of his?

H. T. *The Valley* does interesting stuff with narrative time, narrative perspectives—the way he takes different characters and then writes from those perspectives.

G. A. And what are those books called? Are those the *Querido Rafa*?

H. T. Yes. *Me querido Rafa* and all those works related the *Klail City* series.

G. A. You're going to like my book *Entre Guerras*.

H. T. When I began to read *Borderlands* I was immediately struck by the fact that the question of genre was being deconstructed as I read. I felt like my reading of the book was a deconstruction of genre because there was poetry in there, there was an "I," but it took different forms.

G. A. A "she," a "we." I did that all kind of unconsciously. This other book of stories is a more conscious breaking up of the genres, one genre bleeding into the other. I have horror, mystery, and science fiction blend in this experimental writing. I get frustrated because I want to work more on this stuff and here I am working with more theory. I didn't say it right, because I don't distinguish between the two. But the more imaginative stuff—the fiction—what I call fiction is more fun for me to work with in some ways. Whereas I love the essay writing, once I master—"master," *que fea palabra*—once I get a handle on it I think it's going to be a forté. One of the things that happened last quarter that I'm really excited about is I started writing children's stories. I have a cycle of stories about a curandera's apprentice. The cycle goes from very simple picture books to more complicated children's stories and it's now approaching levels for young adults. Some of the stuff that is in *Borderlands* appears here but for a child because children really need to be exposed to our history. They need to be exposed to bilingualism. They need to be exposed to the issues of Chicanas because they're the ones that are so vulnerable. I'm really excited about this cycle of stories because the curandera apprentice befriends a little Mexican mojadito who has boils on his arms and she tries to help him as she's also trying to keep him from being taken by the *migra*. That book is going to be in the Children's Book Press, a bilingual publishing house. I don't know if you're familiar with it.

H. T. No, I haven't heard of it.

G. A. They do bilingual books. One of the first books they did was called *El Quinto Sol* and it was about the Aztec legend of the sun. And one side was English and the other side was Spanish.

H. T. Where are they based?

G. A. *Aquí* in San Francisco.

H. T. It sounds very interesting.

G. A. Sí. And the other thing I wanted to do was to get into screen-writing because some of the stories that I've written and my poems have a high visual content that's very conducive to film. So I'm trying to do that.

H. T. Goes back to your hieroglyphics?

G. A. Yes. Did you ever see a book *Cuentos by Latinas*?

H. T. I've seen the book but I haven't gotten my hands on it.

G. A. Well, I have the first chapter of a novel in there and several people have approached me about making a film out of it. No one has followed through because of money and stuff but I would like in the future to try young adult and children's literature, as well as screenwriting.

H. T. What kinds of presses are publishing Chicanas?

G. A. The main presses have not been publishing us. It's the feminist presses, for example, my press, Spinsters/Aunt Lute. They had no way of coping with *Borderlands* because they didn't have any Spanish people that could proof. I had to proof. The reason the Spanish is in such poor condition is because for *Borderlands* there never were the usual twelve proofreaders. For the Spanish they had me and I don't know how to proof. I'm not a very good speller, and I don't know where the accents go. So as soon as *Borderlands* came out and it was starting to do well I had all these women's presses come and say, "We're interested in you doing a book with us." There's even been some interest with some mainstream publishers. Suddenly everybody wants to publish me, and yet before all those years of struggle I lived on potatoes for years—Aghhh! Pero the other women that are starting to write, trying to find a voice, they're having the same problem I had—the lack of places for them to publish. So one of the things I do is encourage the process, acting as a referral agency to my press. I feel that I'm finally able to help women of color, especially Chicanas, get published.

H. T. Tell me the name of the presses again.

G. A. They're feminist, small presses like Spinsters/Aunt Lute, Firebrand, and Crossing Press.

H. T. Most of them out here on the West Coast?

G. A. Firebrand is in Ithaca, New York; Spinsters/Aunt Lute is in San Francisco; Crossing Press is in Freedom, California. There's one in Seattle. There's just a handful of presses that have survived. Kitchen Table is in New York. There are some university presses that are interested in our work, but not many. Trying to get writers published is an activism that I've taken up. So that's very gratifying to me because it's passing on to others the help I was given. *¡Pero, ay es mucho trabajo!* Every day people give me manuscripts: "Would you please look at this and tell me what you think?"

H. T. And you still have to write your dissertation?

G. A. Yes. It's been hard.

H. T. You stay busy.

G. A. Sí. Sometimes I think I must be a masochist to be going through all this because it's a killing pace. I was talking to Paula Gunn Allen, a Native American writer, who has a book called *The Sacred Hoop* and a novel called *The Woman Who Owned the Shadows*, and the pace is killing her too. When I talk to Judy Grand and Adrienne Rich, it's the same pace. Whenever I showered, my hair ended up in the bathtub and I was afraid of going bald. It was falling out in chunks and I thought, "I'm going to be the first Chicana bald woman." I went to the doctor and they gave me a thyroid test but it's just the stress. So I have to find a way of slowing down. So, if you have any ideas . . .

H. T. Well, I'm not sure. I can't think of anything off the top of my head. I think I'm just giving you more work, I'm afraid.

G. A. Because I already had a full schedule before you called.

H. T. I'm sure you did.

G. A. But because you were from out of town, I thought, this poor man. You were interviewing other people, right?

H. T. Yes, I've interviewed Gary Soto. I will also interview Ana Castillo before I leave and Arturo Islas, and then Cherríe Moraga will be in New Mexico June 1 so I'll interview her then.

G. A. Well, I wish you luck.

Awards

2001 American Studies Association Bode-Pearson Lifetime Achievement Award
1992 Sappho Award of Distinction
1991 NEA Fiction Fellowship
1990 Lambda Literary Award, Lesbian Small Press Book, *Making Face, Making Soul*
1986 Before Columbus American Book Award, *This Bridge Called My Back*

Primary Works

Llorona, Women Who Howl: Autohistorias and the Production of Writing, Knowledge, and Identity. San Francisco: Aunt Lute Press, 1996.

Making Face, Making Soul/Haciendo Caras: Creative and Critical Perspectives by Feminists of Color. San Francisco: Aunt Lute Press, 1990.

"Metaphors in the Tradition of the Shaman," *Conversant Essays: Contemporary Poets on Poetry.* Detroit: Wayne State University Press, 1990.

"El Paisano is a Bird of Good Omen." In *Cuentos: Stories by Latinas*, edited by Cherríe Moraga, Alma Gómez, and Mariana Romo-Carmona. New York: Kitchen Table Press, 1983.

This Bridge Called My Back: Writings by Radical Women of Color. Edited with Cherríe Moraga. New York: Kitchen Table Press, 1981.

This Bridge We Call Home: Radical Visions for Transformation. Edited with Analouise Keating. New York: Routledge, 2000.

"To(o) Queer the Writer." *InVersions: Writings by Dykes, Queers, and Lesbians.* Vancouver: Press Gang Publishers, 1991.

Selected Secondary Sources

Alarcón, Norma. "The Theoretical Subject(s) of *This Bridge Called My Back* and Anglo-American Feminism." In *Criticism in the Borderlands: Studies in Chicano Literature, Culture, and Ideology*, edited by Héctor Calderón and José David Saldívar, 28–39. Durham: Duke University Press, 1994.

Barnard, Ian. "Anzaldúa's Queer *Mestisaje*." *Multi-Ethnic Literature of the United States* 22, no. 1 (1997): 35–53.

Cohen, Ralph. "Do Postmodern Genres Exist?" In *Postmodern Genres*, edited by Marjorie Perloff, 11–27. Norman: University of Oklahoma Press, 1988.

De Alba, Alicia Gaspar. "'Tortillerismo': Work by Chicana Lesbians." *Signs* 18, no. 4 (1993): 956–63.

De Hernandez, Jennifer B. "On Home Ground: Politics, Location, and the Construction of Identity in Four American Women's Autobiographies." *Multi-Ethnic Literature of the United States* 22, no. 4 (1997): 21–38.

Deutsch, Sarah. "Gender, Labor History, and Chicano/a Ethnic Identity." *Frontiers: A Journal of Women Studies* 14, no. 2 (1994): 1–22.

Elenes, Alejandra C. "Chicana Feminist Narratives and the Politics of the Self." *Frontiers: A Journal of Women Studies* 21, no. 3 (2000): 105–23.

Farrell, Joseph. "Classical Genre in Theory and Practice." *New Literary History: Theorizing Genres II* 34, no. 3 (Summer 2003): 383–408.

Fernandez, Roberta. "Abriendo caminos in the Borderlands: Chicana Writers Respond to the Ideology of Literary Nationalism." *Frontiers: A Journal of Women Studies* 14, no. 2 (1994): 23–50.

Franco, Dean. "Re-Placing the Border in Ethnic American Literature." *Cultural Critique* no. 50 (2002): 104–234.

Hames-Garcia, Michael. "How to Tell a Mestizo from an Enchirito®: Colonialism and National Culture in the Borderlands." *Diacritics* 30, no. 4 (2000): 102–22.

Kaminsky, Amy. "Gender, Race, Raza." *Feminist Studies* 20, no. 1 (1994): 7–31.

Kaup, Monika. "The Architecture of Ethnicity in Chicano Literature." *American Literature* 69, no. 2 (1997): 361–97.

Martin, Biddy. "Lesbian Identity and Autobiographical Difference[s]." In *Life/ Lines: Theorizing Women's Autobiography*, edited by Bella Brodzki and Celeste Schneck, 77–103. Ithaca: Cornell University Press, 1988.

Saldívar-Hull, Sonia. "Feminism on the Border: From Gender Politics to Geopolitics." In *Criticism in the Borderlands: Studies in Chicano Literature, Culture, and Ideology*, edited by Héctor Calderón and José David Saldívar, 203–220. Durham: Duke University Press, 1991.

Torres, Hector A. "Genre, Gender, and *Mestiza* Consciousness in the Work of Gloria Anzaldúa." In *Contemporary Literary Criticism*, edited by Tom Burns and Jeffrey W. Hunter, vol. 200. Michigan: Gale Publishers, 2005.

———. "*Mestiza* Consciousness and dialect(ic)s: Gloria Anzaldúa's *Borderlands/ La Frontera: The New Mestiza*." In *Literatura Chicana: Reflexiones y Ensayos Crítícos*, edited by Rosa Morillas Sánchez and Manuel Villar Raso, 321–32. Granada: University of Granada, 2000.

———. "In Context: Gloria Anzaldúa's *Borderlands/La Frontera:* The New Mestiza." In *U.S. Latino Literature: A Critical Guide for Students and Teachers*, edited by Harold Augenbraum and Margarite Fernández Olmos, 123–33. Westport, CT: Greenwood Press, 2000.

Notes to Chapter Four

1. If the history of genre attests to anything, it attests to a certain inability on the part of writers from classical times forward to keep genres pure—the law of genre as Horace coined it (see Farrell 2003). Indeed, one might take the history of genre and the disposition of writers to mix genres as one more sign that postmodernity is not a simple linear concept in Western history and historiography, but a complex repository of Western memory, an archive of all the materials available to writers at any given cultural moment. This synchronic view of the postmodern might go some distance toward explaining why current literary theory on genre observes that the features defining a text as postmodern are *revenants* haunting contemporary literary production. In his essay "Do Postmodern Genres Exist?" Ralph Cohen observes this aspect of postmodern genres, pointing out that such features as multiple discourses, narrative discontinuity, ironic self-reference, etc., have been present

in Western literary discourse since the eighteenth century (Cohen 11–25). Cohen raises the question of postmodern genres not only to answer it in the affirmative but also to offer a program of inquiry into genre history and theory. The issue as he expostulates it "is not a matter of multiple subjects or discontinuous narration, but of the shift in the kinds of 'transgressions' and in the implications of the revised combinations" (Cohen 16). In this respect, what Anzaldúa does with the genre of autobiography forms part of a history of literary transgressions and more, inasmuch as she generalizes the synchronic status of genre to articulate the uneven relationship that Chicanas have to the social act of writing—the literary modes of production.

2. Biddy Martin, "Lesbian Identity and Autobiographical Difference[s]," in *Life/Lines: Theorizing Women's Autobiography*, ed. Bella Brodzki and Celeste Schneck (Ithaca: Cornell University Press, 1988), 82.

CHAPTER FIVE

Ana Castillo
Two Interviews ⌒

Xicanisma

⌒ When I first read Ana Castillo's *Massacre of the Dreamers: Essays on Xicanisma* in manuscript form I immediately recognized its family resemblance to Gloria Anzaldúa's concept of low theory: critical theory that is easy to understand; borrows whatever it needs from the major critical texts for the furtherance of its project; uses and exposes the contingent authority of personal experience. Straightaway I told Ana I thought she had a very strong manuscript representing this mode of theory construction. Sometime later during Castillo's appointment as a visiting lecturer in the English Department's Creative Writing Program, she set up a meeting at a coffee shop across the UNM campus with Andrea Otañez who was at the time acquisitions editor for UNM Press. I heartily recommended it to Andrea as another powerful example of what French anthropologist Claude Levi-Strauss called the logic of *bricolage*—a species of *la pensée sauvage*—logic untamed by the ideological dictates of Western epistemology but which, nevertheless, can attain great heights of explanatory power.[1] *Massacre of the Dreamers*, thus first saw the light of publication with UNM Press and subsequently went to Plume, a subsidiary of the Penguin Group. The low theory Castillo constructs in *Massacre of the Dreamers* indeed mixes the authority of anthropology with that of personal experience. This mix of theory and practice that Castillo calls Xicanisma is meant to address women of color and contest the hegemony of white

feminism and patriarchy in all forms on the international scene—
a pervasive theme in all the discourses of Chicana feminism. The
introduction to the essays spells out in no uncertain terms the uneven
terrain and field of tension that Chicana feminism enters: "I introduce
here the word, Xicanisma, a term that I will use to refer to the concept of Chicana feminism. In recent years the idea of Chicana feminism has been taken up by the academic community where I believe
it has fallen prey to theoretical abstractions. Eventually I hope that we
can rescue Xicanisma from the suffocating atmosphere of conference
rooms, the acrobatics of academic terms and concepts and carry it out
to our work place, social gatherings, kitchens, bedrooms, and society
in general" (11). "The Ancient Roots of Machismo" exemplifies her
efforts to keep theory close to practice. In this essay, Castillo is intent
on tracing an Arab cultural influence on the formation of Spanish and
Mexican machismo. The argument's major premise that "there is no
justification for machismo" (68) clears out a discursive space in which
Castillo can critique the ancient roots of machismo without the heavy
machinery of scholarship that the Academy demands. Nonetheless,
Castillo's critique takes on an effective global scope as she allies
her language and experience to the texts of Nawal El Saadawi and
Germaine Tillion: the former being an "Egyptian Marxist-feminist
who has written extensively on the oppression of Arab women" and
the latter an anthropologist who "puts forth the hypothesis that much
of what constitutes Mediterranean and Latin cultures, traditions,
and even religious beliefs originated out of a geographical region
and civilization known as the Maghreb" (70–71). Castillo shows her
awareness of the unstable ground upon which her argument will be
built but the politics of restoring dignity to the lives of indigenous
women of the Americas prove too urgent to leave the task to aca-
demicians alone: "My own hypothesis will be scaffolded by Tillion's
argument as an ethnographer. By scaffolding I mean a provisional
structure from which we may try to see across the centuries and con-
tinents how humanity has evolved and connected through migration
and time" (71). Castillo borrows from Tillion in order to illustrate her
own hypothesis that persisting in Chicano/Mexicano culture today
is the "socioeconomic practice of patrimony (the passing down of
property through the father)" (72). It follows that the oppression that

Mexic-Amerindian women like herself have endured is rooted in the economy of patrimony. The logic of the thesis is effective not so much because there is a properly distributed middle term, as classical formal syllogisms demand, but because the major premise is already a universal negation of machismo and its authority in language, the family, and the ideological state apparatus. The mediations of Nawal El Saadawi and Tillion serve as rhetorical devices to generalize the subject onto a global collectivity. In her review of the text, Rosaura Sánchez pinpoints the uneven logic of the text but nonetheless concedes that *Massacre of the Dreamers* is effective on several fronts: "On the one hand, it makes sweeping generalizations about the Chicana populations and, on the other, it provides astute and penetrating insights into specific social problems, including sexism, racism, and 'socioeconomic subjugation' (33)."[2] Castillo's use of the lowercase "i" has surely to be situated in the maelstrom of low theory, and, consequently, in the contingencies of subjective identity, as the first interview situates this imperial English pronoun.

The Mixquiahuala Letters, Castillo's first novel, is a stylistic and generic experiment that, for good reasons, critic Alvina Quintana describes as a literary performative that "functions as an oppositional feminist discourse that challenges the limitations inherent in both Anglo-American and Mexican culture."[3] Furthermore, situating *The Letters* in a postmodern cultural matrix, she shows how this literary performative derives so much of its power and beauty from its exploitation of the resources and models of Western ethnography.[4] The ethnographic component is generalizable to all of Chicano literary and critical discourse inasmuch as this component expresses a desire to represent and for representation.[5] Like Hinojosa's work, *The Mixquiahuala Letters* shows little faith in the model of linear narration. Rather, Castillo chooses a narrative labyrinth of the type Julio Cortázar constructs for the Latin American literary tradition but adapts that technique for her own ends. The labyrinth is necessary if *The Mixquiahuala Letters* is to use the language of patriarchy without bending the knee to the Western *logos*, in whatever cultural/ethnic form it takes, i.e. Anglo, Latino, etc. Castillo's storytelling voice—that voice that has a need to put into story form the lives of the two principal subjects of the *Letters*, Teresa and Alicia—is the voice that first addresses the reader in the opening pages of the labyrinth and is underwritten by the initials A. C. Castillo subsequently delegates that voice to Teresa, who thereafter must tread the thin line between art and politics. In the interview, Castillo gives a nuanced account of how this experiment in the epistolary genre came into being.

So Far From God continues Castillo's experiments in literary ethnography. Castillo performed her "fieldwork" for this novel while she was a visiting lecturer in the Creative Writing Program of the University of New Mexico English Department in 1991, the datemark for the second interview. In teaching this novel at undergraduate and graduate levels, I have encountered the most resistance to both the novel's art and politics from native New Mexicans who feel that Castillo not only does not represent them fairly but who also see her as an outsider poaching New Mexican culture. The classical insider/ outsider problem of cultural anthropology makes an appearance with Castillo's production of this novel. Nativist *ressentiment* notwithstanding, *So Far From God* has generated a lot of critical praise since its publication. Critic Roland Walter praises the novel for its representation of community: "I read Castillo's creation of community—the collective activism that results in progressive change symbolized by 'the sheep-grazing' and 'wool-weaving cooperative,' selling 'hormone-free meat' to food co-ops run by and for the benefit of the people of Tomé—as a utopian solution to the loss of identity, assimilation, and the spread of Anglo culture."[6] Silvio Sirias and Richard McGarry also point to the novel's utopian dimension as an eminent aesthetic and political value in Castillo's ethnographic experiment: "In this tale of the life and death of Sofia's daughter, Castillo destroys several powerful archetypes of patriarchal society in order to build the world anew."[7] Inasmuch as *So Far From God* registers the Gulf War of 1991 in the death/disappearance of Esperanza, the utopian dimension in Castillo's work reminds its readers that the work of critique today must be carried out on a global scale, and still by whatever means necessary. The first interview begins with Castillo already underway in conversation, but without my tape recorder on. I conducted the second interview while Castillo was a visiting lecturer in the Creative Writing Program in the Department of English of the University of New Mexico.

The Death of the Creative Drives and the Academy

A. C. With my most recent book *My Father Was a Toltec* the reviews have been very, very positive, mainstream. Quote, unquote the *literati* without my wanting or trying, has responded very positively to it. One of the things that one reviewer said that pleased me very much was that I make the use of the language look easy and it's very difficult. She compared the writing to an athlete who makes the stunts—very difficult stunts—look very easy, like in the Olympics. It was in a very short passage where she said that, and I thought, "Thank you, because people will read it, because I have chosen daily to use language that's accessible to the people that I want to communicate with, and because I use social issues as the impetus for what I write." The combination of those two things means therefore that I'm a very simple writer. And when I have read people attempting to imitate that style, it doesn't work. It's a big mess. So I see that and I think, "You know, they take so much for granted because of the simple vocabulary and because of the social message"—as if all you're doing is jumping up on a soapbox playing a soapbox orator, which is certainly how I started out when I was nineteen. That pleased me very much because I saw that somebody was seeing and appreciating that aspect of the use of the language. I have seen a couple of examples of people imitating some of the issues that I deal with, picking up on the issues I write about in sort of the same fashion and sort of the same structure, but instead of coming out like a dance, it comes out like a desperate splash of whatever. That's been the dilemma of being a writer like myself, or anybody who's been disenfranchised and chose to be that way, is that you always got treated as if you were sort of a social protest street pole and you're never going to get past that.

H. T. Let me ask you a question to contextualize what I put on tape already. Can you tell me a little bit about your background in terms of education, religion, home, and language? You can take it in any order you want. Just to get a sense of your perspectives, how they got shaped.

A. C. Well, this is pretty standard—at home my first language is . . .

H. T. You're from . . . ?

A. C. Chicago. I was born and raised in Chicago. My mother's from Mexico City and to this day she doesn't speak English. My father was born and raised in Chicago. He's a Chicano and he still is bilingual. My mother speaks only Spanish. My brother and sister were from Nuevo Laredo so they didn't speak any English—they're older than me—when they came here. I was raised by my father's mother who was from Guanajuato. So she didn't speak any English at all. Before I went to school I only spoke to her in Spanish. I was very introverted, very shy during those first years.

H. T. Your father addressed you in both English and Spanish?

A. C. I'm sure he did. I don't have any recollection of it. But I would suspect that he did. He had and has a lot of friends, as you know from *My Father Was a Toltec*. All these guys were Chicanos. I remember them coming and teasing me and talking to me, but like I said if I was with my grandmother all day long and night, which I was, then that was my language. I can remember throughout grammar school not knowing a lot of words in English—common words in English that I knew in Spanish. Education was not a given, except to finish high school so that I wouldn't end up in the factory like my parents. I graduated from a secretarial high school. That would be the thing that I would have to do, although I loved to paint and draw and didn't have any kind of formal exposure to it or encouragement that I could draw very well.

H. T. Did you discover those talents in yourself early on?

A. C. Yes, when I was very small. What I tell people is that there are a lot of things that I don't like to think about because back then I just wanted to leave them behind. But I do remember now, for example, the butcher paper that my mother would give me a little piece of and I'd paint around the blood. I don't like to think about these things, it makes me *triste* remembering this stuff because I have a little boy who's five and a half and he loves to draw so I have stacks and stacks of scrap paper for him and drawing pads. He has markers, watercolors, and all this kind of stuff that for me was a hurdle. If she got junk mail, I'd open up the envelope and paint around the little clear envelope and draw—things like that. So anyway, my first love was the visual arts. The second one I had was a great facility for writing—expressing myself in writing. Once I decided I would go to college after this commercial high school business, I went to junior college. I was kind of torn because I was involved in the Chicano Movement, torn between following the route of sociology, being a social worker, etc., and being in the visual arts. About the third year of going to Northeastern Illinois University, a teacher's college, which I went on to grants and however I could, I realized that Chicago—I didn't realize it then—is such a racist city that by the time I was in my third or fourth year I had been so discouraged, so discouraged by the system, by my white male instructors, that I had lost all my confidence in my art.

H. T. Writing included?

A. C. I didn't show my writing to anyone. I didn't take any writing classes. I did just the visual arts. I ended up getting my degree to teach art, but by that point I no longer had any confidence to do any visual art. I couldn't draw very well anymore. I had a block.

H. T. So you felt a gap in your confidence.

A. C. Well, not a gap, but a pressure. I took classes at the institute when I went to junior college. It was terrible. It was about class, race, sex, everything. I was just out. I could be me if I had money, but I couldn't be me with no money and nothing else. So here I was female, brown, Chicana, political, no money. Certainly there were women of color that might go to Northeastern but they came from countries where there was money. No Chicanas were there. So by the time I was finishing and I was moving more toward the writing of poetry, I kept that away from the institution. To this day I've kept it away from the institution. I never went and pursued any kind of formal degree in English. I would not trust them. They were not there to serve me and who I had to be, and who I was supposed to be, and what they did to me in terms of my visual art was enough to have killed everything. It would have killed an entire artist.

H. T. What kinds of things? What are those traits, those features that build up a constellation of things giving you a clear picture that there's an oppressive method in the system?

A. C. I can tell you as an example what happened in my educational psychology class, because I was going to be an art teacher. And I remember hearing a remark in class about lazy or something Mexicans . . . something about the cultural poverty and the instructor supporting that remark. You can imagine what I felt like being there. On another occasion, we had a tenured art instructor who gave this assignment to us as we were already finishing our courses. It was to prepare a semester of art assignments geared, this is a quote, to "white, middle-class children." Now there was one other Latina who was taking these last classes. She was half Mexican, half Puerto Rican, not politically identified, not dark-skinned. She was just doing her thing. She spoke English very well. She didn't speak Spanish. She had the name Socorro something. I got along with her because she was Latina and that was what attracted her to me. So she worked very hard. She was one of twelve kids in her family. She was getting herself through school and also had a job. So at some point she was going to turn in this assignment late. So she went to the instructor and said, "I'm going to have to turn this in late," and he turned around in front of her and said, "These Mexicans and Puerto Ricans are so lazy." She was so shocked. I mean I would have expected something like that, but she was twenty times more shocked. She wasn't even identifying herself as being Puerto Rican or Mexican. She told me about this, and, of course, we looked into it, but since he had tenure . . . There were some other complaints against him, but there wasn't anything much she could do. Those are just the pressures working constantly against me. I was not getting any kind of attention or supervision from the art instructors, deliberately being barred because I was like this nonentity. They would sit there for three or four hours, devoting their whole studio time talking to some white boy or some pretty white girl. To this day, I haven't been able to go back to it. I wish that I could have. I feel like I missed the real calling that I was supposed to have and writing is sort of a secondary thing. I was really into the Chicano Movement and the Feminist Movement, and I remember working on a painting or drawing in class that had something, probably the Aztecs or something like that on it, and I remember, the only comment that I got from the instructor as he went by was, "That's propaganda." And I didn't get anything on technique. So things like that. It was constantly going through the system of the institution. It was systematically built to assimilate you. And so I have the kind of tenacity that makes me go through—finish things—but at the same time I didn't want to. I decided I knew enough to keep my writing to myself if I was going to maintain it.

Democracy in America: Feminisms

H. T.   What was your experience in the domain of religion?

A. C.   Well, of course, my mother is Catholic. My father is supposedly Catholic, but never practices it. My mother was also that way, kind of. She made sure that we went to church, that we were baptized, that we had our Holy Communion and confirmation, but fortunately, she's not a fanatic about the institution itself, so I sort of found my own way out of it, fortunately. When I was eighteen, I gave it up, did some other type of soul searching. And now at this point I feel that I'm at a place where I can have a very objective, critical, evaluation of it from a Chicana feminist perspective, which is very much needed without being tied into it emotionally. I don't feel anything emotionally, which is very important. I don't think like a Catholic at all. So even though it was part of my upbringing, I haven't practiced it as an adult.

H. T.   How do you define a Chicana feminist perspective?

A. C.   First of all, it involves the need to hold white society to a more democratic process. A democratic process has to be looked upon in terms of a particular society. While Chicanas are U.S.-born, English-dominant speaking, educated in public schools or by

Irish nuns, or what have you, they are very Mexican. Being Mexican, I feel I have a great sensibility about it—that we're still very much living in the sixteenth century culturally. Regardless of being first, second, or third generation, we have that same kind of background. So here we are in the United States, which has a pseudoliberal attitude. I say "pseudo" very intentionally regarding women. So what we are calling feminism does not impress the white woman, obviously. But it's taken within a context of a Third World culture. So here in the United States, we have a Third World culture. Take *The Mixquiahuala Letters* for example. Some people—I would say white feminists—might see it as a kind of neophyte attempt, an updated attempt for some kind of feminist self-understanding. Yet Chicana critics for the most part really love it because they have experienced and understand that process from which it is coming. Even though they may be extremely articulate U.S. doctoral graduates who maybe have never been married, never went that route, never had children, nevertheless, they know that this is one of their conditions—a Third World, sixteenth-century condition. Again, it's going back to the perspective that, for me, for the feminist perspective, comes from that understanding.

H. T. Are there any other defining features?

A. C. Within that, within understanding that, when you asked me that question about religion, I gave you a very personal response which was very clean, but when I think about it in terms of Chicana feminist theory, I don't in any form or fashion underestimate the influence that it has had. Within that, of course, everybody knows the paradigm of the virgin/mother that Protestants don't have, and this country is based on Protestantism, so that's a big difference if you're caught between that schizophrenic dilemma of being a virgin/mother as your ultimate goal and working with Anglo women whose primary goal is to work and succeed. And Mary was just another woman. Chicanas are predominantly from working-class backgrounds, predominantly mestiza, and that's a whole different thing from the kind of feminism that's arising in Mexico right now, which in most countries is usually women who are privileged and white even if they are Mexican and Catholic. So again I feel that I have a great deal more affinity with North African, Arabian women historically and presently than I do with any Anglo feminists here in the United States. Even though we speak the same language and interact in the same society, we have very different experiences.

H. T.   Do you think that would surprise a white feminist?

A. C.   Oh, yeah, because I think that it's been part of the recent gesture on the part of white feminists to incorporate the views of women of color because originally they felt that "we're all women, we're all in this together," while they had housekeepers, Mexican maids—condescending or patronizing, not totally convincing. Some are very sincere in seeing it, and some, unfortunately, are still caught up somewhere in the patronizing way. They can go to Nicaragua and say, "We have so much to learn from the Nicaragua women" and they're not seeing that the experience of the Chicana in the barrio is very similar. It's about surviving; it's about supporting children on your own; it's about interacting with this country that has intervened on our land as well. One of the most moving dialogues that I've had recently was part of this colloquium that Cherríe Moraga and I gave at Oberlin College over spring break and we sort of handpicked our students. There were about twenty students in there: wonderful, young, bright, diverse undergraduates. There was one student in there who was nicaragüensa trying to understand the Chicana experience. She was very concerned about what was going on in Nicaragua and she had a great deal of resistance to feminism even though she probably was without the theory because of the association with white women. I explained to her that the status of a Chicana is what one might be able to perceive maybe fifty, one hundred, or one hundred fifty years from now about Nicaragua if the U.S. succeeds in taking over Nicaragua. It would be the same thing because of what happened here in the Southwest. So we are not at the same place as feminists and as Latinas. We have certain things, practical things, which we have to work on together. Part of the reason why feminists don't acknowledge it is because of what happened to us and to our country one hundred fifty years ago. Nevertheless, circumstances haven't changed that much for us. And we have still been marginalized. Our culture has been capitalized upon.

Chicana Literature and Critique: "i exist"

H. T. What is the role of Chicana literature in that context you're describing—the context of oppression?

A. C. I'm working on a book of essays right now talking about Chicana feminist theory and I have this new literary agent who's very disappointed that I didn't have any fiction to give her. She said, "Well, I respect the fact that you feel you need to do this book even though what I need to get from you is fiction." And then she said, "You know that Dostoevsky did more for the Russian Revolution than any of the essays that came out at that time. We understand this. We know how many poets have been put up against the wall and have instigated revolutions all along." So what this literature can do is a simple question of what art does: what is the purpose of art? This is a nonending controversy between the elitists who feel it's there just for the sake of the dominant, perpetuating their elitism. Then we have the other people who believe it's there to somehow emotionally move and raise consciousness.

H. T. Is there a particular technique you practice in your own prose and poetry to encode that struggle?

A. C. Do you mean language-wise?

H. T. In your use of language, when you sit down to write, to get something out, are there techniques that you're thinking about specifically that you know will capture that struggle?

A. C. Norma Alarcón and I translated *This Bridge Called My Back*. You know in Spanish we have the masculine and feminine use of articles and so at the very last minute we decided to feminize *puente* and we said *Esta puente es mi espalda*, in the spirit of what we were doing, trying to feminize the language as has been done in English. And of course the first thing that we get as Chicanas is that Chicanas don't know Spanish well enough to know that puente is supposed to be masculine. Never mind the fact that Norma, aside from being mexicana, has a doctorate in Spanish—poor Norma. This is her realm, her career. I heard she has like a two-page response now. We barely took that kind of risk again. We're taking a risk as scholars and also as Chicanas who live with the complex of not really understanding Spanish and not really being Mexican and all this kind of stuff. But on the other hand, in *The Mixquiahuala Letters*, when people have asked me about the use of the four endings—that this is so nonwhite male, that it's not linear—that's not stuff that I think about intentionally.

H. T. You don't?

A. C. No. I mean, that's a discovery on the part of critics. However, it is true that I'm not a white male and maybe it's possible that's naturally why I wouldn't write like one. And also again that I have never been appropriated into the white male mentality, by any means. I don't feel like I have any kind of secret desire to even be part of that. So I just do what I feel like doing. I don't think that I have a conscious objective, but I think that what happens is because of who I am—so much of who I am—because I firmly believe so much in who I am that it just comes through the writing. It's easy for me therefore to reject what models there are because they don't speak to me. So I need to create them. By the same token there were no Chicana writer models for me and so I had to create my model. I had to create Teresa and Alicia. It was never there, so I had to do it because I have to say to this world, "i exist." And when that world says all around me, "You don't exist, except by our creation, by our invention; you exist by my invention of you as a female, by my invention of you as an *indígena*, as an Indian-looking woman. You exist by my invention of you as an intellectual, as an artist, or as a writer, and this is the model that you have to follow," that's not a true model for me. That leaves me feeling like a shell because I know that it's only superficial. When I'm objectified as a female, I know that's what's going on and it's a real weird feeling. It's like being a ghost and you slip out of yourself and you say, "Who is that person? Who is she trying to be?"

and it doesn't make me feel good. My search has been a whole merging of those things, and it ends up coming out however it comes out. I think all writers are searching in one project after the next. I see that happening in my projects that I'm searching and I'm getting closer and closer to trying to understand who this woman is. And I don't care to dialogue with dominant society. I don't care, at this point, when there's some interest in quote unquote Hispanic literature. I don't care to fit the bill. I don't care to make a claim on this planet that I've existed and that the people who have been part of my life have existed and they're real and complex and they have the influence of thousands of years of culture that they bring with them here and it's not Anglo, it's not British, it's not Eastern European. It's North African, it's Indian, and it's Spanish, more recently. All of that comes together here, in this crazy place. It's like the new novel that's overdue, *Sapogonia*, where we all live—in Sapogonia.

H. T.   What's that novel about?

A. C.   It's kind of about what I'm telling you. Most of it is told in a first-person male narrative—the epitome of the Latino antihero. Not only is he a jerk in terms of women, but he also will do anything to try to assimilate and make it in this culture. That's one level of it, with a kind of antiromance going on with him and a mestiza who's from the United States and who is just the opposite. But neither one of them are heroes by any means. Real life people make mistakes all the time. And then the other level of it is trying to understand who we are as Latinos throughout the Americas, particularly in our relationship with the U.S. Again, what I needed to do on the social level is talk about how we're excluded from politics. Or, if you get into politics, it has to be a white-male trip. This was a personal goal—what I'm telling you—as a female, as a brown female, I needed to understand that objectification. Therefore, if I have nothing but something that other people have created and if I reject all of those things, what am I in the end? Who am I in the end? And there was no answer for me. Because there isn't. There hasn't been. I have indigenous blood, obviously, but I haven't been raised in that culture, so when certain people ask me, "What tribe are you from?" I haven't been raised in that culture. Obviously I can't speak from that culture. And yet I cannot speak as an Anglo, because I didn't inherit that. There's this big void for me out of which I create and find out who that is. When I say "I," I mean it in the small letter "i." We all need to find out who that is. And so I'm not quite sure that I have the answer yet. It's definitely not in *Sapogonia*. And *Mixquiahuala Letters* didn't have any answers; it just raised questions, raised issues. And *Sapogonia* will do the same thing: raise different questions. It will frustrate people because there are also no she-roes as well as no heroes. Raises more questions without any answers. It just gets frustrating, but that was the point when I finished *Sapogonia*: Who am I, if I'm none of these people, if I'm not this woman? I don't want to be this person in *Sapogonia*, in fact I destroyed her in the book, which I thought was kind of a cliché, a cop-out to kill her. I needed to kill her off for the next novel so I could start anew. But the use of all of that—like the things that you're asking me, they're all so inherent in terms of your perspective. The famous question, "Why do I use the small letter 'i' in *Mixquiahuala Letters*?" I've used it in a lot of my poetry from the beginning. First of all, it came from the fact that I did come from that collective consciousness of the Chicana, so we use the small letter "i" because we weren't speaking as eminent individuals but as part of a collective experience. But the other one has to do with—as I was telling you earlier—the fact that the use of language has very much to do with your perspective of the world. English, as far as I know, may be one of the few languages in which we capitalize the first person pronoun. We certainly don't do that in Spanish. We don't do that in Portuguese and in many indigenous dialects you don't even have a personal pronoun. A translator did a paper on this in my work and tried to figure out what you do when you translate my work. If you know that I use the small letter "i," you go from my use of Spanish to English, do you use my small letter "i" or does the translator use the capital "I"?

H. T. Can you say some more about *My Father Was a Toltec* along

A. C.   It's what I was telling you. I'm just as much a product of him as I am of her. And because the question of gender in society is so hung up with roles, I always acknowledged in a positive-never-being-able-to-achieve way that I am his daughter, in the sense that I have to work hard, and I have to be very self-sacrificing like in the poem "Saturdays": to endure and accept, not acknowledging that there's very much a part of me that just got that way, that just liked it. I didn't have any ill feelings against my father. I liked his free *joie de vivre* way, his youthfulness. He's not a father figure for me, not even a friend; he's more like a pal that I can talk to, and I like his personality. He's a very likeable, charming person. So there were these parts of me, literally. I would be mixed: "I have to work very hard or I'm worth nothing"; and then there's the other side: "You only live once. Go for it. Have a good time." And on the other hand, my father is obviously a traditional man and has a traditional male point of view about women sexually. He doesn't treat me in any of those paternal ways that make women feel terrible about themselves. But he has that deal about women and their sexual objectification. I have this mixture because I am a female and I do sympathize with my mother and the role that was assigned to her by our culture and by society versus the freedom that he gets as a male, which she doesn't get and that I want. So I always related to my father like a boy. Not because he wanted a boy. He didn't want kids. I was just there, and I related. I would say 90 percent of the time, in my interactions with men, I am just like one of the guys because I need to feel that whatever screwed-up condition they have regarding women, I don't want to be part of that. I don't want to sit there and be objectified. I don't want a father. I don't need male guidance. I don't need any of that. But men and women can have a nice interaction—intellectual exchange as equals—respecting and understanding the fact that we have a very different perspective about society and about the world. Men have nothing to tell me about the world because I've lived in that world, and I know what that world is about. I don't want to learn how I'm supposed to work in it. I don't need any advice from them.

the same lines of what you're saying about *Mixquiahuala* and *Sapogonia*?

A. C. The impetus for *My Father Was a Toltec* came when Sandra Cisneros said to me, "Most Chicano writers write about their childhood. You're one of the few who never does." And it hit me at that moment that it was true. I'm just one of those people that wanted to leave it private and let it rest. I saw myself beginning at the age of eighteen, when I was on my own and that was it. So I went back home after that and thought: Okay, this is a challenge. Let me write about that rather than focusing on the traditional, matriarchal legacy—and yes, my grandmother was a curandera; yes, my abuelita meant everything in the world to me, and I ended up at the last of it even dedicating the book to her. We were laughing about this. If we hear another abuelita poem, we're going to scream. That route I could have easily taken. My mother is the epitome of a hardworking, surviving Mexican woman. But what I found interesting for myself personally was my relationship to my father and how he was and how he influenced me. I am very much a product of his indirect upbringing. If you notice in *The Mixquiahuala Letters,* Teresa doesn't have a father figure and I did that intentionally since I'm writing within the Chicano context and the whole thing about women and feminism. All of this has always been kind of rejected, scorned. I was very careful not to mention a male figure because I figured some schmuck, a kind of pseudo-Freudian Chicano scholar is going to say, "Well, obviously, this is where she hates all men because her father beat her up or her father was a jerk or whatever." So I carefully avoided the relationship. What I needed to do was be true to myself.

Gender and Sexuality against Oedipus

H. T. Can you read these last three lines and comment on those?

A. C. "Oh, Daddy, with the Chesterfields / rolled up in a sleeve / you got a woman for a son." Well, what do you think?

H. T. I'm interested in the question of gender, sexual identity.

Art and Politics

H. T. You mentioned earlier that writing was secondary to the visual arts. Do you want to say some more about how you perceived that and what implications it has for your art right now?

A. C. I was talking to this Chicana art and literary critic recently and most of the critics that I talk to obviously are in literature, so it's rare for me to talk to someone who is in visual arts. I said to her that I felt kind of resentful that I didn't pursue the visual arts. I also feel that visual artists have a great edge over us writers along the lines of the Chinese expression "one picture is worth a thousand words." If you can develop your skill, you can express all of that through the visualization of your idea. In terms of literature, we have to learn to use language, to manipulate it, and as a Chicana this is very difficult for us because we're straddling these two languages and the complexes we have in both languages. We need to feel totally comfortable in English and totally comfortable in Spanish. We have to learn the various genres and break new ground in the use of the language.

H. T. You write in both languages, though.

A. C. But I only write poetry in Spanish. I don't write fiction in Spanish. I can't do it. I can talk forever in Spanish. Because my formal education through graduate school is in English, I can compose better in English.

H. T. So you see a difference between the genres of poetry and prose, in the ability of one genre to express what it is you want to say better than the other genre?

A. C. The poetry is sort of my filigree: very intricate work, very small, very concise. It takes a certain care. Maybe that's why I also like to use the Spanish with that because you can't string three words together in Spanish without starting to speak poetically anyway, so it works that way. Prose does go into a different realm. Now I have to go into long elaborations of storytelling and I can do different things. Some of that I do in *My Father Was a Toltec*, where there are stories within stories. You'll see if you read *Sapogonia*. I'm a natural storyteller. So my mind starts a story and then I go into another story, but I always remember my first story and bring you back around to that first story even if it's in the next chapter. Like I said, it's filigree work.

H. T. Is there more craft in poetry?

A. C. I think that would be an extremely controversial discussion because some writers don't do both. They can't do both. And I told myself in the beginning, "If you're going to do it, you're only going to do one thing. So you're only going to do poetry. Once you get the poetry down, then you can do another thing. You can't do it all." I do think that it takes a great deal of skill and attention to do each one. It's not that easy. When I was teaching creative writing this year, many of my students took it as an easy requirement, thinking they could wing creative writing as opposed to taking German. This was the first time they had to learn to do rewrites and I said at the end, "You know, this will teach you as far as your preconceptions about creative writing. Creative writing is not as easy as all that. It's not just writing freehand and saying 'I saw a flower bloom today.'" My son writes poetry like that and he's five years old. Better, in fact. It was like hell for both me and the students because they hated it and I hated them. It takes a certain care and attention to what you're going to do with it.

H. T. You're going to be doing a fellowship at . . . ?

A. C. UC–Santa Barbara. The Chicana Studies Department has a fellowship for Chicanas, which I have applied for. Basically I just have to be in residence, finish this book of essays, and in the spring give probably a seminar in my own work. And I really wanted to get back to my writing so that was just perfect.

H. T. You said some things about the whole question of Chicana identity, particularly your own. It sounds like you see identity as a process and yet, even as I heard you speak of it, it sounds like there is complete dispersal of the subject. Is it fair to say that, or is it wrong for me to draw that inference?

A. C. You know the problem around doing that. I'm fairly certain that if you study any poet of any given time, any sex, any class background, the question of searching for identity is there. It's inherent. It is a process of self-understanding, of going through life. Take Pablo Neruda, ambassador for his country, writing poetry reflecting the issues of his life. What I'm saying is that the difference between me and Neruda is that I'm not a man from a middle-class elitist background. My government is not sending me as ambassador so I can go and write poetry in some other place. What is different with women of color is that they are the very last permitted a voice. What we are hearing now is this very unique, silenced, previously censored voice.

H. T. Is it possible for Chicanos to understand that voice?

A. C. I think there are some Chicano scholars that are making kind of a sincere effort because they have been around Chicanas. Because of their mothers, sisters, wives, and daughters, they're trying to understand the Virgen de Guadalupe dilemma: "My mother's a saint. My girlfriend's a whore. My wife is the mother." So I think there is a kind of genuine understanding, but sometimes it goes to that paternalism and I think one of the greatest offenses that I can get (even though I understand it, therefore, I don't express it; I never express it when it comes up) is that kind of paternalized treatment. They can't help it. The conditioning is such that, "I can't be her lover; I'll be her father. How else am I going to deal with her?" I do notice that, for example, younger men, not all of them, but some of them are different. I think that part of that comes from the fact that now they have a new generation of mothers that may have gone to college or they are in college now and getting literature like *The Mixquiahuala Letters*. And so this is a different time and some of them really open up their minds and think about this. And I would say maybe half, so we'll see what develops in the next ten years.

H. T. One last question. Where does your literature come from? Where does your art come from?

A. C. I don't know. I think that it's all a combination of idea, emotion, and technique. The artist is the one who's trying for the technique. And the other two are who I am as a human being: the intellectual side, the questioning side, and the emotional side. All of those are part of being the artist. Without any of those three things, you can fail as an artist. If you fail with the technique, but you have a lot of passion and ideas, of course you don't succeed as an artist. Also, if you just have a lot of emotion and you don't communicate well, and if you just communicate a lot, then you're an intellectual and you're doing essays. You're not doing literature, storytelling. So I think those three things. What makes an artist? I have no idea. You're born into this world with it. I don't think anybody picks it. So where it comes from is not even a question for me. When you're in your early twenties and everybody is sort of dabbling in poetry, dabbling in things, if ten years later you see them, and they have straight jobs and you're still plugging away, it must be something in you that is truly that. It's about that.

H. T. Endurance.

A. C. Tenacity. Tenacity for sure. But it's the fact. I have talked to Cherríe about this and other people. Cherríe and I are very much the same in that there's no question in it for us. We never think, "Oh, I'll just do it later." It's always of the utmost importance when we have an idea, when we have a challenge. When a question comes to your mind, you say, "How am I going to express this?" and then you have to do it. You have to do it even if you have a job, or if you don't have a job. If the beans are burning, or whatever you have to do, you have to do it. And other people don't quite get it. Other people go for the straight job. Go for the money. I just gave up this appointment to collect more than half a cut in pay and I was going to take a zero cut just to go back to the writing because the writing is my reason for being. I mean, we manage, we eat well, and we have a roof over our heads. It's a matter of priorities. I think that's what it is. And the particulars have to do with the social contexts, as you're saying.

H. T. Thanks very much. I appreciate it.

A. C. It was fun.

DATE OF INTERVIEW 2: January 28, 1991
SETTING: Leon Howard Library, Department of English, University of New Mexico, Albuquerque, New Mexico

From Poetry To Prose: Passages

H. T. Let's begin again, if you wouldn't mind, with a short biography of Ana Castillo.

A. C. I was born in Chicago, Illinois—born and raised—and spent most of my life there.

H. T. What was the date?

A. C. June 15, 1953. And I was there almost all my life, with the exception of one year that I lived in California, and I returned to California in 1985 and lived there until 1990. I moved to Albuquerque in the summer of 1990. Do you want to know about education?

H. T. That's good. Yes. I wanted an idea of salient dates in your life. Can you give us a short history of the works that you've published and the circumstances surrounding the writing of each work?

A. C. *Otro Canto* is a chapbook. There were two hundred copies printed in Chicago, Illinois, in 1977, illustrated by Marina Gutiérrez, an artist in New York. I got a little grant from the Illinois Arts Council, but I was primarily supported by friends who were Chicano-Mexicanos who were working in community arts organizing and publishing a magazine, which they printed in their shop using magazine paper. That day or the day after they printed it, they literally went out of business; their machines were taken away and they left all the copies there. This was in the West Side—in the Mexican barrio of Chicago. And then *The Invitation* was first printed in 1979, and again in 1986. The first print run was two hundred copies, and the second one was approximately six hundred copies. It's hard to tell because this was one of those hands-on projects. I got support from friends to do that book, and the Playboy Foundation that was based in Chicago at that time printed it in their facilities. And in 1986, again I solicited support from friends and people who knew my work and I was able to do that project. In 1985 *Women Are Not Roses* came out through Arte Público Press. Basically, those poems were selected by the editors. They selected a few of the poems from *Otro Canto*, from *The Invitation*, and a few new poems for good measure from *Women Are Not Roses*. In 1986 *The Mixquiahuala Letters* was published through Bilingual Review Press, and in 1990 *Sapogonia* came out. But I wrote *Sapogonia* between the years of 1984 and '85.

H. T. Is there anything about those works, any of the details and circumstances surrounding the writing of those works, that now stand out to you?

A. C. *The Mixquiahuala Letters* is the work I think about the most in terms of my writing because I made my transition from free-form verse poetry to fiction. It took me a long time to teach myself, since I'm a self-taught poet. It took me also a long time to learn to sustain the distance. The writing in *The Mixquiahuala Letters* tends to be more poetic prose. So when I first started to work on that, which was in 1976, I was twenty-three, and I had been writing poetry for about three years. I knew I had the story and I knew what I wanted to do with the time sequence, and all those kinds of things, but I didn't know anything about writing fiction. And subsequently *Otro Canto* came out, and *The Invitation* came out before I was able to really get into that project. I concentrated on it and finished it in '84. I concentrated on it between '82 and '84, off and on, teaching myself the mechanics of fiction writing. In 1980 I really started to concentrate on teaching myself, again, to write short stories.

H. T. So the learning process . . .

A. C. It took a long time. That project took place maybe over seven years, but all that time was about developing myself as a writer, both as a poet and as a fiction writer.

Remembrances of Racial Tensions

H. T. You said you were born in Chicago. What was it like? What was your family life like, things around the house, your relationship with your parents, the languages that were spoken in the house?

A. C. My mother's first language is Spanish. She was from Mexico and migrated north. And my father's mother also was from Mexico. These were the two nurturing figures that I grew up with in my home. Neither spoke any English at all. My father is a Chicano, born and raised in Chicago, and was very fluent in both languages. My older brother and sister, who were born in Nuevo Lardeo, Texas, their first language was Spanish and they learned in English in school. So Spanish is and has always been part of my psyche.

H. T. Did you grow up speaking Spanish first, or a mixture of the two languages?

A. C. I was exposed, obviously, to Spanish at home, and I remember English in school. I remember also being very, very quiet when I first started going to school—panicking—so I have a funny feeling that had something to do with language at that time.

H. T. How did you relate to your parents and to your siblings?

A. C. My mother, until just the last years, has always worked. She did factory work, assembly line work. My grandmother was the one who was raising me since I was a baby. She was a curandera. She was home. We had kind of community traffic there, people coming and going because of her. She passed away when I was going on ten. My brother is eight years older and my sister is six years older, so there was a little bit of an age difference there, so I wasn't quite growing up with them.

H. T. Would you say that Spanish was part of all their psyches, too?

A. C. My sister and my brother don't speak much Spanish, but it's understandable under the Chicago public school system that we went through. But they both understand Spanish very well. As I said, my mother still doesn't speak English to anyone.

H. T. *¿Como se hablaban entre ustedes?*

A. C. I don't remember that my brother and sister ever spoke to me fluently in Spanish.

H. T. No? How about between your mother and your father? Did you speak a lot of Spanish with them?

A. C. Yes, even now, I only speak Spanish to my mother. And my father was bilingual. Mostly he spoke Spanish to my mother and to his mother. And I always recall him addressing me mostly in English, but he felt comfortable going back and forth.

H. T. What about life around the neighborhood and your early experience with education?

A. C. I lived in two apartments, two flats, until I left home. And the first one was torn down when I was ten, and that's where the University of Illinois Circle Campus is—it's right by our house—one of the first Mexican barrios. I went to the same public school that my father went to, and my older sister and brother had gone to, and by the time I went there it was mostly black. And that was a little hard for me. It was pretty tough. It was a very tough little public school. There were some Mexican children there, a couple of gypsy kids, but the majority were black and it was pretty rough.

H. T. Racial tensions?

A. C. Oh, yeah. Well, believe it or not, in that kind of circumstance, I might be considered a little white girl, even though I was Mexican—very Mexican to my own thinking. Then we were relocated by the city, by Urban Renewal, or "Urban Removal" as they call it! These are things I hardly think about now, but in my writing I guess they come up. And one of the things I remember is that they were knocking on everybody's house and we were one of the last families to leave, so they had to move us; they had to find an apartment for us. My father just didn't have that kind of motivation. When the next house was going to be bulldozed down, they put a circle with a cross on it, you know, *un exceso*. I remember the cross on our building. Anyway, they moved us a few blocks over to another neighborhood, which was primarily Italian, just on the border where the university was going to begin. And then I went to the public school there, where the majority of the kids were Mexican because that's where the Mexican kids went whose parents didn't have the money to send them to parochial school. The Italian kids, of course, went to the parochial schools. Or Catholic school. There were at least six or seven Catholic schools and churches in that neighborhood because it had always been an Italian neighborhood and still is. It's called now "Little Italy," that neighborhood. And that was very hard for me. I grew up there, spent my teenage years there, and it was very difficult because of the racism of the Italians against people of color. They were extremely racist. In the middle of that neighborhood is a housing project, which was 99 percent black, and you just didn't go by there without asking for trouble. The Italians literally were hateful of other people of color—Mexicans, blacks, and Puerto Ricans.

H. T. But you didn't encounter them much in the schoolyards, for instance, or in the classrooms?

A. C. The only Italian children that came to my school were the ones who got kicked out of the Catholic school, and they were the bad ones. When they'd get thrown out, as a last resort their parents would have to put them in the public school. But, of course, I ran into all these girls and these guys in the neighborhood. It was one of those city neighborhoods, old-fashioned neighborhoods, where everything you did was there. You go to the cleaners; you go to the eye doctor; you go to the dentist; you go to the market. All of these businesses were all privately owned and they were all Italian merchants. And I did everything there: ice skating or swimming at the park district there. It was pretty insulated, but it was always encumbered by the tension of the racism. And our landlords, who were Italian, were very racist and gave us a very, very hard time. It was a very hard upbringing because of that.

Education in a Racist Climate

H. T. What about your university experience? When did you first decide to go to the university? Tell us a little bit about your educational history at the university level.

A. C. I graduated from high school in 1971. That was during the time of the Chicano Movement. When I was a junior and senior in high school, I went to a secretarial school. I was going to be an office worker. I had absolutely no college prep. In that setting, you worked half a day in an office downtown and then you went to take classes. When I was a junior, I started to develop a political consciousness, when I was about sixteen, and I started working in the Chicano Movement, protesting and tutoring children in the neighborhood, these kinds of things. I was working with a friend of mine, a young black woman who was going to a vocational school, who told me about the Art Institute of Chicago, which I had never heard of. It was a big museum and school. I didn't even know there was an art museum. She was going to go there. I was so taken aback by the fact that another person of color was going to go to college, would consider going to college. That was the first inkling I had that maybe I could go to college. So anyway, when I was a senior, I applied. I couldn't get money.

H. T.   You applied to the Art Institute?

A. C.   Yes, and I was not accepted because I had no training. You have to submit a portfolio.

H. T.   Right after high school?

A. C.   Yes. And also, even though it was a smaller school then, they had a total of seven people with Hispanic surnames.

H. T.   Seven.

A. C.   I know this because I knew someone much older than myself, a Vietnam veteran and Puerto Rican, who was very much a part of the Latino Movement and was trying to do something in the school. I knew there were seven people that were allowed at that time. That was in 1971. And I say Hispanic because they were not—aside from one or two people that I knew—they were not necessarily politically identified; it was just their names. In any event, I didn't get in there. I didn't get any grant money. I was accepted at another university, but I didn't have the grant money. My parents, although they were not opposed to my going to college, didn't see any point in it. They thought I should stay in the office work. And they were not prepared to send me to school. Finally, what I decided to do was go to City College. So I went for two years to City College, and then I went to Northeastern Illinois University, which was originally a teachers' college, and majored in teaching art in secondary education.

H. T.   And do you remember the date for that?

A. C.   I was there from '73 to '75. And I was part of the Chicano Student Union there that had just been organized.

H. T.   And what was that experience like?

A. C.   Again, these were the years of a great deal of political consciousness, so at Northeastern there were, at that time, approximately two hundred people with Spanish surnames: there was the Puerto Rican scene and there was the Chicano Student Union. We made a demand for a Chicano faculty person, as there were none. We did get one, a sociologist, and he was like Our Fearless Leader for a while. He was a very young man working on his PhD and he had a lot of energy, and so my last year there, I do remember the Chicano Student Union, and I remember hanging around in that office with the professor and the other people. And I was already a published poet by this point. From the ages of nineteen or twenty until twenty-two or twenty-three I had already started writing and publishing, so I was also doing readings, and I was known around town for that. But my experience in City College and at Northeastern—and I did take classes freelance at the Art Institute—was that the majority of the faculty were, of course, white and almost always male, except for this one person. There were, again, obvious racist overtones in my classes, so that by the time I was finishing college, I was so discouraged as an artist, I turned to the writing. I literally got a mental block and wasn't able to paint anymore.

H. T. Really?

A. C. And I didn't go for my teaching certificate.

H. T. So that was roughly around '75?

A. C. It was between those years from '71 to '75, my four years of going to school. I also spent one summer in Mexico, which was also a racist experience, because they were all American, middle-class or upper-middle-class, white students.

H. T. Yes.

A. C. It's hard for people to believe in the kind of experiences that I had, maybe because those things aren't prevalent now, but also this is Chicago, and Chicago is known for that. So I had tenured professors who didn't hesitate to be insulting of Puerto Ricans and Mexicans in their classrooms—and they could get away with it.

H. T. And you personally felt that?

A. C. I saw it. I experienced it. I heard it in my classrooms.

H. T. And the net effect was that it turned you away from one form of being an artist, to another form of being an artist, a writer?

A. C. Well, I didn't get any kind of nurturing or mentorship; I was only discouraged, and constantly, whenever I exposed my work, it was criticized or ignored—mostly ignored. I started to write, away from the institution. On the outside, while I was in college, I was organizing in the Latino artists' communities, and I was part of two or three of the Latino artist organizations of Chicago at that time, and in 1974, I was one of the cofounders of an organization of Latino artists that, in fact, did an exposition at Northeastern Illinois University to feature Latino art. But I personally was so psychologically screwed up from trying to get a degree—because most of these artists were not college people, but community artists—that I started to write poetry and I got support from them. I couldn't risk getting discouraged.

H. T.   But you had been writing poetry already, right? You had been writing since '71?

A. C.   I was writing and drawing since I was a child. I could write very easily. When I was in elementary school I would write these little novels, and the teachers would get off on them just because it was me writing them on my own. But my love was the visual arts, and so I started there.

H. T.   So would you say that there was a definite decision that you would concentrate on the written medium?

A. C.   Yes. Somewhere between 1973 and '75, but definitely in 1974, I sat down and said, "I'm going to be a poet," and started doing readings around the city with musicians, accompaniment, the whole thing.

H. T.   You're known as an artist who works both with poetry and prose, and you've already talked a little bit about how *The Mixquiahuala Letters* is a kind of poetic prose. By convention, writers have to work within genres, right? And you're one writer who works very well across these genres. What relationship do you see between the genre of fiction/the medium of prose?

A. C.   Well, when I was just interviewed recently, I was made to think about that, and I felt that it's an extreme advantage to begin as a poet. It sort of "fine tunes" your sensitivity to the sound of language, to imagery, things that you just appreciate. You can appreciate the language that you're writing in much more when you are forced to work with a very—I don't know if "constricting" is the right word—medium. Given only a certain amount of space and time.

H. T. With the poetry?

A. C. With the poetry. And so I think that the poetry helped me a great deal to do the prose. And you see it more visibly in *The Mixquiahuala Letters*, for example, than in other short stories, than in *Sapogonia*, for sure. I trained my ear for this kind of internal assonance. I learned from one of my early critics that I use internal assonance! And I trained my ear for that, so that it comes out in some of my prose, too. And I heard it when I read *The Mixquiahuala Letters* out loud.

H. T. So you're very sensitive to the sounds and rhythms of the language per se. Now, how is that different from the constraints of prose? You seem to be very much aware of the constraints in poetry. Are you aware of any like differences and/or constraints in prose? When you sit down to write prose, do you feel like you're working within certain constraints?

A. C. The example that I just gave you works most clearly with *The Mixquiahuala Letters*. You don't see that as much in *Sapogonia*. And I'm also working on some long fiction now. It's a different challenge; it's a different voice. If you are going to work something beyond twenty pages, beyond the short story, if you want to sustain two hundred to four hundred pages, you find the voice that you are looking for. There the constriction would be—is—maintaining that voice, maintaining that rhythm, maintaining that particularly language to keep your readers convinced of this narrator. And so each project has its own challenge. I think that the challenge for me right now, with bringing new voices into each long piece, is that I sustain them, because they're not—contrary to popular belief—me talking. It's not my autobiography. It's a character I have created, whether I decide to use the first person or not.

Experiences in Storytelling

H. T. Where does Ana Castillo get all her voices?

A. C. [*Laughs*]

H. T. I take it that the voices cut across both the poetry and the prose, right?

A. C. It's just an ear for it. I'll use *Sapogonia*'s Maximo Madrigal as an example.

H. T. Okay.

A. C. I wrote a short story, and one of my first short stories, when I was trying to teach myself to do fiction, in 1980 was called "The Anti-Hero." It was the summer where every day I just tried to write something like that. And it worked very well. It was a first-person narrator and he was this sort of timeless, arrogant, aristocratic Latin American, Latino. And that worked very well for five pages—that's how long that story is. And I ran that across a writer friend and she said I should develop that into a novel. I didn't begin writing that novel until 1984. One of the main reasons was that I didn't know if could I sustain that voice. So for five pages, it's easy, but for four hundred pages it was another story.

H. T. And the voice was something that you just sat down and started to write, and it just came?

A. C. Well, I'll tell you. For example in *My Father Was a Toltec*, Tomás de Utrera is a real person. He knows the poem. I try to keep my ear fine-tuned for people—for their stories and for their use of English. "The Anti-Hero" is based on an individual whom I made into a character whose first language is Spanish. He always speaks to me in Spanish, but occasionally I hear him in English. And I also write a lot while thinking in Spanish and I translate it into English, and you get that sort of "baroque" sound. So I've been able to do that. Tomás de Utrera is a fluent English speaker and an absolutely fluent Spanish speaker, so that voice came out of a conversation, one of the many conversations that we've had. I think it's just a matter of picking things up, having an ear for the idiosyncratic use of an individual's language.

H. T. The experiences in *The Mixquiahuala Letters* that you tell stories about—how many of those experiences are journeys that Ana Castillo herself has taken?

A. C. My standard response to that question—as you must guess this isn't the first time that I've been asked this—is that I would say approximately 40 percent of the final manuscript that came out as *The Mixquiahuala Letters* is based on experiences that Ana Castillo did have. Now what percentage of that 40 percent in the story is something that you'll have to figure out, or let it go. I can say this much: life is sometimes stranger than fiction, and I had to sort of moderate some of it, otherwise it was too unbelievable.

H. T. How long did it take you to write that novel, and where were you during that time when you were writing?

A. C. I wrote it all in Chicago. And, as I said earlier, I started in 1976 and in the process did the chapbooks and then *Women Are Not Roses*, and then taught myself to do fiction.

H. T. So these works were going on concurrently?

A. C. Oh, yeah. I concentrated on it—I would say somewhere between '82 and '84—in the winters primarily, because there were some long, hard, dark winters in Chicago, and I can only remember myself working on them in those periods of time.

H. T. Some of your critics of *The Mixquiahuala Letters* have made the comment that Teresa seems to own a monologic voice in the text, to the extent that she seems to be speaking for Alicia or recovering events for Alicia in the forty letters. Some of your critics had said, frankly, that it seems to them Teresa is taking over the voice of Alicia. How do you respond to those critics? I'm not one of them, of course! But how do you respond to them?

A. C. How should I respond to that?

H. T. I don't know. I'm curious about what you think about that. As I told you, I don't agree with those critics.

A. C. The only thing I can say is that I do remember that Teresa tells Alicia that she is writing this project because she needs to figure it out, because Alicia doesn't want to talk about it. Even when she announces that she's working on this project, or this book, or these stories—I don't know how it's phrased in there—Alicia walks away from her and doesn't want to know. So the only thing I can say, taking it out of that text, is that Teresa needs to do this for Teresa. There's another example in there where she's talking about the Yucatan, and she said, "I know you're going to disagree with me whether it was this hotel room or that hotel room, and let's not get into semantics here" because the point of the story is the psychological experience or trauma that they had, that she needs to work out, and not whether or not was it really here or there. So I think she explains that a couple of times.

H. T. Okay, good. Teresa is the one who needs to put into story form all those events.

A. C. Also, Alicia is a visual artist and there is a letter in which Teresa goes to her opening in New York, and she is told the story visually.

H. T. Thank you, that's wonderful. Now I want to take that same idea and apply it to Ana Castillo. We know that between Alicia and Teresa, Teresa is the storyteller of the two, in terms of words, which is what you just said very clearly. Now, what about Ana Castillo? What is it that makes her tell stories? What is it that makes her into a storyteller? Why did she want to be a storyteller in the first place? When did she find out that she was a natural storyteller?

A. C. Like I said, now that I have to think about these things, I know that I was telling these stories in picture form, and in my own way, as a child, writing out very long, long narratives with illustrations, stories that I made up in my head as my way to survive my childhood. But when I think about it now, looking back—you don't know how much you're putting on for who you are now—my father was a talker. He always loved to talk, to tell stories; it didn't matter if you were listening or not. Even though I'm more quiet than he was—he was a pretty open person—I did in writing what he did when he would go on and on and on and tell stories over and over in a social context and over the kitchen table. I get a lot of that desire to be with people and tell stories from that because it was a very pleasant experience for me. I think there is a tendency for that in the Mexican culture, so it's part of our oral history, I suppose. I'm isolating him, but if I get my mother by herself—she was a very quiet woman—she'll tell me all kinds of stories about her upbringing and her family and great grandmother.

Chicana Language(s)

H. T. Do some stories come easier to you in one language or the other?

A. C. Because I was educated in English, that's the language that I can write in.

H. T. But you do a lot of writing in Spanish in *My Father Was a Toltec*.

A. C. Again, I think that I have battled the known dilemma of the bilingual Chicano in this country, so that I felt insecure for a great deal of time with both languages, writing both languages and not necessarily speaking them. And I have developed the English more so. I started writing Spanish as a child, too. It's one of our traumas and one of our dilemmas in this country.

H. T. The two languages?

A. C. That the two languages exist for us in our thinking processes and in our perspectives on life and the world and they're very different realities, as well. And yet we don't usually have the privilege of hearing or seeing that language in its best, where it's most articulate, where it's even its general, standard form. My father was a fluent English speaker but he spoke Chicago, urban working-class, street English and Spanish. The Spanish that I know is not, obviously, an educated Spanish—it was a Spanish that was among working people.

H. T. Have you had any formal education in Spanish, or just from your travels? Is that where your Spanish takes on different layers?

A. C. My mother started to teach me to write in Spanish when I was about ten. But I never studied Spanish. I studied Portuguese in graduate school.

H. T. Was there some motivation for that?

A. C. I like the language. I really did, and majoring in Latin American and Caribbean studies at the University of Chicago, you not only had to speak English and Spanish fluently, but you had to choose another language that's used in Latin America, so I chose Portuguese.

H. T. Is Vincent Das Mortes related to that?

A. C. Who is he? Well, it was written not long after I finished graduate school. Between all of that—starting to write *The Mixquiahuala Letters*—I also went to graduate school and majored in Latin American Studies, and then went to Brazil, so there was a time in the early eighties when Portuguese was easy for me.

H. T. You have a Master's in Social Science?

A. C. Yes.

H. T.   And then from there you went to Brazil?

A. C.   As soon as I finished.

H. T.   A Master's in Latin American Studies?

A. C.   Latin American and Caribbean Studies, in the social sciences.

Art and Politics Made Anew?

H. T.   Let's talk about the relationship of art and politics and your views on that relationship. I notice, for instance, that in *Sapogonia*—as one example of many—you experiment with your prose, with your language, as when in your opening chapter of *Sapogonia* a dramatic pronoun shift occurs.

A. C.   It does!

H. T.   And thereafter, the perspectives are signaled by shifts in pronouns. And other interesting things, too, are going on—that's just one example of many. Do you see a relationship between this way of experimenting with language and your political views?

A. C.   I think maybe, in a very broad, global way, I would say that that's absolutely true, in the sense that I have always been a rebel against the institution—the university—as far as creating something different. That goes with the time element, and so, I think that in the broad sense, yes. It's about bringing down some of that and introducing something new in the twenty-first century—a new way of thinking. It's all connected—the language and what's going on in society at a particular time.

H. T.   I'm asking the question for many reasons, but one reason is that obviously, when you experiment in that way, you do it at the risk of leaving some readers behind. So I guess another dimension to that question, is how do you anticipate that? How do you reconcile your need to do this artistic experimentation with the need to be read?

A. C.   When I started to write poetry, I was writing from the social-political impetus, not to write love poems or "personal" poems but to write about the politics of being Latino or Latina, of being Chicano. So it was important for me to write a kind of poem that wasn't esoteric, that wasn't going to be off-putting to people in general, people who would not normally be attracted to that genre. And I feel that to a certain degree *The Mixquiahuala Letters* maintains that, but I cannot explain to you all the complexities and the workings of my mind, and why I start to do what I do. But I do think, still, that despite the complexity of *Sapogonia*, that we shouldn't underestimate a general readership. Therefore it's different like much of the literature that I have enjoyed reading, that I enjoy reading and learning from—which was written by Latin American writers—when I was eighteen and nineteen and twenty years old. And it was very different. I've always been attracted to experimental literature.

H. T. Which writers were you reading back then?

A. C. One of the first people I read was García Márquez and *One Hundred Years of Solitude* when I was about nineteen or eighteen. And Julio Cortázar. I read all of Jorge Amado. I can tell you I read everybody and everything. And they would drive me nuts! But I was compelled to it. I was driven to the mechanics of what they were doing. When García Márquez won the Nobel Prize for *One Hundred Years of Solitude*, they said it was a writer's book. I read and reread Julio Cortázar to try to learn from the writer the labyrinth of his style.

H. T. What did you learn from Cortázar, if you could summarize it in a nutshell?

A. C. Well, I think he is one of the best examples of playing with time. When I was going to write *The Mixquiahuala Letters* I was twenty-three, and I had this idea about playing with time— that time was fluid—and I mentioned this project to a friend of mine, who was getting his Master's in Spanish literature, and he said that's already been done!

H. T. Teresa tells a story called *"Un cuento sin ritmo* / Time is Fluid." Is that related, in terms of the need to get it down on paper?

A. C. I really wanted to do that, and the editors modified some of the playing with the tenses in that particular little section. That was the only section in that book in which I really deliberately tried to do that.

H. T. The time is fluid.

A. C. Yes, and that was the only section where I was trying to play with the tenses deliberately, in one sentence. And, as I said, the editors modified it somewhat. Not so much from sentence to sentence, but within the sentence, I think they probably felt it was a little too confusing.

H. T. Do you see your desire to work that way as a political decision?

A. C. That's why I said earlier that I think in the broader sense, in my feeling of a global commitment, ecologically, and all the other ways that we are all connected on this planet, yes, I would say that, but not in the very specifics that I work in.

H. T. So you strike a balance between a global political commitment versus a local commitment to some kind of aesthetic perspective of your own?

A. C. No, I think the aesthetic is just me. And I think the specific is that—if I am talking—I have a very conscious commitment to Latino people, here in this country. I feel very motivated by the fact that, as a Chicana, we are torn into a rather countryless state of existence—not to have a point of reference—which works on your head philosophically, spiritually. I was not born in Mexico. I was born in Chicago with a very heavy Mexican orientation. Those are my specific ways of dealing, and those are the stories that you hear. I have a commitment to that. I have a commitment to many of my major characters who have brown skin. That's a commitment to the story of a different character that you're not used to seeing in literature. In Julio Cortázar's work, for example, I can deal with his Latin American history, I can deal with the language, but his women have white, porcelain skin. They're Argentine, probably from a European background. My people, for the most part, are mestizos. And so I get into the kind of trappings of that mestizaje, and what that's like. So I do that on a very conscious level. The aesthetic—I think playing with my medium—comes from my artistic orientation. If I had stayed in the visual arts, I don't know what I would be painting now. I probably wouldn't be painting the Aztec figures that I was doing in 1975, but I'd probably be doing something with paint, and my medium would be multimedia, probably because as an artist you continue to challenge yourself with your aesthetic and with your medium. So that part, I think, really is me as an artist.

H. T.   That's an interesting idea.

A. C.   Another way of putting that is that I have found my voice. You usually encourage a young writer to find her voice, to find his voice—a place in which they feel comfortable and strongest.

H. T.   And one interesting aspect about the body of work is that your voice seems not only to reflect but also to refract a very diverse reality and through your storytelling voice you create a Chicana feminist subject. In other words, your works have that political edge to them, but they never lose sight of some kind of story-telling aesthetic emphasis.

A. C.   Because I'm all of those things. I didn't start out as an essayist, for example, in which I would have extracted that feminist idea and just discussed it. I identified with the Chicano politic, the Latino politic. So that came into play. All of those things have been part of my personal learning experience, my quest, and also my commitment to society. So, how do I make that com-mitment? Well, as an artist, I make it by creating. In creating— and I have chosen to write stories, whether they are in poetry or in prose—all of those lessons, all that comprehension that I pick up as a socially conscious human being comes into those sto-ries, always. Maybe the fun thing about something like a novel is that you can split it up in ten characters, or five characters, so one character doesn't have to say or do all of those things that you want to say. You can have different people, and not every-body has to be politically correct, which is the way the world is. So I can do that, and I can play it off and set up the scene for it. You know, it's that early radical feminist adage of the personal being political. So you set up a scene—it's a home, or it's a love story—and in there you have the dynamic of those two or three characters playing off each other.

H. T.   How is the voice of Maximo a refraction of Ana Castillo?

A. C.   [Laughs] I think that he is representative, in many ways, of a particular time in our history as Latinos in the U.S. and Latin Americans. As I said, coming from the early Chicano Latino Movement, which was dominated by men, I was compelled to understand this individual. I found him seductive and at the same time repulsive, but someone who dominates. It was very important for me, as a woman and as a feminist, to try to get into the workings of this kind of person's mind and try to understand him.

H. T. Does that mean that you are breaking down the way the subject is gendered socially, and that you are able to move across the skins, so to speak, between man and woman? You can understand what it is like to be a man, for instance?

A. C. I don't want to be so presumptuous just because I wrote four hundred pages on it, but that was my attempt.

H. T. Is it possible for a woman to understand a man? Is it possible for a man to understand a woman?

A. C. What has been said in our society, in which we do live with a hierarchy, is that the oppressed or the subjugated have the advantage of understanding that group that they are subjugated or oppressed by, because that culture—that way of thinking— dominates. I look around the world, and I see we're at war. I see the language of the battles, the equipment that's being used, and all of that is unequivocally a man's world. The structure of the buildings, the projectiles—everything has been based on that kind of thinking. So I don't think that it's too presumptuous or unfair for me to say that it's easier for a reflective woman to understand the male world, maybe not a particular individual man or all individuals she runs into, but the male world. That's what I was trying to do in *Sapogonia*. I hear—as a challenge back to *Sapogonia*, for example—writers say, "I'm going to write a book in the voice of a woman," and so, of course, I have some problems with that because even I, as a woman, when I wrote *Sapogonia*, found it much easier to understand the male character than I could understand who woman is. Who is woman? If she has been so distorted for so many thousands of years, how can I say that who I think I am is not more than just a reflection of the society or history?

H. T. Let me ask you this. In light of that point, which I think is very persuasive, how are we to read the ending of *Sapogonia*— which is also the beginning—but also in light of the epilogue to *Sapogonia*, in which we have an almost idyllic picture of Pastora at some level embracing some sort of existential peace about her life? Do you see some relationship between those two possible endings?

A. C. Again, it goes back to my inability to have a conclusion in life. I do see it that way, that kind of circular motion. I didn't want to just kill her off because that's too easy. It was the thing you would expect: she has to die, she's rebelling, let's kill her. And so, therefore, I could not see him destroying her because that's what he has to do either figuratively or actually. He has to get rid of her in his mind. But at the same time, I thought it was too much of a cop-out for me to just follow that and kill her off. That's part of my feminist philosophy of history—human history—that continues.

H. T. So the sacrificial act works on the side of showing the patriarchy that destroys women. Is what I'm calling "existential peace" possible for that Chicana subject?

A. C. Well, I'm not sure if I understand or agree exactly with her "existential peace." As a conformist, there's a superficial peace that she has, but underlying that we know that she's still driven by this dynamic in which she knows that she is simply a projection of his creation.

H. T. Thanks, that's great. Let me ask you a little bit about the present: what it is you are doing now, what brought you to Albuquerque, and what we can expect from Ana Castillo in the future?

A. C. Well, in California I worked. For five years I was teaching, doing readings around the country, and some of my books came out at that time. Three of my books came out at that time. I was a single parent and I worked on *Massacre of the Dreamers* at the University of California at Santa Barbara, my first nonfiction thing.

H. T. What's the status of that? Can you tell us?

A. C. This is January 1991, and I would like to go back into it, polish it up, and hone it for publication. Hopefully, at some point this year, I'll have it ready to go out to some publishers, and we'll see what happens.

H. T. So you'll be striking out into new territory?

A. C. It's not new for me, but it's new for readers.

H. T. For your readers.

A. C. Yes. And so with getting the NEA, I came here to . . .

H. T. When were you awarded the NEA?

A. C. Last year. I split my stipend up for two years.

H. T. And before that, you were at UC–Santa Barbara?

A. C. As a fellow.

H. T. For a year?

A. C. Yes.

H. T. What was the date on that?

A. C. '89 to '90.

H. T. And before that you were at Chico?

A. C. Yes, as an assistant professor. I was working full time there, teaching.

H. T. And the date would be?

A. C. '88 to '89.

H. T. So you've been moving a lot?

A. C. I've been moving every year.

H. T. And now that you are here in Albuquerque, what are your plans?

A. C. I was really hoping to take advantage of this very unusual time that I have to myself that as I said I have not had for many years because I was caught up in four book projects. I also have *The Third Woman* issue that I coedited on Latina sexuality overlapping some of these. And I also translated *This Bridge Called My Back*, which took over two years, which overlapped with the teaching and the other books that I was working on. So then I threw myself into *Massacre of the Dreamers*, and that took everything out of me. So I couldn't just say, "I think I'll work on some poetry here this afternoon." I was working seven days a week on this. Not only was I attempting to write theory, but I was attempting to write theory in a new genre. I'm always introducing something in a poem or in prose, but you don't have to prove any of that; you just go and do it. Anyway, what I was hoping to do here—and I think I'm going to be able to do it—is to have some solid beginnings toward a new novel by spring, which I'm working on now—a new fiction project and a new collection of poetry.

H. T. Any prospective publishers for those works?

A. C. No. I'll send them out together as a package deal. Actually, my agent will do that for me, so that I'm no longer trying to represent myself in the world, so that I can have both of those out at some point.

H. T. Ana, I want to thank you for granting me this interview, and you were very generous in giving us so much of your life in your work.

A. C. Thank you, thank you.

Awards

1998 Sor Juana Achievement Award by the Mexican Fine Arts Center Museum in Chicago 1994 Mountains and Plains Booksellers Award

1993 Carl Sandburg Award

1990 National Endowment for the Arts Fellowship for Poetry

1987 Before Columbus Foundation American Book Award

Primary Works

Carmen la Coja. With Dolores Prida. New York: Vintage Español, 2000.

Esta Puente, Mi Espalda: Voces de Mujeres Tercermundistas en los Estados Unidos. Eds. Cherríe Moraga and Ana Castillo. San Francisco: ISM Press, 1988.

Goddess of the Americas/La Diosa de las Américas: Writings on the Virgin of Guadalupe. New York: Riverhead Books, 1996.

I Ask the Impossible: Poems. New York: Anchor Books, 2001.

The Invitation. Berkeley: Third Women Press, 1979.

Keats, Poe, and the Shaping of Cortázar's Mythopoesis. Amsterdam: John Benjamins, 1981.

Loverboys: Stories. New York: W. W. Norton, 1996.

Massacre of the Dreamers: Essays on Xicanisma. Albuquerque: University of New Mexico Press, 1994.

Massacre of the Dreamers: Essays on Xicanisma. New York: Plume, 1995.

The Mixquiahuala Letters. New York: Anchor Books, 1986.

My Daughter, My Son, the Eagle, the Dove: An Aztec Chant. New York: Dutton Books, 2000.

My Father Was a Toltec: Poems. Albuquerque: West End Press, 1988.

My Father was a Toltec and Selected Poems, 1973–1988. New York: W. W. Norton, 1996.

Otro Canto. Chicago: Alternativa Publications, 1977.

Peel My Love Like an Onion: A Novel. New York: Doubleday, 1999.

Psst—I Have Something to Tell You, Mi Amor: Two Plays. San Antonio: Wings Press, 2005.

Sapogonia: An Anti-Romance in 3/8 Meter. New York: Anchor Books, 1990.

The Sexuality of Latinas. Ed. with Norma Alarcón. Berkley: Third Woman Press, 1993.

So Far From God. New York: W. W. Norton, 1993.

Watercolor Women, Opaque Men: A Novel in Verse. Willimantic, CT: Curbstone Press, 2005.

Women Are Not Roses. Houston: Arte Público Press, 1984.

Selected Secondary Sources

Derrida, Jacques. "Structure, Sign, and Play in the Discourse of the Human Sciences." In *The Structuralist Controversy: The Languages of Criticism and the Sciences of Man*, edited by Richard Macksey and Eugenio Donato, 247–65. Baltimore: The Johns Hopkins University Press, 1970.

Elenes, Alejandra C. "Chicana Feminist Narratives and the Politics of the Self." *Frontiers: A Journal of Women's Studies* 21, no. 3 (2000): 105–123.

Gonzáles-Berry, Erlinda. "*The* [Subversive] *Mixquiahuala Letters*: An Antidote for Self-Hate." In *Chicana (W)rites: On Word and Film*, edited by María Herrera-Sobek and Helena María Viramontes, 115–24. Berkeley: Third Woman Press, 1995.

Heide, Markus. "The Postmodern 'We': Academia and Community in Ana Castillo's *So Far From God* and in Denise Chavez' *Face of an Angel*." In *U.S. Latino Literatures and Cultures: Transnational Perspectives*, edited by Francisco A. Lomelí and Karin Ikas, 171–80. Heidelberg, Germany: Carl Winter Verlag, 2000.

Levi-Strauss, Claude. *The Savage Mind (Nature of Human Society)*. Chicago: University of Chicago Press, 1968.

Martinez, C. Elizabeth. "Crossing Gender Borders: Sexual Relations and Chicana Artistic Identity." *Multi-Ethnic Literature of the United States* 27, no. 1 (2002): 131–48.

Mermann-Jozwiak, Elisabeth. *Postmodern Vernaculars: Chicana Literature and Postmodern Rhetoric*. New York: Peter Lang Publishing, Inc., 2005.

———. "Gritos desde la Frontera: Ana Castillo, Sandra Cisneros, and Postmodernism." *Multi-Ethnic Literature of the United States* 25, no. 2 (2000): 101–18.

Paredes, Raymund. "Review Essay: Recent Chicano Writing." *Rocky Mountain Review of Language and Literature* 41, no. 1 (1987): 124–28.

Porsche, Michael. "*So Far from God*: Ana Castillo's Telenovelistic Xicanista Reassessment of the Paulinian Triad." In *U.S. Latino Literatures and Cultures: Transnational Perspectives*, edited by Francisco A. Lomelí and Karin Ikas, 181–90. Heidelberg, Germany: Carl Winter Verlag, 2000.

Quintana, Alvina. "*The Mixquiahuala Letters:* The Novelist as Ethnographer." In *Criticism in the Borderlands: Studies in Chicano Literature, Culture, and Ideology*, edited by Héctor Calderón and José David Saldívar, 72–83. Durham: Duke University Press, 1994.

Rodriguez, Ralph E. "Chicana/o Fiction from Resistance to Contestation: The Role of Creation in Ana Castillo's *So Far From God*." *Multi-Ethnic Literature of the United States* 25, no. 2 (2000): 63–82.

Sánchez, Rosaura. "Reconstructing Chicana Gender Identity." *American Literary History* 9, no. 2 (1997): 350–63.

Sirias, Silvio and Richard McGarry, "Rebellion and Tradition in Ana Castillo's *So Far From God* and Sylvia Lopez-Medina's *Cantora*." *Multi-Ethnic Literature of the United States* 25, no. 2 (2000): 83–100.

Torres, Hector A. "The Ethnographic Component in Chicano/a Literary Discourse." *Aztlán: A Journal of Chicano Studies* 25, no. 1 (2000): 151–66.

———. "Story, Telling, Voice: Narrative Authority in Ana Castillo's *The Mixquiahuala Letters*." In *Chicana (W)rites on Word and Film*, edited by María Herrera-Sobek and Helena María Viramontes, 125–45. Berkeley: Third Woman Press, 1995.

Walter, Roland. "The Cultural Politics of Dislocation and Relocation in the Novels of Ana Castillo." *Multi-Ethnic Literature of the United States* 23, no. 1 (1998): 81–97.

Notes to Chapter Five

1. Claude Levi-Strauss, *The Savage Mind* (Chicago: University of Chicago Press, 1966), 16–33. See also a necessary complement to this discussion involving mythical thought/la pensée sauvage: Jacques Derrida, "Structure, Sign, and Play in the Discourse of the Human Sciences," in *The Structuralist Controversy: The Language of Criticism and the Sciences of Man*, eds. Richard Macksey and Eugenio Donato (Baltimore: The Johns Hopkins University Press, 1972), 247–65. In this reformulation of what Levi-Strauss variously calls mythical thinking or bricolage, Derrida generalizes this form of thinking to include the mathematical logic of engineering on the grounds that both are forms of practical problem solving and hence both involve creative thinking.

2. Rosaura Sánchez, "Reconstructing Chicana Gender Identity," *American Literary History* 9, no. 2 (1997): 358.

3. Alvina Quintana, "Ana Castillo's *The Mixquiahuala Letters*: The Novelist as Ethnographer," *Criticism in the Borderlands: Studies in Chicano Literature, Culture, and Ideology*, eds. Héctor Calderón and José David Saldívar (Durham: Duke University Press, 1991), 74.

4. Ibid. Quintana generalizes this double-edged relation that Chicana writers have to ethnography: "Chicana literature functions as a bold cultural intervention, which ironically enough resembles what we have come to respect as interpretative or experimental ethnography" (74–75).

5. Hector A. Torres, "The Ethnographic Component in Chicano/a Literary Discourse," *Aztlán: A Journal of Chicano Studies* 25, no. 1 (2000): 151–66.

6. Roland Walter, "The Cultural Politics of Dislocation and Relocation in the Novels of Ana Castillo," *Multi-Ethnic Literature of the United States* 23, no. 1 (1998): 91.

7. Silvio Sirias and Richard McGarry, "Rebellion and Tradition in Ana Castillo's *So Far from God* and Sylvia Lopez-Medina's *Cantora*," Multi-Ethnic Literature of the United States 25, no. 2 (2000): 87.

CHAPTER SIX

Sandra Cisneros

Two Interviews

Stories Not Written Before

Sandra Cisneros's *The House on Mango Street* is widely recognized as a Bildungsroman. Chicana critics Tey Diana Rebolledo and Erlinda Gonzáles-Berry delineate certain differences between the Chicano and the Chicana Bildungsroman: "In contrast to the young male hero who at the end of the Bildungsroman comes into a complete sense of integration and freedom, the female adolescent is carefully schooled to function in society to lose her freedom and her sense of individuality in order to become a loving wife and mother. She thus integrates her destiny with that of a man who will protect her, defend her, and create a life for her."[1] Cisneros rejects this trajectory beginning with her first work of prose, *The House on Mango Street*, while a young graduate student at the University of Iowa Writers Workshop. There, as critic Robin Ganz puts it, she had an epiphany: "Although Cisneros claims that the Iowa Writers Workshop failed her, she experienced an epiphany there that she frequently designates as the moment her writing acquired a voice."[2] Cisneros retreads those steps at Iowa in the interviews and talks more about the sense of alterity upon which that epiphany arrived. Threading the variables of race, gender, and class, the sense of difference she experiences at the Writers Workshop vis-à-vis her classmates begins shaping the deconstructive voice of her storytelling protagonists throughout her work. The alarmingly simple voice of Esperanza in *The House on Mango Street* is deconstructive in force. Her critics consistently attend to this voice in *Mango Street* and in *Woman Hollering Creek*, where the storytelling voices multiply.

Despite its allusion to Virginia Woolf's *A Room of One's Own*, *The House on Mango Street* differs from that classic of Anglo feminism precisely because the tradition in which the former text stands systematically ignores the variables of race/ethnicity and class.[3] In the sense of otherness that Cisneros experiences at Iowa resides her desire to represent disempowered voices. It is that sense of difference/alterity/otherness that gives Esperanza's voice its deconstructive edge. The ring of deconstruction can be heard in the titular story "The House on Mango Street" expressed in the desire for a house that isn't on Mango Street. At the moment that the nun asks Esperanza where she lives and the little girl points to the house, Cisneros brings the reader into a deconstructed space: "*There*. I had to look to where she pointed— the third floor, the paint peeling, wooden bars Papa had nailed on the windows so we wouldn't fall out. You live *there*? The way she said it made me feel like nothing. *There*. I lived *there*. I nodded" (8). The repetition in italics of the word *there* points to a building in disrepair. Matching this disrepair is the sudden loss of being Esperanza experiences with the *there* issuing from the nun's question. This emptiness is not on par with the emptiness that someone such as a nun would seek to fill through the spiritual practices of the Church. Rather this act of discursive violence suspends Esperanza over the abyss of her desire to have a "real" house: "I knew then I had to have a house. A real house. One I could point to. But this isn't it. The house on Mango Street isn't it. For the time being, Mama said. Temporary, said Papa. But I know how those things go" (9). Esperanza knows that her desire is somewhere else inasmuch as she can't even raise her arm to point but remains frozen in her desire for the real house. The real house is to come but first she must cross all the delays of time, being, and their evanescence.[4] The social act of writing will carry Esperanza/Sandra over those delays and when she arrives not only must she return to Mango Street, she must do so with a sense of justice the nun did not have. Cisneros addresses extensively in both interviews the ethical commitment to others/the Other that she developed as a consequence of her experiences with the discursive violence that registered in Esperanza's psyche. The parallel to her experience in the Iowa Writers

Workshop is unmistakable. Cisneros does not tire of encouraging her students to seize the literary modes of production, telling them to write over the obstacles that the dominant culture places in front of them. "The Three Sisters" reiterates this ethical commitment. These figures/ *comadres* allude to the three Fates of Greek mythology: one to spin the thread, the second to measure it, and the third to snip it. Like the figure of the Shadow Beast Anzaldúa posits in *Borderlands/La Frontera*, the three comadres appear to Esperanza from her unconscious as creative drive, making a demand of her: "When you leave you must remember always to come, she said" (97–98). While the ethical demand to return clashes with Esperanza's desire for a real house, making her feel guilty for the desire, Esperanza/Sandra also knows that the demand really springs from her own need to mete out a life that makes a difference to others/the Other. When Esperanza says, "I didn't understand every-thing they had told me. I turned around. They smiled and waved in their smoky way. Then I didn't see them. Not once or twice or ever again," (98) Cisneros is suspended over her commitment to the social act of writing from birth to death—a fruitful delay.

Woman Hollering Creek broadens that commitment as Cisneros's storytelling voices multiply. In her reading of this text, critic Harryette Mullen goes some distance toward tracking this exponent in the work of the unconscious: "The repression of subordinate cultures and lan-guages by the dominant culture and language is paralleled by, and frequently associated metonymically with other repressed elements that erupt from the 'unconscious' of the text to disturb, contradict, or at least complicate its conscious signification."[5] This critical statement is in synergy with Cisneros's sense in the second interview that the multiplicity of voices that go into the stories of *Woman Hollering Creek* were always there. Mullen carefully tracks the generic and linguistic plays that make *Woman Hollering Creek* resonate with the voices of the Mexican multitude: "Searching for and validating folk and popu-lar articulations often excluded from 'the literary,' Cisneros employs throughout the entire text of *Woman Hollering Creek* a network of epi-graphs taken, not from the literary traditions of the United States or Europe or Latin America, but instead from Mexican ballads and romantic popular songs that circulate throughout, and indeed help to constitute, Spanish-speaking communities through dissemination of recordings, through jukeboxes located (along with *tortillerias*, *mercados*, *cines*, and *botanicas* [sic]) in Latino neighborhoods, and through Spanish-language radio stations broadcasting to cities or geographic regions with large Spanish-speaking populations."[6] In the second interview, Cisneros comments at length on the process she goes through to internalize the multitude of voices she hears daily so as to transform them into literary form. In a brilliant reading of "Never Marry a Mexican," Mullen shows how the signifier "Mexican" has multiple references, rendering the advice of mother to daughter at best indeterminate: "While on the surface it seems unequivocal, her mother's advice is actually cryptic, ambiguous, and certainly ironic, in part because 'Mexican' frequently is used to refer not only to Mexican nationals but also to naturalized and native-born U.S. citizens of Mexican descent."[7] At its worst, the advice of mother to daughter misfires when daughter Clemencia is seen as unmarryable by Drew, her Anglo lover, because she is Mexican. Mullen takes Clemencia's act of vengeance—placing gummy bears throughout Drew's apartment where his wife will find them—as the point in the telling where she is most Mexican.[8] Whether Clemencia's act of revenge is a sign of how Mexican she is or not, Cisneros's story certainly speaks to the difference between Anglo and Mexican/Chicano patriarchy—virtually none.

DATE OF INTERVIEW 1: June 1990
SETTING: The home of Sandra Cisneros in San Antonio, Texas

Educational Faultlines

H. T. Can we talk about the whole issue of education? Could you give us the history of your education and then talk about this whole question of gaps in your education?

S. C. I was educated in Chicago Public Schools for the first year and a half of my education and then we were quickly ushered into Catholic school for the rest of my life, it seemed, because of the neighborhoods we grew up in. My brother had gone to school for a year in Mexico and was used to a very disciplined form of education. My younger brother and I had stayed in Chicago and we were in the public schools. When he came back and moved into the neighborhood there was a lot of chaos in his classroom and he came home saying the little kids are all crazy and he couldn't learn because of the way he was used to a disciplined, military-school-type atmosphere in Mexico. So my mother and father took us out and put us into Catholic school, and that was in the middle of second grade, and from then on, I went to Catholic school not because my parents were devout but because there wasn't an alternative to getting your kids an education and not getting them beat up in the schoolyard. So we went to Catholic school not because they wanted us to have a Catholic education. My mother is kind of a freethinker. My father is a lazy Catholic. "You go [to church]; light a candle for me," he would say. All the women in the family were devout Catholics and the men stayed at home. So he didn't really care if we went to Catholic school but that system of education continued 'til I was in high school for the same reason that the Catholic high school was in the neighborhood. That was the alternative to going to public school where we would wind up with all those bad kids, the riff raff, hanging around there. So because I grew up in the mean neighborhoods there wasn't a choice for parents like ours. Then, when I graduated from high school, I went to Loyola University of Chicago, and this is curious. The reason why I went there was the nostalgia for my childhood; that is, my older brothers and I hadn't gone to the same school in years and they were enrolled at Loyola University of Chicago because they were in the sciences and the school has a good premed program. I went because I thought it would be nice to be in school with my brothers and I was just an English major and every school had an English Department so what did it matter, right? So I went off to Loyola University for that curious reason. Also, because it was a city school, you didn't have to go anywhere, just stay in the city and there wasn't even a question of going anywhere at that point. There was money also for me to stay in the dorms if I had wanted to. That would have been real brave for me to step out of my father's house, but my father made it very clear that under no circumstances was I going to live in the dorms.

H. T. How about your brothers? Where did they live?

S. C. In the dorms, because there was money there. Not me! I was always very, very protected to the point where I could never stay at anyone's house for a pajama party or anything like that, which, as a child, you don't understand why. You have no idea why your father is so adamant about that, but again my father said, "No, under no circumstances" and I was still very much under his control and I didn't know to question it. I'd just say, "Okay, I don't care." I had to take a very, very long public transportation route to get to school. Later on, my boyfriend—I had a boyfriend in college—would pick me up even though it was out of his way. He didn't like seeing me take that long route so he would come to get me, yelling and shouting because I never woke up on time. I was still sleeping. I was still dreaming and I had to get dressed in the car on the way there, pulling up my pantyhose. He was always yelling, "You're always making me late!" And then from there I went to school at the University of Iowa, the Writer's Workshop. My junior year at Loyola I met a writer who was recently hired there and he sent me to his teachers in Iowa and that's how I wound up in Iowa. If he had not been hired, I probably would have been teaching high school English and trying to write on the side and not even knowing where to start. So that's my education down to the University of Iowa and with no sense of what I was getting into.

H. T. You got your MFA there, right?

S. C. Yes, but I had no idea that it was a prestigious place or that it was difficult to get into, or that my getting in meant something good about myself. I thought they felt sorry for me and had some sort of affirmative action quota to meet and that I must have been there by mistake because how could I have gotten into the University of Iowa, coming from the type of education that I came from, the poor, Catholic schools that didn't have money for art supplies or any extra things, you know, very poor schools? I didn't realize how prestigious that school was 'til I got there. That's where my race- and class-consciousness began. As long as I was at Loyola University in this multiethnic city you could think that the world was like that and things were happening to you, yes, little things that left their barbs in your heart, but that you could attribute to something else. You didn't have the language or consciousness to articulate it and it wasn't until I got to Iowa that I started realizing, "Hey, wait a second."

H. T. What happened in Iowa?

S. C. Something happened that had never happened—well, it happened all the time but I had attributed it to being a new kid because we moved around a lot—and that is, I felt other. I started thinking that I wasn't very smart or that something was wrong with me. I would say something and the teacher would look at me; everyone would look at me like I was a Martian, so I didn't say anything after a while. My friend Joy Harjo and I got very quiet in those sessions. And that was when we'd sit in the back and once she looked at me and joked and said, "Just like the Indians!" and I laughed and I thought "No wonder the Indians don't say anything!" I didn't know why people jumped on me or were very antagonistic when I said something. I just thought "Oh, now I really stuck my foot in my mouth or I'm just not being smart about this, talking about things I don't understand."

H. T. At the workshops?

S. C. Yes, and they didn't really like what I was doing or what Joy did. On the other hand, I was very young; I was too young to be in the Writer's Workshop because the average age of the workshop members was about twenty-eight. I was twenty-one years old and I didn't know shit. So I was just kind of muddling around, trying to read everything everybody else was reading and trying to sound like those writers. It always seemed like when I was an undergraduate it was my voice that came through because I wrote about what I knew. But when I got there I tried to write like my teachers, but that had started happening already my last year in Loyola. In Iowa I stopped writing about what I knew and I tried to write like my teacher, like my classmates, like the writers who the teachers liked. It was just like when I was an English major and I was trying to write this paper sounding like someone I'm not. If someone had only told me, "Talk your paper through and then go back and revise it and that will bring out the real personal part." Now I tell my students, "Write this as if you're in your pajamas. How would you say this if you were wearing your pajamas?" There's something about wearing your pajamas and saying something. You don't try to sound like [*laughing*] Walt Whitman. "How would you say this if you were at Dunkin' Donuts?" is what I say to my students. They always joke about that and call my school the writing of donuts, but to me, making language something alive is already happening in this day and age and in public places. For instance, talking to the woman behind the cashier register, would you say this to her? If you would not, then there's something wrong with your writing. That's what I say to my students now. How would you say this if you were talking to someone at Dunkin' Donuts? Use that voice. That's your voice. And even if you have to dress it up a little—that's your first draft to start something—say it the way you would say it. You don't have to hesitate when you want to talk to someone across the room, when you want to communicate with someone who's sitting across the table from you. You don't think, "Oh, how am I going to introduce this thought?" You just open your mouth *y sale como sale* and that's usually the purest way. Sometimes you make little stammers but that's okay; you put that all down and that's your first draft. Our minds have a very logical way of putting thoughts together again, but if we have to think about it, it's like trying to think about how to breathe—you know you're going to do it all wrong and get nervous and think, "Oh my God, what if I forget to exhale!" Relax, it's very natural. And that's how I base all writing. It's all based on speech and we all can talk. We all can communicate and if we can stay really close to the speech we use when we're in our kitchens, or in our pajamas, or at Dunkin' Donuts, not trying to impress anybody, but just coming from some real heartfelt part of you.

H. T. So did Iowa help you learn that? Or did you have to learn it independently?

S. C. No. See, it's funny. Iowa taught it to me in a naïve way when they shut me up. For a year when I was fumbling around and the break came between first and second year, it was that summer between those years when I think things started to gel. It happened actually in the second semester of the first year when I took a course in memory and the imagination and the books we were using were Isak Dinesen's *Out of Africa* and Nabokov's *Speak Memory*, books I really love. And then we had *Poetics of Space* by Gaston Bachelard, and I still don't understand that book, but the thing is, I came to class and everyone was so enthusiastic, talking about it and that's when it all hit me in that classroom. I remember my face feeling hot, *como cuando te sientes avergüenzada*. Even though you're brown, you feel browner. I felt hot and it occurred to me at that moment when they were talking about Gaston Bachelard's *Poetics of Space* that there was something about me that was different from everyone in the room and the thing that triggered it was that they were talking about houses. They were talking about the house of their memory, the attic of their memories, and the basement of their childhood. Well, I don't want to talk about the basement of my childhood because there were rats there! [*Laughing*] I don't want to go near those basements and we lived in third-floor flats and we didn't have attics. Who in the hell had an attic! And then all of a sudden it occurred to me in that moment that I don't have a house of childhood. All I have are some apartments. That's when everything slammed into me at that moment. I decided then that I didn't even like the stuff they were writing and trying to imitate. I'm going to do just the opposite. I'm going to write about stuff that none of these kids that come from all these schools can write about. I would make comments about Isak Dinesen. I'd say, "I think this is a wonderful book. I can't wait to share it with my mother if she read." I remember this East Coast writer turning around and looking at me with this kind of cut-and-dry advertisement face and he said, "Oh, yes, my mother liked it very much when she was seventeen." And I thought, "Wow, his mom read it when she was seventeen." I couldn't believe it! And that's when I realized what had happened! [*Laughing*] These people's parents weren't reading *Familia Burrón* comic books, *Este* magazines and *¡Alarmas!*

Some people had books in their house but, *se me incendio en ese momento cuando me dijo eso.* Now it pisses me off, but *en ese momento*, I thought of him like a gardenia or an orchid. Their whole family were orchids and I was a dandelion and that's when *me di cuenta.* But then I thought, "Well, there are some things that dandelions know that orchids and gardenias don't." That's when I started writing *The House on Mango Street* and the first section of *My Wicked, Wicked Ways.* All of a sudden all this stuff gushed out and I would pick what I would write about by looking at the worksheets and I'd write about the opposite of what they were writing about. It suddenly occurred to me then after that breakthrough that whatever they wrote about, I'd write about the opposite. If they wrote about swans then I would make sure I'd write about a rat in my poem. If they wrote about a cupola, then I was going to write about a porch to counter them. That's when I found my voice. It was at that moment that I realized I had a lot of stuff to write about. I made this circular route because I started that way in college. I always wrote as a child, but in college my strong points were directed in a new way and I had to come back. Something very negative like Iowa turned out to be very positive because by taking that really antagonistic and very angry stance, I found what it is I could write about and no one could tell me otherwise.

Against the Invisible: the Creative Drive

H. T. What happened after Iowa?

S. C. From Iowa, I came directly to my job, literally. Over a weekend I found a job when I came home to Chicago. I found out about the job through Carlos Cumpián, a Chicano writer. In fact, let me give you one of his books. This is for you. Some of my students are in here.

H. T. Thank you.

S. C. Anyway, Carlos Cumpián told me about a job at Latino Youth Alternative High School, which was this little fifty-student school that worked with high school dropouts. It's almost like Carlos was divine providence; I don't see it as an accident that

that happened. That job was there so that I could come into the neighborhood, so that I could go from Iowa into the barrio because I hadn't grown up in that barrio. I grew up in the Puerto Rican barrio in the North Side. I did not grow up in the South Side Mexican barrio. We only went there on Sundays to get our *carnitas* and our *dulce*. So all of a sudden I found myself working in the opposite environment of Iowa City. I had been fascinated in Iowa with speech rhythms and in those writers like Luís Pales Matos, a Puerto Rican writer who's working a lot with poetry in various wonderful languages. Luís Pales Matos and I worked in the barrio and I was like a kid that you gave a new drum to. I was trying to find how many different ways this thing could make sounds so people would say things and I would always use spoken English as my trigger at that point for writing. That was a reaction from Iowa and I was going to take an antipoetic stance using an esoteric voice and write antipoems using street people's language, slang. Of course, the people that I admired at that time were Carl Sandburg and Gwendolyn Brooks, who is kind of a formal voice but is still taking very city, urban antipoetic subjects and she's still one of the poets that I admire most. It helped also that they're from the Midwest, which has always been kind of antielitist, no? So I went from Iowa to the barrio and I just was stealing poems because I had these kids that were probably illiterate but wonderful talkers. And you know, when you don't have anything else, you become very good with language, just sharpening your language. If you're standing around on corners, that's all you do. And so these kids were wonderful for me to learn from. I taught them something I knew, but I also have to say I learned a lot from my experience there, from the years of working with them. It was a very small, liberal school with a lot of do-gooders from the '60s. Everybody had a different kind of philosophy and here I had no theory, none of this consciousness that I was working with anarchists, Marxists, socialists—all these really politically conscious people. And I was there like a *sonsa*, just kind of absorbing it. They kind of thought of me as being frivolous and an artsy-fartsy type, but I was developing my consciousness and I developed it from being there. There were some things, of course, that to this day I can't put into an -*ism*. Working in that school I realized the need for me to be there. Looking at photographs taken by Juan Rulfo you see the same kind of images that come up in his writing. He's photographing the same images that he writes about and I think that's also true if you look at the types of people that I'm drawn to just in my everyday life—I'm photographing in my head. If I'm at a restaurant I'm not looking so much at the other customers; I'm looking at the woman who's picking up the plates, or in a group of people I'm looking at the child. I'm not looking at the child in terms of longing. I'm looking at children as identification because I see them as being powerless. Of if you put me in town, I'm always going to look at the people that don't quite fit in because I didn't fit in for so long. The fact that I'm vocal now makes up for all the years that I was silent, and Iowa made me silent again. I was silent the first eleven years of my education. I only started talking when I got some confidence and some rewards for being a writer. I was very talkative through college, but they shut me up again at Iowa, where I came back as myself at eleven. It was the same me, being shut up by the nuns who were making me feel as if what I had to say wasn't good enough. Now I realize that it was because we were very poor children, though these neighborhoods had middle-class families and some poor ones. And there was a lot of racism there. I see that now. I thought it was something I did as a child, but I wanted very badly to be accepted and to be loved as a child like all children do. We had this unconditional love at home and then all of a sudden we go to school and we are treated very badly. We want other children to love us and we want our teachers very badly to love us. I remember always having these little daydreams of the teachers loving me because I felt so ugly and dumb. I felt like, *no sé porque no me quieren*, but I couldn't articulate it. I just felt it. I remember even coming home and telling my father, "I don't have any friends" and it was true. I don't think anybody ever talked to me. It wasn't like they disliked me; it's that I was so quiet I became invisible. I was invisible for so many years that I think all those years of being invisible still makes me think I'm invisible now. So I go down the street and I stare at people like a sonsa and all of a sudden they look at me and *me da susto*, "Oh, I'm not invisible anymore!" I was invisible for so long that I could stare at people at will, always looking at the new kid that came in the classroom or the one that had his hair cut by his mother or the one whose shirt was dirty. I was looking at these little *mocosos* because that's what I was and I could feel what that person felt. Those are still the people that I write about. You know those are still the people because *y tantos años*, so I'm still writing about invisible people from so many years of being invisible. It shocks me every day when I realize I'm not invisible; that people look at me; that people listen to me; that I can give a lecture and rouse people up and make people mad if I want to make them mad, or make them happy that they can laugh at the things I have to say. I always feel real grateful that they want to hear me, especially having come from a family of seven children. Nobody listens to you when you got that many kids talking at the same time. All the awful things, I tell my students, all the terrible things that happen in your life, that hurt you so much, think how they've changed you, how they alter you. You would not be the person you are if those horrible things hadn't happened to you. Fortunately, I can see now those horrible things were for a reason because *esas cosas horribles me ayudan entender y tener simpatía para el mesero que esta recojiendo los platos*. I'm looking at those rooms that you pay for by the week. I'm looking at that sign. I know who goes up there and lives there. I know those are the things and people that I have to write about because nobody else sees them.

H. T. At Iowa it seems like you developed, you identified a voice through some kind of countervoice.

S. C. Yes, a counterstance. That's exactly what I did.

H. T. From that experience, those years, you seem to have found a resource for creative energy. How are you channeling that creative energy now?

S. C. I'm still doing the same thing. I'm still writing about the invisible people and not only the invisible and silent people. I'm still doing it all the time.

H. T. Can you still find that source?

S. C. Well, I'm still angry. All you have to do is look at the *New York Times Book Review* and see what's selling. I look at Texas/Tejana literature to see who's not being heard. Every day you can see people who are not being heard that should be heard. That's where my stories come from—things that happen every day to invisible people. I'm very intuitive, so when I witness something and that person stays in my heart for a long time and I'm thinking about them either from my childhood memory or from my recent life, I know to trust my heart and write about that person and usually in the writing process I find out why I'm writing about that person. I don't know why until I finish writing. I wrote about one of those children that I said was in my classroom with the dirty collar and the crooked hair and it occurred to me one day that I always think of him and even remember his name and ask, "Why do you haunt me?" I decided to write about this little character and realized when I wrote the story that the reason I wrote about him was because he was me, too! I had crooked hair and I was so *chamorroza*, not for the same reasons as him, but you know we were the same species and we recognized each other. I was poor, he was poor too, and that's why I wrote about him. The same goes for the story "Woman Hollering Creek." That woman that I gave a ride to stayed with me, and she was actually from a town between Austin and San Antonio. She stayed with me for a long time and I wrote about her because she haunted me and that was also me. I've also been the victim of violence like that. I had not been beaten to the degree that she had, but I'd been the subject of physical abuse by lovers that I'd had and I had put that in a drawer—don't open this file—and then all of a sudden she touched some very deep part of me that I didn't even realize was there until I wrote it. I said, "Oh my god, it is so scary to realize that I am writing about myself," which is why these people stay with me.

H. T. You're able to turn those experiences into a social voice that doesn't stay circumscribed within those experiences, but which you're able to turn outward into a social critique, a social voice. Any response to that?

S. C. Well, I can because it's fiction, and I think with fiction you can do that. I can't do it in poetry.

H. T. Why not in poetry?

S. C. Because it's a different process.

The Poem: a Classical Theory

H. T. Can you say something about those differences?

S. C. With *Wicked, Wicked Ways*, I think some people felt it was too personal a book. After coming out with *House on Mango Street*, they wanted something like that work. They didn't realize there were a lot of poems in *Wicked, Wicked Ways* turned into stories for *House on Mango Street*—the failed poems—or that the poems from *Wicked, Wicked Ways* came before *House on Mango Street*. Half the book did, and then half of the book came after, so the response that I get is rather cool for the poems because people want *House on Mango Street*. I have to say this again. I don't choose what I'm going to write about when I write a poem. In a way that's also true of my fiction. I don't choose what I'm going to write about; the subjects kind of haunt me and then I write but I also can say what I feel in the case of fiction and I can envelop or change or embroider or take several characters and come out with my conscious viewpoints. That's not true with a poem. In a poem, I write about something that doesn't have a language; I feel something and I don't know what it is; I don't have any language for what it is. I feel and it might be just a wonderful feeling of well-being or it might be a kind of hurt feeling, a kind of sadness or shock. I don't know what it is. I'm always at a loss when I'm arguing with people because I can't argue. I'm not linear. I shut up only when I'm arguing because I don't know what I feel until I write it down. That's why poetry is like that. Sometimes people won't get a response when they have confrontations with me but my response is to go cry. I can't argue. I'm feeling all this stuff and then I go and I write and I get beyond all the *llantos* and I can find what it is. But when I find something, it really does explode in my brain like shrapnel. That to me is the poem and my students know that when I teach writing. Unless you come to that little door, to that arrival of learning something, then it's not a poem. You're still searching for the poem. A lot of student writing is just that searching. They haven't gotten deep enough or honest enough or sat with the poem enough. And then they see. They can see what a poem is, but you don't choose what that little door is. *Vas con un hilito*, like Theseus, and then you're just winding it up and sometimes you go to a dead end and you've got to go a different way. When you find that Minotaur, that horrible Minotaur, sometimes it's so horrible that you don't like it, but you don't have a choice what that Minotaur is, whether it's a Minotaur or a maiden. You don't have a choice. That's the poem. The rest is just the meandering. That's where you stop. That's the end when you get to that.

H. T.   And do you keep that poem put away until you get familiar with the Minotaur, or do you put it out to the public right away?

S. C.   No, no, no. That is the poem. I have arrived. I need to revise it and clean it up, to work on it, and that's the hard part. The discovery of the Minotaur is what makes you want to write, but unfortunately, I know I have to work and revise and change things and then after a long time of revising, it's as tight and the best that I can make it and it all works and holds together. It usually doesn't go beyond that. When I've gotten to a poem, when I haven't had that kind of discovery, then it's not a poem to me. It's just not a poem and it's a very different process from fiction. With fiction I'll say, "Oh, this character stays with me so long, I want to write about this character," and there's a surprise about why these characters or these voices are trapped in me. But it's not like the poetry where things really do explode in my head—like a bullet in the brain—it's horrible and that to me is poems and I don't have any say in what I'm going to say in poems. To me poems are much more autobiographical, even if I'm writing in a persona. If you really want to see some part of me that I don't show anybody, all you have to do is read my poems. Our truest selves, I think, come out in poems and it's very scary. The most courageous thing you can do is to write a poem because you're showing someone some part of you

moving to the Southwest. Even though the proximity to Mexico is greater here, in Chicago our ties are stronger because we're first-generation, second-generation from Mexico. It's a real port of entry so we have very close ties. I was shocked when I came here and I would do things that are *costumbres mexicanas* and people would look at me and make fun and say, "Oh, you do that," and I would say, "Yeah, this is Mexican" and they didn't know that. They hadn't been farther south than Monterrey. It startles me that the people don't cry when they hear the Mexican national anthem. They don't have an alliance here to Mexico. They don't go there and visit their relatives; their alliance is to here; they've been here forever. And to me, on the other hand, I have the nostalgia of immigrants, though of course it's a false nostalgia because in some sense, perhaps being of the generation that I am, I'm more patriotic to Mexico than the Mexicans but that's because you have nostalgia.

H. T. But you were born in . . . ?

S. C. Chicago.

H. T. But you still feel that nostalgia?

S. C. Oh, yes, and in some ways maybe my ties are stronger than my brothers' because I lived and spent a lot of time in Mexico. I've chosen to live here, which puts me close to Mexico, and as an adult I've spent a lot of time looking for my relatives and spending time to learn my cousins' names and learn about those family relationships. It's very important to keep those ties, so I'm kind of inheriting my father's interest of going to *casas de familia* when we go to Mexico. I do it because I've always enjoyed listening to those family stories and now I take a tape recorder and I tape it to try to dig up as much as I can. Relatives are very, very good about writing to me or sending me *memorias*, testimonies. They write to me partly because they know *es mi oficio como escritora*—that what I'm doing when I'm talking to them, sitting at tables, talking like you and I, is research. It's real interesting because I've had to reintroduce myself to some of these relatives as an adult when I go there now and I find that they'll tell me some things that my father would never tell me. The thing that's very curious about being here in Texas is that I'm learning how those Mexican stories are finding their way into my book. This current novel, a lot of it takes place in Mexico. I've never written about that because only being here jostled some of those memories. Suddenly I started talking and realizing how much of Mexico has stayed in my mind—those trips, being in my grandmother's house, and witnessing the fights and seeing if the fights were fights about classes and my father supposedly marrying down. It was a real class war and those are things that I didn't like about my history, but they're coming up in my current novel.

Canonical Differences

H. T. What are your feelings about questions of gender in Chicano literature?

S. C. I have to take that question and redefine it as how I see myself as a woman historically, okay?

H. T. Sure.

S. C. That's a really big question. I don't know that I can answer that question because maybe I don't have the distance, or it's hard for me to remove myself from my identity as a writer and step back to see myself in this process of Chicano literature. It's difficult for me since I am a writer and also I don't have that kind of analytical perspective that you or someone in your field would.

H. T. When you read other Chicana and Chicano writers, for instance, and the canon that is being constructed, do you have perspectives on that?

S. C. Yes, but I think that the canon is Chicano literature now. I think the canon is Chicano literature since 1975.

H. T. So something is changing, something's shifting.

S. C. Well, if you ignore the women's voices then you're not looking at current Chicano literature.

H. T. Can you talk about that?

S. C. I think that it's hard for me sometimes to get some perspective on it because I'm in the woods and I'm part of it as it's all happening, but since 1975—and this is very personal—I think the most exciting literature is coming out of the women's voices, because you have a group that has been silent for so long. It's a very exciting time to be alive and to be writing. I was never excited by the earlier voices that I was hearing, even in Chicano literature, though I have to admit I was very naïve about Chicano literature. I discovered all those voices at a very late age by myself and not in an institution because, in a way, I was isolated at Iowa and in the Midwest. Of course, you have to realize at that time in my life I was really firmly entrenched in paper, on writing being written down on the page and on working on the page and not necessarily appreciating it in an oral way. That was my whole education. I've come to a whole different philosophy now that I've been out of school for ten, eleven years and I understand that some poetry works better performed. There are some poets that are oral poets and some poets that are paper poets and there are some that do both. I'm willing to acknowledge that all of these thousand flowers can bloom in the same garden without killing each other. We shouldn't have to be battling each other, but what I saw at that point and at that time in my life, Chicano writers didn't appeal to me. I have to admit now as an older poet, an older writer looking at these early Chicano writings, they still don't appeal to me very much. I can acknowledge them and their importance historically and socially and see where they were coming from, but I don't think that the best Chicano writing came out of that period. I think a very emotional voice and social voice came out of that time with a real need to create Chicano identity and so they're important to me in a historical sense, not in a literary sense. I think that since 1975 you have writers that are much stronger. This is my viewpoint and I'm not saying it because I'm from that generation. I think you have writers that are technically stronger getting away from the rhetoric and who are still performing poets. These writers are more conscious about being strong on the page as well. We're becoming products of our education so that we're more paper-conscious since we evolve from poetry from that vein. This writing has shifted so that it's meant to reach an audience via books as opposed to simply via public rallies. I think for those of us who are committed to our communities—and that's the majority of us, though not necessarily all of us—we still continue to do oral readings and that is still how we reach the class we want to reach, which isn't used to buying books or wouldn't know how to buy one even if they wanted to, even if they could find our books. We've become adept at performing our poetry as well as publishing it and reaching an audience on paper. Technically the work is tighter and stronger now. Also, it's much more exciting to me as a woman because the subjects and voices that we're hearing are voices that we never heard before. I didn't feel any sense of identity and I did not feel emotionally moved when I read these early Chicano writers. They didn't have anything to say of my urban experience or my experience as a woman and I could read them and just throw them away.

H. T. So who or what are these new voices?

S. C. These voices are the products of people who have honed their craft in or out of a workshop. There are some writers who are very good writers who haven't been in writers' workshops. You're seeing people who have taken more time with the craft and who are more conscientious about their writing. You still have the grassroots writers, but you also have writers that are well-read honing standards of excellence. Before I think you had writers that did a little bit of everything and there's more of a specialization in writing now. The women's voices appeal to me so much because they're meeting a real need. They're nourishing some real hunger that I had not only as a woman but also as a Mexican American woman, as a Chicana. I have to use Mexican American as opposed to Chicana sometimes because I'm using Mexican/American, not Mexican hyphenated. Growing up with a Mexican father and a Chicana mother created this unbalance in my life. Working-class women's literature, women of color, specifically Latina women's writing like my friend Ana Castillo's, or my friend Cherríe Moraga's, Helena Viramontes's, Elena Poniatowska's, and Marguerite Duval's sends me all the way to my typewriter as much as Manuel Puig's stories. I can read those other writers and within a social and historical context understand where they're coming from, but they don't make me want to write. They don't even make me want to read.

H. T. What do you think has happened?

S. C The women have found their directions. They know what they have to say is valid. Maybe they're finding through each other and through other women's writing permission to say these things that they always felt but haven't seen on pages. By our very existence we give each other permission to write. That's why it's such an exciting time to be alive because you know you're not only writing about being Mexican or being a Chicano—meaning Mexican American—you're also writing beyond that. It's exciting that you're filling in all those gaps there, but you're also writing about being a Mexican American woman, about being a Chicana, or being a Mexican/American woman. These things haven't been written about! There are all these virgin subjects that you could just tap into and it's so exciting to me.

H. T. And that's different, would you say?

S. C. The women for one thing have gotten an education so that we have the tools with which to write. I think that we've fought for and succeeded in getting in our spaces, our rooms of our own to write in, whether it involves a divorce or education, or husbands that are supportive sometimes. Whatever. We have fought so that we have rooms of our own instead of supporting someone who has a room of their own, or living vicariously through someone else's career. It's taken a lot for us to fight for this space so that we have our own rooms to work in. In my case it took a lot of that wandering through the desert in my twenties. You realize that you don't have to live your mother's life; there are alternate routes you can take. That realization has allowed us the luxury of indulging in our writing. It's hard to indulge in your writing if you don't have an education and have to work a job that brings you home exhausted. But if you can get a job that allows you a salary so that you can support yourself and not have someone support you, you can determine your own self. Self-determination has been a key thing for a lot of women to come through. Even though we had college educations there were still some things that as Mexican women we have to fight. My writing, for example, has led me to the type of life I'm leading now and I'm seeing this is the life that I've chosen and as a consequence it means that I'm not going to have any children. I don't have time in my life for children and I don't foresee a time in which I'll have time. I do not foresee myself having a child unless I have a wife and I don't see myself having a wife, nor do I see myself being a wife. To me that's incompatible with writing. I see other women are able to balance that, but not without a lot of llantos and frustration and I'm too selfish to put anything in front of my writing. I can be a writer. It is feasible. I realize that what I'm doing is okay, that I can do it, that it is possible for me to be a writer, that I don't have to *soñar* or do it when I come home or do it in between flipping tortillas. I do not have to flip tortillas; I do not have to have children and I do not have to live in a man's house. It takes a long time to figure those things out in your life, to realize that your life is complete by yourself. It goes beyond our culture—being something that is antieverything the planet teaches us. It's something that our gender teaches us, that our society teaches us. The alternative to being old maids—we choose it because we're not missing something in our lives. Our lives are too full to manage anything else, which is something that's very novel for our families to deal with. You waste a lot of energy going through all these emotional tugs-of-war within yourself. It's taken a while for women to realize that the space they have to write is something they can value. Even white women come to me and say they've never met anybody like me whose big concern in life isn't to marry. That kind of question doesn't come into my life.

Feminisms Apart

H. T. How does that make you feel when white women approach you?

S. C. I'm learning something because for a long time I didn't have anything to do with white women. I did in the early part of my life and then when I came to Texas that didn't concern me at all. They didn't have anything of interest for me that they could teach me and that's when I went deeper and more fervently

and militantly into being with Chicanas and there was nothing white women had to teach me but I think that I'm learning
something. Everything and everyone that comes into our life
does so because we need to learn something. If we're smart
we're going to learn something from it and we're going to incorporate that into being the balanced human being that we want
to be. If we're dumb, then we're just going to let the lesson go.
I don't feel a commitment to speak for middle- or upper-class
women, but I think that by what I write, by being who I am,
and by living by my heart, those women are learning something about women of color and working-class people. So, in
a sense, even though what I'm writing about and who I wrote
for doesn't have anything to do with them, it doesn't exclude
them, but rather it teaches them and I would much rather have
them learn from me than the media or other mainstream writers, no?

H. T. Do you think that white women are open to what Chicanas
are saying?

S. C. It really depends, if they come and meet us, if they find us. It's
not our obligation for us to teach them, but on the other hand
if our books are difficult for our own people to find, you can
imagine the difficulty for mainstream writers. Feminist writers
are looking at us and reading and learning and as our distribution grows, our readers are going to grow too, because what
Chicana women are doing is of an international caliber. It is
developing and maturing to a caliber that's going beyond just
American women's voices. I believe in the strength of what we
have to say, though perhaps what we have to say is a little bit
farther ahead than our skills in saying it. It's a maturation process. For instance, I don't think that we've come to the level of
black women writers, technically.

H. T. What do you think has caused the gap between black women
writers and Chicana writers?

S. C. One of the things has to do with education and another is just the
autonomy that black women writers have. We don't have models like that in our communities or in our families and I think
black women writers have always been more independent and

used to going by themselves and living with that community of women, surrounded by each other. We come from a very male-dominated culture and we have had to deal with all the guilt and all the tears and the frustration that that means—feeling alienated from our culture because of who we are. We have our battle wounds from that. Just by existing, though, and being there for each other we as writers have become each other's support group. In turn we are inspiring a whole younger generation of women just by our mere existence, just by being, just by stepping into a classroom or by having my stories out there or my stories reaching somebody else. It's a ripple effect that's going to help those eleven-year-olds out there reading *House on Mango Street* in a way that will save them from being lost in the desert. I think all those things account for the difference between us. We're still at an infancy stage right now, coming toward our own self-determination.

H. T. What's going to happen when this generation of women gets to be fifty?

S. C. The technical proficiency that is necessary to be in the league of black women writers is going to be there by then. I think that right now just a few of us have made it so that we can fight and call ourselves writers and make space for our writing. But some of us do have children and we all have the economic problems of being women writers. It's real hard for us to get jobs. It's very difficult for institutions to acknowledge us. I always use the term "illegal alien" to name this lack of acknowledgement. What good does that do you if the university won't hire you for a position that gives you some financial security? You always have to be running around worrying about jobs. It's very stressful, especially if you're going to be a self-determined woman and support yourself. That's the only way I can see myself being a writer. I can't imagine having children and a husband. Those women I see who have children and husbands have a lot to contend with. They're not writing as well or as much as women who don't. So I think you have to look and ask who's in the forefront of Chicana letters and do they have children, or are their children grown, and do they live by themselves? When you start looking at that you start seeing the ones that have more books are the ones that are living by themselves or have had to live by themselves or have realized that they can't live with a lover because your lover is your art and that lover is very egotistical and selfish and takes up the whole house. It takes a lot for lovers to understand that you already have a lover and that if they come into your lives, to realize that they're not the center of your life. Like Jean Rhys you have to be very, very selfish to be a writer. It takes a lot for us to discard all of those cultural and gender stereotypes that we've grown up with. That's what I call the period of being lost. It wasn't a period of being lost only from our culture and class, but also from gender. We have to be crazy—schizophrenic—for a decade or so until we find ourselves and have the space that we've fought for and then from there we can go on.

H. T. What kind of battles do you think that men in general, and Chicanos in particular, are going to have to fight in order to understand Chicanas better?

S. C. Well, that's a big question. The way I always explain it to Chicano men is by bringing up the parallel of the struggles of the Chicano Movement. When they say something, I'll say to them, "Listen to what you're saying: it's the same things that white people said about the Chicanos." It's that same battle, but they don't acknowledge it. I'll be involved with men who are working strongly with human rights issues, but they don't realize that human rights also deal with the person in your bed. They will laugh about it. How could they laugh about their sisters and their mothers and daughters? How could you laugh about half of your culture? To them it doesn't matter because it doesn't affect them, so it's not real. And I'll say it's just like the white people that used to think black people or Mexicans were just being overly sensitive. If it doesn't affect you as a man, it doesn't mean that it doesn't exist.

Values and Essentialism

H. T. What kind of "values" have to be dismantled?

S. C. I think this is a real touchy subject with Chicanos because

Chicanos feel very strongly about their Chicano values and they don't see those values as being sexist and they accuse us of being *malinchistas* when we do dismantle and reinvent ourselves. They accuse us of being influenced by these foreign, strident, upper- and middle-class feminist ideals that don't have anything to do with the Chicana woman. My brothers see Chicanas like me as being traitors to our culture. They don't realize there's no way that you're going to keep some traditions if they oppress you; there's just no way you can survive and that is first and foremost what you have to realize. You have to start examining Chicano culture. Examine that culture and be critical of that culture and not swallow it whole and complete. Start realizing that some of this has to be revised if it has been and continues to oppress half of our own raza. It is at the point right now where this consciousness has to reach the women as well as the men. A lot of the women aren't even aware they fit into that system of oppression that they're victims of. They're not aware of it. It's a matter of education, always, and part of that education is being met with the stories that they are writing.

H. T. Through their own narratives?

S. C. Yes, we're bringing up those issues. We're questioning and bringing those issues out. Education addresses these issues in what we write about. Perhaps women and men, Chicanos and Chicanas, can read what we write and learn from it.

H. T. In your own stories, for instance, are there any certain values that you can point to as examples of the kind of thing that's going to have to be dismantled in order for women to have the space to reinvent their own identity?

S. C. I'm writing about things that have never been written about, one because they're about Chicanos but beyond that because I'm writing about Chicanas as well: things that have never been written about, voices that haven't been heard and that we don't see in history, stories that haven't been told on paper. Therefore since they're not on paper, they don't exist, supposedly, according to historians. Unless it's written, it's not history. It doesn't exist. We're invalid. We're invisible. We're not heard. The stories that I'm doing always seek things that haven't been written about. Stories precisely about this battle between the sexes. How could a revolutionary man forget issues of women if he's fighting for human rights? How could you forget about the rights of your wife? That's precisely what I'm addressing in my story "Ojos de Zapata." I'm writing about one of Zapata's wives, and she's talking. I couldn't find anything about Zapata's wives. You don't know how many books I read! I've read over thirty books and I found a couple of paragraphs. One essay dealt with his wives and gave me names and children. It was not within the context of talking about his wives; it was the context of his progeny and how they have been victimized by the revolution. No one has ever written about the wives of Emiliano Zapata.

H. T. They're invisible.

S. C. Well, what was their story? Do you think they liked being part of a harem? According to historians he lived with three women at one point in Tlaltizapan and all with the utmost cordiality because they were sisters in the cause. Did he ask them? No! I think that we are all part of harems in a sense. It's easy for me to write this story because I've been in love with warriors like that too, and have had to share that warrior. How could that revolutionary even think about the rights that he was talking about and still oppress the women that he oppressed? I think about it when I research the dates and see a woman, a common-law wife, and then the year he married someone else and then went back, he had a child with his common-law wife. What did these women think? Those are the type of stories that I'm really interested in writing about. I can take my own viewpoints, personal viewpoints, and put them through the mouthpiece of this historical character because, of course, those are going to be the questions I ask as a woman when I read these books about Emiliano Zapata. This story started because I'm very much attracted to Emiliano Zapata as a character and as a figure and I thought there must be some reason why Emiliano Zapata haunts me. It's because he's the type of man who lives his political belief; he's not going to be talking about it. He lives it. I have always been attracted to those kind of men that have *mucho coraje*. I saw him as a true Mexican. But then I realized as I was reading all of these books that all this criticism kept floating up and I wasn't going to write this love story about Emiliano Zapata. I'm writing about things that are real close to my heart—the character of Inéz Alfaro, his common-law wife before he married María Jesusa Espejo. I took her as my character. The story may fall flat on its face because it's so hard to do a historical thing. How could I write about a woman in 1909? What kind of self-determination for a woman existed at that time? I had to make her into a bruja because that's the only way that I can make a woman have power and some autonomy. Only the brujas had power, so that meant I had to read books on *brujería*! Everything leads to something else. In *Woman Hollering Creek* I had to write about women who save each other because those are the stories I'm not seeing in Chicano literature. I'm writing about men who beat their wives. I'm writing about Chicanas saving mexicanas. I write stories that haven't been written before, stories you can recognize because they're based on a true story. Those stories are her story and my story too, because in some sense my helping that woman was a vindication for the times *que yo fui golpeada*. But now I have the consciousness and I have the language and I can do something. Language is much better than throwing stones; language is much, much stronger. Some of the things we have to say may offend some of the Mexican men, but they can't deny violence exists. My newer stories are to me more exciting technically. *House on Mango Street* was the first time I wrote a book of fiction. I'm more excited about the things I'm writing about today, form- and contentwise.

H. T. What can Chicanos do to read and teach with more understanding what Chicanas are writing?

S. C. Well, I think the one thing they can do is read. [*Laughing*]

H. T. Just plain read it. [*Laughing*]

S. C. A lot of Chicanos who are in positions of power aren't reading us. The critics are not reading us. A conference like NACCS is a good example. I went to a NACCS conference and I'm never going to go again because I saw the real lack of interest, mostly on the part of the sociologists. These people in fields other than literature don't realize that all the issues they're bringing up are being talked about in literature with a rich and accurate testimony.

H. T. So read the literature first, right?

S. C. Yes!

H. T. What about in terms of teaching it?

S. C. In terms of teaching it, I don't know what I can say. I suppose you know journals like *Third Woman* and reading critiques and reviews and criticism by women writers is going to help in teaching it. I think that is foremost.

H. T. Is there anything else you want to say about Chicana literature and gender, or anything that you think would be interesting to your general readership?

S. C. It really hurts me to go to lectures at universities where Chicanos and Chicanas who teach there don't attend our readings. In some ways those first ten years of Chicano writing have hurt us because a lot of people don't want to hear us. Chicana literature isn't just strident, angry rhetoric, but literature resonating on an international level. When I talk to Chicano students on university campuses they don't know any literature post-1975. That tells me that Chicano critics aren't really introducing these voices to this younger generation that needs to hear us. There are some Chicano teachers that aren't Chicano by birth but they're Chicano in their hearts and their surnames are Wong, or Benton, or Smith. Then there are some people whose surnames are Martínez or Sierra who are not Chicanos but they get chosen to be spokespersons. A Spanish surname doesn't necessarily make them Chicano.

H. T. What makes someone a Chicano or a Chicana?

S. C. I think someone who has the political consciousness, and that means the class consciousness to write about things that haven't been written about because they're issues that mainstream society doesn't necessarily want to hear. They're writing about struggles and working-class people and oppression and pain. Chicana and Chicano writers have a commitment to this community of people and they look to serve it whichever way they can. A Chicano or a Chicana writer makes a commitment to our culture, writing in a politically conscious way.

H. T. Shall I risk a closure to this conversation for now? We can talk again when you come to visit Albuquerque and UNM.

DATE OF INTERVIEW 2: July 15, 1991
SETTING: Barelas Coffee House, Albuquerque, New Mexico,
at the conclusion of Sandra Cisneros's appointment as visiting
lecturer in the Creative Writing Program, Department of English,
University of New Mexico

The Movements of Home and School

H. T. Sandra, can we begin again by talking about biographical information, your background and your family life? When were you
born, and where?

S. C. I was born in 1954 in Chicago, Illinois, and I lived in Chicago
for all of my growing-up years until I went to graduate school
and I was twenty-one. Then when I was finished with graduate school I went back to graduate school for lack of funds and
imagination. And then when I won an NEA when I was twenty-
eight, I did what I always wanted to do and left town. I've never
lived there since, except for brief stays in my brother's house.
But I haven't really lived in Chicago. When I lived with my
brother during those times when I needed some income to survive those six-month periods we were outside in the country,
outside of Chicago. I really haven't lived in Chicago since I won
the first NEA when I was twenty-eight in 1982.

H. T. And what about your family life? Your relationship to your parents, what was that like, growing up in your house?

S. C. I'm the only daughter, so I'm my father's favorite child and
everybody knows that. Mexican only daughters are *princesas*,
so I'm real *consentida*. In my family the men were raised to
believe they had to take care of me and I was raised to believe
that I couldn't do things without them taking care of me. My
father raised me in a very typical way and my mother taught
me just the opposite—that I should study and learn a career
so that I could take care of myself. She wanted me to have that
option and not be stuck in a marriage. So my mom raised me in
a kind of atypical way. I was the only daughter but unlike my
friends I didn't have to stay home and do all the housework.
I didn't learn to do all that housework at all. In fact, I'm still

pretty bad at it. As long as I had a book, I didn't have to be in the kitchen and since I was an only daughter I spent a lot of time by myself reading.

H. T. Were Catholic values very strong in your family?

S. C. No, no. Again, I lived in a kind of atypical home. My father was a Catholic and for men that means you never have to be devout until you die and my mother was a daughter of a real freethinker, a small-town campesino man, a country man who was raised during the time of the Mexican Revolution and was very cynical and antichurch. His wife was a real devout Catholic. My mother didn't admire her mother, but she admired her father and took after him. She had the formal Catholic education but pretty much dismissed it once she stepped out of their doors and the control of the nuns. And she let us, just like my father, sleep on Sundays, as long as we had the Sacraments. We all had First Holy Communion and had been baptized. That was the extent of it. We didn't have to go to church or anything. We weren't raised with any statues or *santitos* or *altares*; the only thing we had was a Virgen de Guadalupe picture that my father's mother gave to him and my father out of some kind of *cariño* for his own mother kept it and believed it should always be important though he never went to Mass or anything. One time we had some priests and nuns visit us while I was in high school and we were all real embarrassed because we never went to church but they came to visit us. The whole family was uncomfortable having them there, but thank God we had that Virgen de Guadalupe on the wall.

H. T. What about the Spanish language in your household? Was it strong?

S. C. We always spoke Spanish to my father and English to my mother because my mother's first language is English. We never did speak to my mother in Spanish, but we always spoke to my father in Spanish. We grew up with both of them.

H. T. What would you say were the attitudes toward both languages around the house? Do you have any memories of that?

S. C. Around the house we never even thought about it. I think my relatives in Mexico City were concerned that we would forget our Spanish and part of that concern made my father come to a decision about allowing my older brother to study in Mexico for a year so that he would have the Spanish. For the rest of us they were rather lax, maybe not lax, but indulgent with us. There wasn't anything really formal or set down about the languages. We just always knew to speak to my father in Spanish because that was his language. It was just a given. We could be talking to both of them and we would look at my mother and say something in English meant for my mother and my father could understand it. But we never would think of speaking to him in English because that would be odd. And it didn't seem unusual to us to be switching like this and speaking to two parents in two different languages.

H. T. In terms of your decision to become a writer, are there any things along the way in your life that helped you to make that decision?

S. C. I always liked drawing and writing and to me the drawing and the writing come from the same part of myself, but I think that the Chicago Public Library is what encouraged me to be a writer because I really like books and I wanted very much to have my name in the card catalog. You know we used to have card catalogs at that time and I just thought it would be so wonderful to pull up my name and to see how many people had taken my book out. You could tell that if the card was dog-eared and dirty that people had been fingering and looking at it. That to me was so wonderful, so I wanted to be part of the Chicago Public Library and I knew that when I was very little, but I never said it to anyone.

H. T. Did you used to go to the library often?

S. C. Oh, yes. Once a week and I never told anybody that's what I wanted.

H. T. Where did you go to school?

S. C. I went to public school for the first year and a half, and then we had to change schools because the schools we went to were in bad neighborhoods. It was chaos and there was a lot of violence so we had to change schools. After that I went to Catholic schools from mid-second grade to mid-third grade. Then we changed and I went to the school where I had the most negative experiences with the nuns there that I write about in *House on Mango Street*. From the mid-third grade 'til mid-sixth grade I went there. Then I went to a real poor school from mid-sixth to the eighth, a poor parish where the nuns were rather nice. Across the street from that grade school was the high school I went to. We moved a lot so we changed schools a lot.

H. T. So your parents were something like middle-class?

S. C. No, my father comes from a middle-class home, but we weren't middle-class when we were growing up. My father comes from a very middle-class home in Mexico City and my mother comes from a real working-class home and when we were growing up it was not a middle-class at all. We were living in poor, working-class neighborhoods. They live in a poor neighborhood now, but by the standards of their neighbors and of that neighborhood they live a very middle-class existence. So sometimes when you drive in the barrio you'll see a house a little fixed up or really nice, and that's my mother and father's house. But they live in a bad neighborhood and they know it. They could move, if they got their act together, but they are all settled. They live by middle-class standards today but when we were growing up we really were not in a position that you could call middle-class.

Academic Culture and Power Relations

H. T. Let's talk about your work. I'm interested in getting an idea of the events surrounding the creation of each work. For instance, how did you get the idea for *House on Mango Street* and how did you begin to work on it? What kind of surroundings were you in when you started that work?

S. C. Actually, I wrote a precursor short story for *House on Mango Street* that a lot of people have never seen and I don't even know where it is. Only a handful of people saw it when I was an undergraduate. It was the very first time that anyone in my undergraduate school knew that I was a creative writer. I had been a writer in high school, but by the time I got to college I was so busy with my requirements and living . . . there wasn't really time, nor was there a course offered for creative writing, so I was busy being an English major even though my whole reason for being an English major had nothing to do with the courses and the criticism. I was interested in writing, but I was an English major. So I wasn't a very good English major because I'm a not very logical, critical thinker or linear person. I wasn't a bad one; I just wasn't great. I was a B-student. It wasn't until I started taking writing classes that I got As in English. The first time was in an expository writing class in which we had to write argumentative essays. Finally we got to do a creative writing assignment and I whipped out with no trouble at all a story that was a precursor to *House on Mango Street*. It was actually a story with a person that had no name. A girl, a young girl that has the voice of Esperanza and her brother, these two children, witness a death that has happened in a Mexican neighborhood that would anchor *The House on Mango Street*. I wrote the story in the child's voice and handed it in and the teacher was so amazed. She said, "These remind me of Bernard Malamud's stories, his Jewish community, but they're in a Mexican neighborhood." I think she was surprised that I could write these things, whereas I knew that I had millions of them, but no one had ever asked for them. I wrote another one called "The Dog Lady" within the same community, the same voice, and there were two of them that I wrote as an undergraduate that were precursors to *House on Mango Street*. I don't know what happened to them. I didn't come back to that theme of *House* until I was in graduate school, but I was so busy writing poems and trying to write poems like my teachers that I really strayed away from where I had started—stories from that community. I was trying to write like James Wright, like Richard Hugo, Donald Justice—my teachers. Well, Richard Hugo wasn't my teacher, but Donald Justice was, as was Marvin Bell. I was trying to write like them.

H. T. Was that at Iowa?

S. C. At Iowa and at Loyola. My teacher at Loyola sent me to his teacher at Iowa. They hired a writer at Loyola when I was a junior. And he in turn was my teacher for creative writing during my junior and senior years as an undergraduate.

H. T. Of course, you went to undergraduate at Loyola.

S. C. When I finally found a creative writing class and these writers, I found I kind of fit. It wasn't until this creative writing class with these other people that were writing, or trying to write, that I realized who I was and where I fit. I stopped hanging around with my friends who had been my friends until then. That was to me a big departure—a big juncture—right there in that junior year. A lot of things happened to me that year that were explorations—of sexuality, lifestyles, just everything that happened that junior year when I was in college.

H. T. How did you finally decide to go to University of Iowa?

S. C. I didn't know what the University of Iowa was. I didn't even know there was a writers' workshop there. My teacher sent me there.

H. T. Marvin Bell?

S. C. No, Marvin Bell was my graduate schoolteacher. My undergraduate teacher, who was a poet, had studied with Donald Justice and he sent me to Iowa.

H. T. What's his name?

S. C. I don't want to name him. I don't like him very much. He eventually was fired from the university because of a sexual harassment suit and rightly so. He was just a very young man, very insecure, who wanted to be the cool, poet professor. I don't name him only because I have a lot of bad things to say about him and I don't mind saying those bad things or why I have those bad feelings. *A mi me da mucho asco* to remember that time because I was his best student and he should have been there for me as a teacher. *Se pasó* from just being a teacher to being my lover and I was very young and naïve in ways that maybe most women aren't at that age, but I was. I was very protected at home, so it was a real distorted type of relationship I had with him and he should have been just my teacher. I wrote about it in my poetry when I was at Iowa. I was too close to it. I'm going to write about it. I've written about it in some bits and pieces. The character in "Never Marry a Mexican" is part of those bits and pieces. I remember being in love, but I don't remember the love. Have you ever have that kind of relationship where you're so in love, you remember being in love, but I don't remember the love? I have nothing but a lot of contempt and no respect for this person.

H. T. Well, I'm glad you're not naming him.

S. C. It embarrasses me when I meet people that knew us, or knew me from that time because I think, "What a bimbo I was." I really was very young and a real idiot. I have a lot of things to say about it as far as exploitation and the cultural exoticism that was going on—there was a real abuse of power.

H. T. Do you think he was turning you into an exotic object?

S. C. Yes.

H. T. Because of the color of your skin?

S. C. Yes, and because of my age, and because he was a man turning thirty, in his first teaching position at a big university and to him it was cool to have this mistress and it was this really public thing so it was a real sexually and culturally exploitative deal that I was too young at that point to figure out.

Works: Gender, Class, Ethnicity

H. T. What about *My Wicked, Wicked Ways*?

S. C. *My Wicked, Wicked Ways* were poems that I wrote at Iowa. *My Wicked, Wicked Ways* is the title of my thesis. Norma Alarcón was going publish the *Rodrigo* poems, but there weren't that many so she took the rest of my poems, including my Europe poems and my old poems from my early twenties. In essence *My Wicked, Wicked Ways* came from my graduate school poems, the poems I wrote before *House* and after—the Europe poems. That's why some documents say *The Rodrigo Poems* is forthcoming. Susan and I thought that was going to be the name of the book.

H. T. Tell me what kind of research you did for *Woman Hollering Creek*.

S. C. I guess the oldest one is "One Holy Night." I wrote that story in 1980 and I wrote it every year since then. That's the oldest story in the whole book.

H. T. You rewrote it for every year.

S. C. I can never get it down. I still feel like it's not done, but if I don't publish it, it will keep haunting me. So "One Holy Night" is the oldest and it was written before *House on Mango Street*. I wrote *House on Mango Street* when I was twenty-eight. I got the NEA and I finished it with that award. Then there's one story called "Salvador, Late or Early," which I wrote at the Dobie Paisano. The rest of them, the initial ones, were all written either in my brother's guest room in Elborn, Illinois, or when I was living with Rubén Guzmán, my compañero, in the little garage apartment on Twelfth Street in Clarksville. The longest one, one of the longest ones in the early part, was "Woman Hollering Creek," which I wrote there all that year of 1987. The rest of the stories I wrote starting in January 1989.

H. T. And what kind of research did you do?

S. C. I wrote two at Berkeley in the fall of 1987: a story that didn't get into the final collection called "Divine Providence," and another called "My Lucy Friend Who Smells like Corn." I wrote that in Berkeley. What kind of research did I do? Some of them required research of going out to the community. I'd be writing and I'd have to stop and go to a Mexican religious store to go look up the names of herbs, plus to confirm that the spellings were correct. I had been looking up in herb books the names of those plants because a lot of them were spelled by ear. Then I would sometimes have to go to my grocery store to look at the *veladoras*. Some of the research happened when I had to go to the Valley to write about the Central American refugees. That story died but I did do the tapes of those voices and that took me to the shrine of Don Pedrito Jaramillo and that in turn led me to a lot of research by either gathering names through my phone book or gathering information about saints through books about the saints. I did research using my own letters, going through my own letter file looking for letters either I wrote or letters people wrote to me. I found the letters would create voices by the way people sound on paper. Especially for the "Little Miracles" story, I had to work to try to get each one to sound like someone had written it. I went to churches, too, and to the religion boards in the back where they pin the notes and I looked at the notes themselves. I noticed a lot of the issues were from my own neighborhood conversations or again from letters that my relatives sent me relating problems they were having. I did research on certain patron saints that you pray to if you have acne. I would then have to create a voice that would need that prayer. I collected names of towns on my trip to south Texas when I went to collect the testimonies of Central American refugees. So everything is my research, especially letters.

H. T. Between *House on Mango Street* and *Woman Hollering Creek,* there is this kind of quantum leap in terms of narrative voices that you project and create. I'm thinking here about *House on Mango Street* where the voice of Esperanza tells the story, whereas by the time we get to *Woman Hollering Creek* the voices just seem to multiply. What happened?

S. C. I think I always did have those voices. My earlier poems are monologues. That's what I was fascinated with in Iowa. I was always fascinated by speech rhythms. All those poets who were doing things with vernacular speech just flipped me out. In Marvin Bell's class we all had to write a statement of what we were trying to do and I remember writing in my statement that I was interested in these vernacular voices. All my poems, whether those that died or finally made it, were pieces especially triggered by someone talking. The majority of them turned out to be this child's voice because that was what I had: both familiarity and distance. I couldn't write about being sexually exploited by the older man because it was too close. But I was always interested in voices in my poems. The *Rodrigo* poems are very different from my early poems, which were much more rat-a-tat-tat syllables and language. I never thought that I was limited to the child's voice in *House on Mango Street*. It made me very angry that people thought that was all I could do. They trivialized and dismissed this book cause it's just a kid's voice, but that was the voice I needed for that story. I had to work to make each of those pieces work but they just trivialized the book by calling just a kid's book, saying, "Anyone can do that." But it was hard writing those pieces. Each one took me a very, very long time—months—to craft.

H. T. So you would tend to disagree with the characterization that the voices multiply? You think they were already there in some kind of form. In that case, what would you say was the catalyst that brought them into the foreground?

S. C.   Manuel Puig says that first you have to extirpate your past before you can write about the present. I needed to get rid of that thing that made me figure out my class difference in that class at Iowa. The house I had to write about was a terrible obsession. Only a younger voice could give me distance from it. Afterward I got into the poems that had to be in my adult voice. And this is all the more fascinating because I can't direct what I'm going to write a poem about. I can't write about political issues I want to address in my poems because I don't pick what the poem is going to be about.

H. T.   When you work on your poetry and your prose are you consciously aware of building into your text a political dimension?

S. C.   Only in fiction. Yes, in fiction, but not in poetry because you don't pick what you're going to say in poetry. It picks you. In fact some of the stuff that gets said in poetry you don't even want people to know about. It comes out and there's nothing you can do about it, but with the fiction it's different. In fiction you can say, "This is an issue that needs to get said so I'm going to write a story about this." That's how *Mango Street* changed as I was developing. It's really a book about the author's search for identity and gender and class and ethnicity even though the persona is a young girl, twelve or so. In real life I was twelve politically, going through that questioning period, looking at the negatives. I was going through a real crucial period of post-Iowa twenty-eight.

On the Autonomy of Poetry

H. T.   Why do you think there is this different between poetry and prose you're proposing in which you say that poetry's exigencies pick you?

S. C.   Because that's how it is.

H. T.   But can you elaborate a little bit on that?

S. C.   Anybody will tell you that! When you write a poem you may say, "I'm going to write this poem and I have this first line or

I want to write a poem about this man who just disturbed me because he came over here and left a note and it really upset me and I want to write something in response." You think that's what you're going to write about, but what you actually end up with, where the poem ends up going, is what I call the door it takes you to. It's not a poem until it takes you to that door, to that discovery. That door that it takes you to isn't where you thought it was going to go. If you direct a poem, it's not a poem but a piece of junk, and it usually winds up in a dead end. But if you say, "This is what I want to write about" and then let that lead to the next line and to the next line, then like fishing it pulls up all this stuff inside your heart. You don't know what it is. You feel the tug and you think it's a fish, but sometimes it's a boot, sometimes this gold chest, sometimes a monster. You don't know what it is that's on the other end. A poem is in the making when you feel that tug, but you don't know it in advance. It's not premeditated in the way that fiction is.

For a Moving Chicana Aesthetic

H. T. Can we turn to your views on the relationship between Chicano and Chicana literature and the canon of Anglo-American literature? What relationship do you see there and is there a relationship with Latin American fiction as well?

S. C. I think it has less to do with Latin American literature than with first generation groups such as, say, Asian American writers, than with the Anglo-American literary scene. Even with black writers I don't see commonality.

H. T. So the commonalities are with Asian American literature?

S. C. And working-class groups. The point of contact with black writers for me would be perhaps with what a working-class writer was. But the difference for me is that Asian American writers are living simultaneously with two cultures many times in conflict with each other. African Americans have been here for so long and were so colonized that they don't have a point of reference to that other culture. I find the parallels in writers like Yamamoto or Kingston.

H. T. Where do you see yourself situated in relationship to the Anglo-American canon?

S. C. Where do I see myself situated? I'm too close to tell; it's a big question.

H. T. What about within Chicana literature? What do you think are the aspects of Chicana literature that make this literature so innovative, so fresh, and so new?

S. C. Forms—one of the innovations for me is forms. I'm always very intrigued by writers that are doing something innovative in forms. In some sense it has nothing to do with the canon of American literature, because the canon seems so spiritless or passionless right now.

H. T. What is it that makes Chicana literature innovative?

S. C. The forms make it very innovative. The risk that the writers take.

H. T. Let's talk about Chicana writers.

S. C. Of the male writers only the younger poets call my attention for innovating with form, cross-pollinating the stories, crossing in a lot of ways, crossing forms, crossing the languages to do something new. This is not to say that the crossing of the languages wasn't there with the early writers but it was there in a way that was meant to create an argot; it was there for political purposes, to exclude people and to create a kind of identity in Chicano writing, whereas now, when I see the mixing, it's not to close doors but to open them and to borrow from the two languages to add something new to the English language. It's very innovative and exciting to see that you can do something new to English by adding the *sabor* of Spanish; that's the little thing *que le da un* little kick. Even if you're only writing in one language, it doesn't have anything to do with code-switching. Although that's certainly allowable, it's only one little boring thing that you can do. Asian American writers like Maxine Hong Kingston are aware of that too: that you can think in another language and borrow from its sensibility, from its syntax and idiomatic phrasing to add something new to the English language. I'm really bored to death by writers that are writing a traditional story. I'm always looking for a writer's writer, someone that's doing something a little bit different. I have to say I like the women writers because they take those risks, mix genres, or do something to a story that is exciting for me.

H. T. What writers do you like to read among the Chicanas?

S. C. I like reading Gloria Anzaldúa. I like Cherríe Moraga. I like reading Ana and Helena.

H. T. And on the stage of world literature, where do you see Chicano literature in relation to writers from around the globe?

S. C. The writers that are influencing us are not the American writers, but marginalized women of color, small press, working-class writers. If I'm going to look at any women's writing in the U.S. it's always going to be the Asian American writers. I'm also looking at working-class writers like Carolyn Chute or Grace Paley or Pat Ellis Taylor—American writers coming from a real different America. Latin American writers that I read include women writers like Elena Poniatowska, Merced Reda, and Manuel Puig a lot. I appreciate Gabriel García Márquez, but he's not my favorite. I like Manuel Puig better. I like Eduardo Galeano. I like Clarice Lispector, Marguerite Duras, Harriet Dower, and Maria Dermout, a Dutch writer. I take all these different writers from where I find them, different places on the globe.

H. T. Can you say something about politics and art? How you think your art affects the political landscape?

S. C. All art should make you think in ways that you haven't thought before. That to me is exciting when art does that. I'm real fierce as far as I always want art to address, move, and change people. I follow what moves me, *lo que me emociana mucha*, what "emotions" me a lot. That's what I write about. It's not just about writing about your own self, which is what happens when you write poems, but writing for a collective. I feel that responsibility to think in a collective form when there's so few of us that have been able to get upstream: my family, my raza, and by my family I also will extend it to other people. Everyone has an obligation to speak up and to act when there's an *injusticia*.

H. T. So how does art address those injustices?

S. C. By writing about the issues that I write about. I feel so privileged that people read my stories, that people invite me to come and speak. That's a very big responsibility. You can't take that lightly. I tell my students, "You are a responsibility. You are in a position of power; don't waste that power." When people are listening to you, you're aware of this power and privilege when a whole room is listening. You shouldn't waste that power when you've got it triplefold in front of an audience at a university or in front of a classroom of thirty students or in a newspaper article, or in a story, or in a poem. Anywhere where people listen, you have a responsibility not to say some *babosadas*. You have a responsibility to take that opportunity when people want to listen to you and do something to help make the world better. You have that responsibility to make the world better before you're dead. As Jean Rhys would say, you have to earn your death. You have to earn your death. In my life, writing is the gift that I have and I've taken that gift and worked it to empower the community by representing it in a way that's going to help communication between the community and the mainstream in a more truthful dialogue.

H. T. You mentioned your writing is a gift. Do you see a spiritual dimension there?

S. C. Absolutely. I really do. I feel that everybody has some gift, some reason why they were put on the planet. If you're doing what you should be doing then you get blessed, and if you're not there's a lot of resistance and pain. I have a great belief in Divine Providence. There is nothing arbitrary about the idea that people come into our lives for reasons, why things happen to us, and why pain happens to us. All that should have kept me from becoming a writer is precisely what makes me the kind of writer I am. So I do feel a sense of strong spirituality in my work, all the more now that I can articulate it better than a couple of years ago.

H. T. What happened in those two years?

S. C. Since 1987, the last four years, a lot of things happened. One, I went through a year of near-death experience in '87 when I got very sick and went through a period of self-doubt that I told you began at Iowa and then persisted at Chico. I came very close to dying. It was a very reflective year afterward, in which I read everything to find out how I'd come that close to destroying myself. I wanted to know how I could prevent it from happening again. That year I read all kinds of books, including books on spirituality. It was the experience of writing my last book that allowed me to go into churches and not feel my revulsion that I had for the Roman Catholic Church. It allowed me to witness something I had overlooked—the faith of our community. I articulated what I learned in that child's monologue, and in the "Milagritos" story. I had to balance out some things that I had thrown away.

H. T. From traditional religion?

S. C. Yes, I had to rethink things and relook at ways in which I had defined power.

H. T. Patriarchal power?

S. C. I mean a woman's power, the power of my grandmother, whom my mother had dismissed as being weak, submissive, always in the church. When I looked at her again I could also look at the Virgen of Guadalupe in a different way, incorporating her with her pre-Columbian precursors. If we redefine the power to be silent not as weakness, but a source of real strength and endurance, we can see that as the ability to understand someone else's pain. When I was in my late twenties and early thirties, power was about protecting yourself. *No te dejas.* You fight and sometimes that just creates more problems. You waste a lot of energy biting each other's ankles like dogs. I don't have to fight with anybody anymore. I write instead. That, to me, is my power.

H. T. What you're saying is not a retreat into art but into action.

S. C. But to me art is action because my art is a challenge to the patriarchy.

H. T. How?

S. C. Everything I write about, how I write it, who I'm writing about, where I write it, the myths that I take, and the way that I revise all of these male myths is a challenge. It's a revision. To me, art is my politics because that's what I was given in my lifetime, but regardless of what your life is, you can be a terrorist or you can create anarchy whether you're a waitress or a painter, right? And for me that's what I must do, but I'm not saying art is a retreat. I don't think it's a retreat. I think it's a different way of choosing a weapon, you know, a different way of fighting. Everything that I write about, even the way that I write it, to me is an act.

H. T. The way that you write it?

S. C. Yes!

H. T. How's that?

S. C. The shapes of the stories I write aren't like anybody else's. The forms of those stories, the way of piecing a story together, the way of telling the stories that I'm telling, the people who are telling the stories, the language they use—everything that I've done since I was at Iowa has been a move of resistance. All of that has been my act of resistance against not only white writers but Chicano writers too.

H. T. How so against Chicano writers?

S. C. I read a poem about someone writing about their barrio and I'd say, "Shit, that's not how my barrio was." It was not a wonderful place that I wanted to go to. *House on Mango Street* was about rewriting that view of the barrio. Or, if I read something about the women, I'd say, "That's not how women are!" Somebody would write about Llorona, and I'd say, "I'm tired of this. I'll do my own." Or, somebody would do a Tejana story and I'd say, "Those aren't the Texas girls I know." I remember at Iowa I'd always been trying to do something different from what people around me were doing.

H. T. Tell me what you're working on now.

S. C. A novel. I have a novel that was a short story that got too big. The ideas are too big for the short story so the short story got aborted and it's going to be the next book.

H. T. What's it about?

S. C. It's about Mexican princesses and their fathers and how fathers love their daughters as opposed to how they love their wives. It's about my father's generation that came to the United States and it's what I witnessed front-row-center seat when I was growing up between the mexicanas and the Chicanas, with one foot in Mexico and one foot in the United States. It's a very unique position I have as a Chicana because a lot of Chicana writers don't have that intimacy with Mexico and because I grew up with one Mexican parent, I do. I don't feel divorced from Mexico like Lorna Dee or Cherríe. Relatives are still there. In this novel I want to go back to Mexico so I can investigate the two countries and that part of my past that has to do with the class wars I witnessed growing up but could never mention in *House* because I was too young of a writer. I want to write about issues of Latino men and love and how our fathers teach us to be the lovers we are. I'm real concerned about fathers and daughters. I'm not so concerned about mothers and daughters. I'm concerned about fathers and daughters and men that we love and how they love their daughters, or how they love us, or how they love their mistresses and wives—those are the triangles that I'm real concerned with. I want to force America and Mexico to look at themselves from a different perspective.

H. T. Well, it sounds really wonderful.

S. C. That's what I say it's going to be, but watch, it will be something else! I don't know what it will be.

H. T. A little bit of poetry in there? It sounds like the project is submitting itself to your theory of poetry, which is that the poem chooses you.

S. C. Yes, and in some ways that's true. In some ways I have a very conscious idea of what I want, but I always allow things to go where they will. I know I'm going to get to Z, but I don't know how I'll get to Z. I allow a lot of things to float up. I know what the story's about but the route that I take to get there isn't linear. Maybe I'm cross-pollinating genres even though it looks like prose—a lot of my stories are poems that I wrote out longways.

H. T. *Muchas Gracias*, Sandra.

S. C. You're welcome. I appreciate it very much.

Awards

2004 Mountains and Plains Booksellers Spirit of the West Award
2003 Texas Medal of the Arts Award
2002 Honorary Doctor of Humane Letters from Loyola University, Chicago
1995 MacArthur Foundation Fellowship
1995 Mountains and Plains Booksellers Association's Regional Book Award for poetry
1993 Honorary Doctor of Letters from the State University of New York at Purchase
1993 Anisfield-Wolf Book Award
1991 Lannan Foundation Literary Award
1991 PEN Center West Award for Best Fiction
1988 National Endowment of the Arts Fellowships for fiction and poetry
1988 Roberta Holloway Lectureship at the University of California–Berkeley
1986 Chicano Short Story Award from the University of Arizona
1985 Before Columbus American Book Award
1984 Texas Institute of Letters Dobie Paisano Fellowship
1984 An Illinois Artists Grant
1982 National Endowment of the Arts Fellowships for fiction and poetry

Primary Works

El Arroyo de la Llorona y Otros Cuentos. New York: Vintage Books, 1996.
Bad Boys. San Jose, CA: Mango Publications, 1980.
Caramelo, or, Puro Cuento. New York: Knopf, 2002.
The Eyes of Zapata/Los Ojos de Zapata. With Cristina Pacheco. Mexico: Instituto de Mexico San Antonio, 2003.
Hairs/Pelitos. With Terry Ybáñez. New York: Knopf, 1994.
The House on Mango Street. New York: Vintage Books, 1991.
Loose Woman: Poems. New York: Knopf, 1994.
My Wicked, Wicked Ways. New York: Turtle Bay Books, 1987.
Woman Hollering Creek, and Other Stories. New York: Random House, 1991.

Secondary Sources

Carbonell, Ana Maria. "From Llorona to Gritona: Coatlicue in Feminist Tales by Viramontes and Cisneros." *Multi-Ethnic Literature of the United States* 24, no. 2 (1999): 53–74.
Derrida, Jacques. *Margins of Philosophy*. Chicago: University of Chicago Press, 1982.
Doyle, Jacqueline. "More Room of Her Own: Sandra Cisneros's *The House on Mango Street*." *Multi-Ethnic Literature of the United States* 19, no. 4 (1994): 5–35.
Estill, Adriana. "Building the Chicana Body in Sandra Cisneros' *My Wicked, Wicked Ways*." *Rocky Mountain Review of Language and Literature* 56, no. 2 (2002): 25–43.

Ganz, Robin. "Sandra Cisneros: Border Crossings and Beyond." *Multi-Ethnic Literature of the United States* 19, no. 1 (1994): 19–29.

Gonzáles-Berry, Erlinda and Tey Diana Rebolledo. "Growing up Chicano: Tómas Rivera and Sandra Cisneros." *Revista Chicano-Riqueña* 13, nos. 3–4 (1985): 109–20.

Kaup, Monika. "The Architecture of Ethnicity in Chicano Literature." *American Literature* 69, no. 2 (1997): 361–97.

Klein, Dianne. "Coming of Age in Novels by Rudolfo Anaya and Sandra Cisneros." *The English Journal* 81, no. 5 (1992): 21–26.

Mermann-Jozwiak, Elizabeth. *Postmodern Vernaculars*. New York: Peter Lang Publishing, Inc., 2005.

Morales, Alejandro. "The Deterritorialization of Esperanza Cordero: A Paraesthetic Inquiry." In *Gender, Self, and Society*, edited by Renate von Bardeleben, 227–35. New York: Peter Lang Publishing, Inc., 1993.

Mullen, Harryette. "A Silence between Us like a Language: The Unstranslatability of Experience in Sandra Cisneros's *Woman Hollering Creek*." *Multi-Ethnic Literature of the United States* 21, no. 2 (1996): 3–20.

Olivares, Julián. "Sandra Cisneros' *The House of Mango Street* and the Poetics of Space." *The Americas Review* 15, nos. 3–4 (1987): 160–69.

Poniatowska, Elena. "Mexicans and Chicanas." *Multi-Ethnic Literature of the United States* 21, no. 3 (1996): 35–51.

Rios, Katherine. "'And you know what I have to say isn't always pleasant': Translating the Unspoken Word in Cisneros' *Woman Hollering Creek*." In *Chicana (W)rites on Word and Film*, edited by María Herrera-Sobek and Helena María Viramontes, 201–23. Berkeley: Third Woman Press, 1995.

Rojas, Maythee G. "Cisneros's 'Terrible' Women: Recuperating the Erotic as a Feminist Source in 'Never Marry a Mexican' and 'Eyes of Zapata.'" *Frontiers: A Journal of Women Studies* 20, no. 3 (1999): 135–57.

Sanborn, Geoffrey. "Keeping Her Distance: Cisneros, Dickinson, and the Politics of Private Enjoyment." *PMLA* 116, no. 5 (2001): 1334–48.

Notes to Chapter Six

1. Tey Diana Rebolledo and Erlinda Gonzáles-Berry, "Growing up Chicano: Tomás Rivera and Sandra Cisneros," *Revista Chicano-Riqueña* 13, nos. 3–4 (1985): 109–20.

2. Robin Ganz, "Sandra Cisneros: Border Crossings and Beyond," *Multi-Ethnic Literature of the United States* 19, no. 1 (1994): 23.

3. Jacqueline Doyle, "More Room of Her Own: Sandra Cisneros's *The House on Mango Street*," *Multi-Ethnic Literature of the United States* 19, no. 4 (1994): 6. Doyle puts it succinctly: "Cisneros's *The House on Mango Street*, dedicated in two languages 'A las Mujeres/To the Women,' both continues Woolf's meditations and alters the legacy of *A Room of One's Own* in important ways" (6).

4. See Jacques Derrida, *Margins of Philosophy* (Chicago: University of Chicago Press, 1982). Deconstruction attributes a structure of delay to the linguistic sign proper: "When we cannot grasp or show the thing, state the present,

the being-present, when the present cannot be presented, we go through the detour of the sign. We take or give signs. We signal. The sign in this sense is deferred presence. Whether we are concerned with the verbal or the written sign, with the monetary sign, or with electoral delegation and political representation, the circulation of signs defers the moment in which we can encounter the thing itself, make it ours, consume or expend it, touch it, see it, intuit its presence" (9). Deconstruction seizes upon this structural property of the linguistic sign not necessarily to endorse a way to get around it but to demonstrate to what ends and interests the delay is being put to use.

5. Harryette Mullen, "'A Silence between Us like a Language': The Untranslatability of Experience in Sandra Cisneros's *Woman Hollering Creek*," 21, no. 2 (1996): 4.
6. Ibid., 12.
7. Ibid., 9.
8. Ibid., 8.

CHAPTER SEVEN

Pat Mora
I Was Always at Home in Language ⌐

⌐ Pat Mora's work creates a form of mestiza consciousness commensurate with the varieties that have surfaced since Gloria Anzaldúa's proposal in *Borderlands/La Frontera*. Like Anzaldúa, Mora traffics between the borderlands as geography and the borderlands as a spiritual site of practical disposition. Like Anzaldúa, Mora also puts the experiences of Chicanas at the center of the sociopolitical stage her literary productions occupy. Mora has an equally deep identification with Mexican women who cross the border daily from Juárez to El Paso to earn their living as maids. This identification brings in its train the Spanish language, which was such a strong presence in her family household. Mora's sense of being at home in two languages stands in marked contrast with the experience of Richard Rodriguez for whom life in two languages was not only traumatic but was made a matter of choice—either English or Spanish. Along with the other Chicana writers in this book, Mora seeks to redress the radical absence of Chicana voices from the canons of American and Chicano literatures.

Mora performs her literary craft in the genres of poetry, essays, and children's literature. Her books of poetry include *Chants, Borders, Communion, Agua Santa/Holy Water,* and *Aunt Carmen's Book of Practical Saints*. In *Nepantla: Essays from the Land in the Middle*, she writes essays in poetic form, and in *House of Houses*, her family biography addresses issues of gender oppression, class divisions, and racial and ethnic prejudice operating at the U.S.–Mexico borderlands. The upwelling of writing that Mora describes in the interview attests to the power of her art to emerge even in less than optimal circumstances. In *Chants*, Mora composes a poetic discourse that traces a path of identification between indigenous Mexican women and the experiences of modernity characterizing contemporary Chicanas. While the desert geography of the American Southwest predominates in the poetry, the literary trope is inclusive, stretching over all topoi where indigenous women suffer patriarchal and economic oppression. *Chants* opens with an invocation to her desert muse to help her weave her words into flower and song, the Aztec trope for poetry and ultimately the vehicle for keeping the dead in the land of the living through the work of memory. The invocation reaches back to the rich symbology of the Aztecs, as in the tradition of Alurista, but puts the focus on the land itself for the sake of establishing solidarity with Chicanas/Mexican women. "Unrefined," the poem following the invocation, pictures the desert as a woman whose desire to break the confines of refined behavior leads the sun to look on her with fascination. "Mexican Maid" delineates the different relation that Marta, the titular figure of the poem, and her Anglo boss/*señora* have to the revolutions of the sun. The sun tans her Anglo boss, a sign of her class position and leisure. However, for Marta, the revolutions of the sun signify her daily trek over the borderline to and from work. Class privilege is here twin skin to white privilege. Read in line with these opening poems in *Chants*, "Mi Madre" reminds the reader that the borderlands desert has cradled mexicanas and Chicanas from time immemorial. The mexicano/mexicana presence cannot be eradicated from the borderlands. In "Curandera," Mora puts her faith in the creative act when she equates the poet and her creations with the work of healing carried on by curanderas. This is in keeping with the emphasis she puts on the notion of a writer or any individual coming to grips with her calling, which she talks about in the interview. "Elena," the persona poem that Mora refers to in the interview, harbors some of this vision of coming to one's work. Elena buys a book to learn English against the frowns of her beer-drinking husband. The lengths that Elena will go to learn English speak to the economic issues wrapped up in the language of the global dominant, as well as hints at Mora's pursuit of her own calling to write and make a difference in the lives of other women, mexicanas and Chicanas alike. The poetry in *Borders* weaves a tighter tapestry of identification with women living their lives under gender, ethnic, and economic oppression. Linda Fox points out that the nature of this identification stretches across time and place: "It is evident that from the vantage point of the adult lyric speaker the bonds between women of differing generations and retrieved cultural heritage are intertwined."[1] Significantly, Mora's identification radiates from her homespace. Section II of *Borders* contains poems for her children and other family members. "Oral History" in particular is a paean to her maternal aunt, Lobo, a prominent figure in *House of Houses*. The poem practices *flor y canto* in the sense that it brings Lobo into the land of the living to commune with Mora and her family: "*Lobo*, as you dubbed yourself/when you claimed four of us/ as your *lobitos*, little wolves/who even now curl round the memory/ of you and rest peacefully/in your warmth." The middle ground of *Nepantla* is the poem itself, in which to rest in peace is to remain/rest in the memory of Lobo. With *Communion*, Mora enlarges the scope of her exploration into the lives of women living on the borders of gender, ethnic, and economic oppression to take in that suffering as it occurs on a global scale.[2] This widening in scope corresponds to her travels abroad and the keen observations she brings back about the plight of women in other parts of the world.

House of Houses is a tribute to Mora's family history. In both *Chants* and *Borders* Mora had already evoked this family history but *House of Houses* transforms that evocation into a genealogical, autobiographical record of great strength and beauty. The winner of the 1997 Premio Aztlán, this prose work can easily be described as an epic spiritual narrative, a kind of ethnography of the Chicana historical experience and aesthetic sensibility. I say that the work is a kind of ethnography because Pat Mora walks among her narrations as a figure with pen and paper, collecting narratives from her family. The result is a generous revelation of Pat Mora's family, and beyond that a history that is not reducible to a single self or family. Like the revolutions of the sun with which Mora opens her first book of poetry, *House of Houses* takes the reader through a narrative timescape comprised of twelve months mapped to twelve chapters. This does not reduce the composition of the story to a rigid timeline. Rather, the genealogy is supplemented by a circular conception of time and together they resonate with multiple memories. B. Marie Christian states: "The notions that time is concentric rather than linear and that all our past is simultaneously available to us are reiterated throughout *House of Houses* by the foregrounding and generations. Viewing her family as a 'house' in her imagination, she describes a home of concentric design."[3] Christian points to the multiple strategies Mora uses to spark the work of memory, among these are references to the *Popol Vuh.* At work also is a silent but recoverable influence of Gaston Bachelard, theorist of poetic space.[4] Bachelard advocates the freeplay of the imagination between both the absences and presences composing the linguistic sign in a motif that encompasses the poststructuralism that has sunk its roots into American soil since the late 1960s. That Mora brings all of these discursive traditions and motifs to bear on the production of *House of Houses* signals the mode and variety of the mestiza consciousness that Mora is constructing through the work of her imagination.

Mora's discourses on the formation of the Chicano canon as well as the mainstream American canon match closely those of other Chicana writers such as Ana Castillo and Sandra Cisneros in this volume. The challenge to the exclusion of the literary works of these Chicana writers from the Chicano canon is a call to keep the question of aesthetic value open and contingent.

DATE OF INTERVIEW: December 13, 1999
SETTING: The home of University of New Mexico Biology Professor James Brown, where Pat Mora resided during her visiting professorship in UNM's Honors Department

Language

H. T. We're here at the home of James Brown to conduct an interview with Pat Mora, Chicana writer, and we want to know something about her life. This is wonderful fictional ethnography. Thanks so much for being so generous . . .

P. M. My pleasure.

H. T. I'm really happy that you're doing this. This kind of interview I hope will be helpful for teaching and helping readers understand more of the context of your work and where it comes from.

P. M. Great, great.

H. T. Why don't we begin by asking a most fundamental question? Where were you born?

P. M. I was born January 19, 1942, in El Paso, Texas.

H. T. Do you have brothers and sisters?

P. M. I'm the oldest of four, so I have to two sisters—two younger sisters—and the youngest is a brother.

H. T. What was it like growing up in the Mora household with your brother and sisters?

P. M. It was great as far as I'm concerned. I'm keenly aware that we all have selective memory, and I never know why we remember what we do, but I grew up in an incredibly loving household because I had not only my parents, but also my maternal grandmother and a maternal aunt about whom I've written a great deal, and who I refer to as Lobo in *House* at different times. There was always somebody there to spoil us; there was always someone there to pamper us, and those are important parts of my memory. I always thought of my house as a very safe place to be. I suppose given all that we read today, I'm keenly aware that not all children have that experience and that's why I was fortunate enough to have had it. It was a safe place.

H. T. Are you thinking of recent events like Columbine?

P. M. Like that, and also the level of both abuse and the number of children growing up without really strong family structures that I had.

H. T. What was life like growing up with two languages in the Mora household?

P. M. Well, of course, the thing about an experience like being bilingual is that you have no idea what it's like not to be bilingual; you cannot imagine, to some extent, not having two languages sort of streaming in and out of your mind. I'm keenly aware that it was a blessing in that it allows me to name the world in two different ways and also it gives me two registers in which to work when I'm writing. At the time I thought nothing of it; it was normal.

H. T. It just enveloped you?

P. M. Absolutely. I've no memory of not speaking both, all my life.

H. T. Are you saying that Spanish and English coexisted in an equal, balanced way?

P. M. Yes, I would say equal and balanced, though particularly as my siblings came along, probably there was a move toward more English. That would be my guess because my grandmother who lived with us never spoke English and never had any interest in speaking English.

H. T. What was her name?

P. M. Her name was Amelia Delgado; we called her Mamande. And so as long as she was alive, there was that presence of someone who was a Spanish speaker. That maintained Spanish as a presence in our home. Lobo, when she came into this country, spoke only Spanish. She became more bilingual; she would read *Jane Eyre* in English when I was young. You could speak in either language to her, but Spanish was definitely a presence at home, and my parents always moved back and forth.

H. T. Is there an accent that you remember that was distinct to the family language?

P. M. Well, two thoughts come to mind. One was not an accent in the traditional sense, but the role of my father's humor. If you want to associate accent that way, I would say I associate my father's fantastic sense of humor in both English and Spanish. That might come to mind. The other thing that would come to mind would be thinking of accent in terms of level of affection. *Muy cariñoso.* Just as I was bathed in both languages, I was also bathed in a lot of affection.

H. T. So you're equating the language with an intense affection?

P. M. Yes, because I think family-Spanish doesn't have to, but can often be a very affectionate language. Because of the interest in both the children and the elderly, I think it can have a very affectionate component.

H. T. How do your parents address each other in Spanish?

P. M. My mother would call my father Raúl, and my dad would refer to my mother as Estella.

H. T. *¿Hablaban Español entre ellos?*

P. M. *Ingles, también.*

H. T. *En inglés en el trabajo?*

P. M. *Y Español.*

H. T. Two languages.

P. M. Two languages all the time. After they moved to L.A. and I'd go visit, I used to love lying in bed as an adult listening to them because it brought back what it was like as a child when you're hearing your parents in another room. And depending on conversation or mood or topic, it might be in English; it might be in Spanish.

H. T. In your work *House of Houses*, you talk about a migration from El Paso to Los Angeles. You stayed in El Paso?

P. M. Right. By the time they moved in 1963, I was married, and the sister after me, Cissy, was at the university and she also stayed in El Paso to finish and moved into the home of an aunt and uncle. So it was the younger two siblings and my parents who moved to L.A.

H. T. So it sounds like Spanish was completely comfortable for you.

P. M. It was. I think what happens is that when your educational experience is in one language, whatever language that may be, that language begins to occupy a greater part of your mind as your vocabulary keeps increasing, as well as your ability to express complex thoughts. It so happened that later on in my life, when I was a university administrator, I did some work with colleagues in Mexico, and that gave me a chance to work on my Spanish. I always define myself as English-dominant. I'm bilingual, but I'm English-dominant.

H. T. You began with Spanish offering you a sort of comfort zone with family. With friends, too, or just within the home? How far did it extend? Did it go outside the doors of the house?

P. M. I would say more in the house.

H. T. Do you recall at what point English started to take over areas where Spanish was previously being used?

P. M. Well, again, I would associate that in part with education and also in part with friendships. The children in the neighborhood where I lived probably all spoke English.

H. T. Anglo and Mexican kids, Chicano kids?

P. M. On my block, they were probably all Anglo that I'm remembering. When I went to school it was probably a mix. I went to a

Catholic school; it was a parish school, and it was probably a mix. But I would say we probably spoke English. My friendships were in English. It's interesting that at this point in my life, I so revel in my friendships that are also in Spanish. But I went through many years when that wasn't true. I didn't have those. I would tend to stay in English. And now I love being able to have friendships in Spanish.

H. T. Do you have a sense of how that transition started to take place, or is it lost to memory?

P. M. If I do it's totally unconscious because I always spoke both. It was as easy for me to have friendships in English. I never went through that transition, that someone like my mother did, who spoke only Spanish in the home but English outside the home.

H. T. That's neat, the way the languages coalesced with each other and coexisted in a sort of sameness. Did you feel like there was a sameness to them? Or am I reading too much into that experience?

P. M. I think there is a sameness. It is seamless when your parents move back and forth.

H. T. That's certainly a shot in the arm for universal grammar. Do you recall any special encounters with English that might recall a suture in that seamlessness?

P. M. Never. Never with English. I think what does happen, and did happen, was that you realize that Spanish doesn't belong in school. It's not that anybody ever said anything. But when I was in high school it was a big issue because there were boarders from Juárez and they'd get demerits and all of that. But in elementary school, it's possible that the nuns said to us, "Don't speak Spanish," but I don't have any recollection of that.

H. T. That seamlessness, I take it that includes the melodic structures of both languages. Somehow the melodies of both languages work together.

P. M. Right. Particularly since I heard them both every day, I probably didn't have a day when I didn't hear both. My parents would fight in English and Spanish, or they would express their pride in you in English and Spanish. I would say I experienced on a daily basis the multiplicity of roles in which language can function. Also, I had the gift of an inordinately articulate mother in both in English and Spanish. Throughout my home experience, I was exposed to a real sense of how well language could be used. She has, and had, a real feel for language.

H. T. Maybe a hint of your own poetic voice?

P. M. Who knows? But I credit her with my love of language. It's really thanks to her.

H. T. So Spanish in your household was generally a positive thing?

P. M. It was normal. It was normal the way my family always had dinner together. One could stand back and think of all the good reasons why that was a positive experience, but when you're in it, it is just that experience.

H. T. It sounds like this experience stands in such contrast to the experience of a writer contemporary with you, Richard Rodriguez, for whom the transition was very marked, and the attitudes toward English and Spanish themselves were very marked. As you say, for you, with Spanish, you can't pin down if there was something negative attached to it. But for a writer like Rodriguez, there is that sense that Spanish was heavily marked, negatively marked, in the public sphere. Not for you. Not so in Pat Mora's experience.

P. M. Not until, in a subtle way, I realized that it's not like that at school. There is no punishing or scarring moment, just awareness that it's not there. And one of my interests is in the importance of bilingual education, and in the importance of some education in the home language, particularly for students coming from monolingual homes, monolingual Spanish, or monolingual Vietnamese. I would be so concerned that they would feel that their home language was not a resource for their educational experience. The perception that the home language could be a handicap is what concerns me.

H. T. You don't have that now?

P. M. No, no. I mean my concern for the generation of children in school now. I know that I didn't have that experience, and I ache for them if they do.

H. T. What are your feelings right now about bilingual education as a federally funded program?

P. M. I'm a very strong supporter of it. I get quickly irritated when people cite studies why we should not be investing in this. My response usually is to say that we have studies that tell us what an inadequate job we're doing in the teaching of science, but it doesn't mean we stop teaching science. It alerts us that we need to do it more effectively, or that we need to look at the instruments we're using, and I feel the same way about bilingual education.

H. T. It's an interesting analogy, because it says something to the effect that when it comes to language, language is politically charged.

P. M. Absolutely. It's about politics, not education. And a history of repression. Some people are frightened that we could have a multiplicity of languages that are educationally sanctioned. I think that makes some people terribly nervous.

H. T. It sounds like your bilingual childhood was a very positive experience.

P. M. It was a very positive experience.

H. T. What are your fondest memories of growing up bilingual?

P. M. Well, one comment might be that it gives you two ways to be loved. And I think that was part of the experience. Again, thinking of this grandmother who was a very quiet, gentle person, and because she spoke only Spanish, one of the things I equate Spanish with is this sort of stream of kindness. She becomes symbolic of a lot of the Spanish language for me because she was that one steady presence within the house.

H. T. Mamande?

P. M. Mamande. Lobo also. It's very hard to talk about it objectively because it seemed so normal.

H. T. Did you encounter negative attitudes toward your accent?

P. M. Accent in English or Spanish?

H. T. In either one.

P. M. I've never been aware of having either.

H. T. You just had that nice, complete experience?

P. M. Yes, and if you met my mother you would know why. I would say she had a beautiful accent in Spanish, if we want to think about it as having an accent, and the same thing would be true in English. I had a good start.

Education and the Question of a Calling

H. T.   Let's talk about your education. Where did you receive your primary and secondary education?

P. M.   I went to Catholic schools K through twelve. I went to a parish elementary school, St. Patrick's School, which is the school attached to the cathedral in El Paso. My mother would always tell the story that my father would say to her that "there's a great school right by the house. Why would we have to . . . ?" because it meant they would have to drive us to the Catholic school. But even though neither of them had gone to Catholic schools, she felt we would get a better education. She would always say that, though Daddy would ask the question, deep in his heart, he felt great pride in his heart that he put all of us through Catholic school. That was a considerable sacrifice to have four children going through Catholic schools. It meant that my father worked really long hours. He would be on the seven o'clock bus in the morning, leaving the car for my mother so she could drive us to school. And then if he had a lot of work at the optical company he owned, we might either take him dinner, or he'd come back and have dinner with us, and sometimes he'd have to go back and work again. Sometimes she would go back with him. Not every night, but there were times in our lives when that happened. Both made considerable sacrifices for our education. And that was part of the impetus when I wrote the corrido for my father. I wanted to do one totally in Spanish because it was going to be hard for me and I wanted to do something hard. But I wanted a deal with a different kind of hero. You don't have to have a pistol in your hand to be a hero, and there are thousands of Mexican and Mexican American parents who have sacrificed for that education for their children.

H. T.   The connection between Catholicism and education seems really strong, the way your mother insisted and your father's secret . . .

P. M.   . . . taking pride in it. Yes, though I wouldn't describe either of them as what I might call fierce Catholics. I was the fierce one. I was the terror when it came to Catholicism. I would say my father in particular was devoted to Our Lady of Guadalupe.

I would say that, and we went to Mass every Sunday, but it was because that was really being reinforced at school. My mother was not the kind of Catholic, for example, that would have been praying the rosary all the time or anything like that. In many ways she was a modern woman, rather than maybe that image of relying on religion to save the day. I would say my mother tended to rely on herself to save the day.

H. T. Very active?

P. M. Active. She had her hands full with four children, plus two relatives at home, and she also helped my father; she took care of all the bills and all the payroll accounts with some help from her brother. But also she was very active at school, again sort of shattering some of those stereotypes. My mother was president of the PTA. She was always involved in our elementary school.

H. T. You graduated from which high school in El Paso?

P. M. From Loretto, which was a private girls' school that was even farther away, so it was even a bigger sacrifice.

H. T. Was there a bus that came by to pick you up?

P. M. No. Either Mom would take us, or by that stage, we would take two buses. We would take one bus to get downtown and then another bus to get to Loretto. I really loved school and so no sacrifice was going to be too much. I would stay after school and work and get home late, and my parents sort of tolerated it. I'm sure they sometimes wished I didn't spend so much time at school. Sometimes Saturdays I would go back. I went through a stage where I really loved science. I had a nun who was a chemistry teacher that I was very fond of. I'd go over on Saturday, and we'd do experiments and things like that.

H. T. After high school, what happened?

P. M. Then, although neither of my parents had the opportunity to go to what was then the local college, which is now UTEP, I think it was very important to my mother that her children go to college. I never considered not going. I would never have considered not going.

H. T. Where did the funds come from for your education?

P. M. I was fortunate to get small scholarships. I lived at home, and I worked. If you had a certain grade point average, you could often get a little scholarship that would cover your books. That was all I needed because I lived at home. My mother was always good about dropping me off or picking me up whenever I needed. At a certain point my father started having a lot of financial problems because a lot of the bigger optical companies were coming into town and it was going to be difficult for a small optical company to survive. And that was why my family left El Paso. My father had to close his business, which was a great blow to him. A great blow.

H. T. Did you stay for reasons of education?

P. M. No. By that time I was married.

H. T. You had already graduated?

P. M. Yes. I was able to go through college in three years, not because I had planned it. I actually had planned to go away my last year. I had a good friend, and she and I first thought about going to one of the colleges run by the Sisters of Loretto; it was the Sisters of Loretto who taught me all twelve years. Then we had decided we were going to go to UT–Austin. We even had arranged for a dorm and everything, and then my friend was killed in an auto accident.

H. T. Who was your friend?

P. M. Her name was Mary Sammons. Of course that was a terrible blow; she was my dearest friend in college. When I added up my hours, I realized I could graduate a year early. So I ended up graduating in three years, and then getting married, and I then worked on my Master's in the summers.

H. T. How old were you when you got married?

P. M. Twenty-one. Too young.

H. T. Very young. You graduated from college very young, too.

P. M. I don't think that young.

H. T. Twenty-one?

P. M. Maybe today because some people take longer because of the nature of the degrees.

H. T. Is there a connection in your mind between your education at the university and your education in Catholic schools?

P. M. Totally different. I dedicated *Aunt Carmen's Book of Practical Saints* to the Sisters of Loretto because they were such a strong force in shaping my life. My mother loves to joke about the fact that I loved the nuns so much that I would wake up and take the bus to school even though she was going to drive the rest of the siblings. But I knew she'd usually get there late, and I couldn't bear that, so I would go early. I loved to help them. I was what you'd call today a very nerdy student. I think one difference was that I went to a school at a time when in Catholic schools you were taught primarily by nuns, and if you weren't taught by nuns, the lay teachers shared a certain ethos and a certain set of values. To some extent, I think that's changed just from my brief brush with some Catholic schools. One, you don't have the presence of nuns and priests because they are in short supply. But part of the experience was not only, I think, high standards in terms of learning, that is, lots of homework and lots of scoldings. I have all these memories of nuns with their arms folded at the front of the room, giving us these fierce lectures about what we hadn't done—our behavior—but also the whole emphasis on having high aspirations for your role in life.

H. T.   The nuns imparted that?

P. M.   A strong sense of vocation. A word you just don't hear much. What was your calling? What are you called to do? I think that became one of my essential questions. If we all have some essential questions, I would say that is one of mine.

H. T.   The question of calling?

P. M.   The question of calling. In fact, I'm one of these people who is very compulsive about New Year's resolutions. So when I was writing down my resolutions for this new millennium, the first one was to deepen my understanding of my work in this world. I think that really is an echo of that sense of "What is your vocation?"

H. T.   That's a wonderful question.

P. M.   Yes. Let's hope that I can deepen the understanding.

H. T.   What was your degree in?

P. M.   English, with a speech minor, both in a Bachelor's and a Master's. Again, I credit my mom with the interest in public speaking. She always loved public speaking, which utterly fascinates me about this child who came from two very quiet parents. I never knew my grandfather, who was the judge in Mexico, Eduardo Delgado, but my mother and my uncle always talk about how he was a very quiet, reserved man who communicated with a look. My grandmother, and I knew her very well, was a very quiet person too. Never, I mean never, did she raise her voice. How did these two very quiet people raise this extrovert that is my mother who goes to school, loves being in the band, loves being on stage? She is aware when she talks about it that the principal did not like the attention that she got. But some of her teachers I think saw her potential and her talent, so they would encourage her. She goes through public schools feeling intensely her difference. She's the one who goes on speech trips and sees the sign "No Dogs or Mexicans" when the speech team is going in and she's hoping nobody is going to realize that she's Mexican so they won't ask her to leave the restaurant. Of course it just pains me no end that my parents both experienced that kind of nonsense. Anyway, to get back to the university, my university experience was about amassing credits. It did deepen, I would say, my understanding of literature and language, in part because of the public speaking component, because I credit my mom. When I started doing public speaking, which was in elementary school, I had this great coach at home. If someone had to volunteer to give a little talk on the rosary, Pat was going to give it and Pat was going to get to try it out on her mother first, who would say, "Did you think about this? Did you say that?"

Coming to Writing

H. T.   When did you first realize that you wanted to be a writer?

P. M.   Of course, it's a question that young writers ask often. Soon you tell the story so often that you hope it's the true story, or you don't know if it's a true story. I was never much of a diary-keeper, but when I was a young, married person with young children I would occasionally write little notes: "This would make a good poem; this would make a good essay; this would make a good children's book." It's interesting to me that it is in the three genres in which I write. But I really didn't pursue it very much. One time when my children were little, I sent off an idea to Hallmark, and they paid me a hundred dollars. It was the first money I ever made writing.

H. T. Do you have a date for that?

P. M. That's an interesting question. I don't know that I know when that was. But my son was young, so I should be able to place it. So then, nothing succeeds like success. That's the power of the editor and the power of publishing, because when something is accepted, that writer all of a sudden has ten good ideas, or thinks that he or she has ten good ideas. So I began to submit more, and then I got nothing but rejections, and I sort of shut down.

H. T. For how long?

P. M. I think for a long time. We'll have to look at that date.

H. T. Two or three years?

P. M. I'm going to say more. But maybe it's less. My son was born in 1967; I'm going to say I didn't go back to it until about '79. Again, the power of rejection was so strong I literally thought, "No one's interested in my writing."

H. T. Does it sound like you came to writing as an accident?

P. M. No. I think of coming to writing as sort of an upwelling. If you're a reader, you keep taking language in. You keep taking language in, and then it's almost like there's an upwelling. Now the upwelling can be assisted by everything from joy, sadness, confusion, to frustration. I had found such intense pleasure in language; maybe that would be an interesting point that I had never thought about. I didn't have negative experiences with language, verbal or written, but was always praised for it because it was something that I could do well because I was getting this assistance from home. So we could say I was always at home in language.

H. T. Nice way of putting it.

P. M. I never thought of that before. I might not have been at home in history, and I might not have been at home in math. I was at home in language, written or spoken.

H. T. How did the idea of becoming a writer become attractive to you?

P. M. I think what happened was that at a certain point, in the late '70s, I begin to think, "Gee, in a few years I'm going to be forty and my life may be half over." I always think that the notion that my life might be half over was a factor in my deciding I wanted to invest time in this. Also about that time I was considering a divorce and it could be that—and again I haven't explored this a lot. It could be that the intensity of emotions that I was dealing with made language attractive as a way to help me deal with it. So those could have come together: age, this intensity of emotion, and that language for me had always been a way out of situations.

H. T. So as you moved toward this calling to write, was there any conjunction of factors that made writing attractive to you? You said, "Nothing succeeds like success."

P. M. I'm very goal-oriented, so once I decided that I was going to do this, I decided that I needed to start setting aside time. I had three children who were all excellent students and just as my mother had always helped me with my homework, I always liked to help them, so it would usually be after they were through with their homework, or on the weekends, that I could work on this. There was another factor that I have never really gone back to explore, and that is that in 1981, when I went through a divorce, I started teaching part-time at what was then UTEP. I had taught part time at the community college, and when my youngest started kindergarten, I started teaching composition classes part time at the university.

H. T. Freshman English?

P. M. Freshman English. So let's say the late seventies, a couple of years before my divorce. You sure are getting a lot of information. One Valentine's Day one of the other part-timers came into the office and said, "Happy Valentine's Day" and we started joking. It turned out that he was ABD from Columbia and was a writer. Circumstances had him in El Paso. We started talking about writing and he said, "Would you be interested in exchanging writing?" And I said, "Oh, I could never do that." I had always written for myself and I really didn't show it to anybody. He said, "How are you ever going to get any better if you don't show it to somebody? Why don't you show it to me?" I remember so clearly that day that I handed over a folder with some of my poems to him. That was probably important—his presence in my life, which was very brief because he died a few months later.

H. T. What was his name?

P. M. His name was Larry Lane. He was a New Yorker who was very intense about language, and loved poetry, and probably had had some advantages I hadn't had, advantages of classes in poetry and literature and the kind of library that I really didn't have. But we started exchanging poems. And when he died, I was enough on my way that I decided I would audit a poetry class at the university, which was a very awkward experience for me. My recollection—and it could be inaccurate—is that I was the only non-Anglo in the class.

H. T. This is at UTEP?

P. M. At UTEP. I have since had a few creative writing classes, but they tended to be very alienating because there has been, from my perspective, no place for another voice.

H. T. Another voice?

P. M. Meaning the Chicana voice. The presence of mainstream American literature has been so pervasive and oppressive that I had to psychologically push myself through the class. I hadn't thought about it until now, but that has been true.

H. T. Give us a brief history of your publication record. What was your first work?

P. M. The first work was published was in 1981, and it's interesting that later in my life I go live in the state of Ohio, a state I knew nothing about, certainly had no connection to, but my first poems were actually accepted by a tiny press in Ohio. I had submitted things to an ad in *Poets and Writers* that said this press was looking for work by women, and so it was a tiny, feminist publication. I remember coming home with my children—it must have been summer—and here was this envelope, and it said, "We would like to publish your poems." I can still remember it. I couldn't believe it.

H. T. What was the name of that work?

P. M. The first one was called "Disguise." The other one that they accepted was a poem called "Migraine." Both were these intense, personal poems. I was talking to a good friend today about the fact that I think that's often where early poetry begins: with very intense, personal experiences. And then over time, some writers are interested in—and I certainly am interested in— persona poems. But some writers prefer to stay with intense, personal poems.

H. T. Persona poems?

P. M. Persona poems like "Elena," a poem that is trying to adopt the voice, or hear the voice, of someone whose experience is very different from mine. And of course, I've had a particular interest in hearing the voice of a Mexican woman. *Chants*, for example, my first work, is really about women in Mexico.

H. T. *Chants* is your first work?

P. M. My first published work as a collection. So the voice of women of Mexican heritage in this country, particularly those whose voices have not been heard, became and remain a very intense interest of mine. Not my only interest, but an interest.

H. T. And after *Chants*?

P. M. I'll always be grateful to Arte Público Press and to Dr. Nicolás Kanellos, the publisher, who called me up one day and said, "We published some of your work and I have to think you have a collection." Indeed, I'm very goal-oriented, and my goal for that year was to get a collection published, and here he calls in January and says, "We have funds to publish a collection and we'd like to see yours." I can't say enough about the importance of small presses. I might never have had a career as a published writer had it not been for Arte Público. They published my first three collections: *Chants*, *Borders*, and *Communion*. I had also returned to my interest in children's books. I had mentioned that I was interested in all three genres. I had, when my children were little, submitted essays to women's magazines. They were never accepted, but I submitted them. I had tried children's books, and I had ended up having success with poetry. But, I think it was after *Borders*, the second collection, that I began to resubmit children's books. That is a very, very difficult field to get into, and it remains that way. People particularly in the Southwest tend to go to a bookstore and they see an array of Chicano writers or books by Southwest writers and they think everything has changed, but the fact is, five thousand children's books are published in this country each year, and only 2 percent are by or about Latino children. We know the demographics in terms of the population, and we still don't see Latino editors at major houses. That hasn't happened. And I think that's what has to happen for things to change. So sometimes people think I have some success in children's books. I would say I experience weekly or daily frustration about what I am still unable to place. It's very, very difficult.

H. T. You continue to write for children?

P. M. I continue to write for children; I love to write for children. I think there is a very close connection between picture books and poetry. I think that's why I love it; it's very spare. You really have an opportunity to play with music, to play with cadence, to play with repetition. A number of editors have talked to me about middle grades, but up to now it has held no interest to me. Again, I love the spareness of picture books. It's a great thrill to think of a child, a young child, early in their language experiences savoring what you wrote. It's an incredible experience.

H. T. Is there a political element to that delight in the writer and in the reader?

P. M. There is certainly a political element. There is delight that comes from being part of inserting these voices, these stories, this language, and this culture into what is being defined as American literature, whether for children or for adults. But there is another kind of delight and it may be even more intense for me, and that is the personal delight when I see a child hint to me, "Oh, I'm like that," or "My family is like that," or "My abuelita is like that." I would say that the intensity of that pleasure is even greater than the political one because the political pleasure is an intellectual pleasure. It has an emotional component, but it comes from that sense of justice. We, and by that I mean Chicanos, but also Latinos in general who have Spanish in our background, have our place in the Americas. It is colonialism and racism and oppression that have suppressed that voice. So there is that intellectual sense that it is right that our stories be part of this. But I'm very interested in the emotional component. And the emotional component comes from the little girl who approaches me after I've done a reading and says, "I speak Spanish, too."

H. T. So you write in Spanish?

P. M. I often give my presentations for children bilingually so that if I'm going to be at a school where I'm going to have children who are monolingual in both languages, I'll often do a slide presentation where I go back and forth, so I'm talking about the books and about writing. Even if I did the whole presentation in English, I will always include Spanish, and I will always talk about how lucky I am to be bilingual.

H. T. Code-switching languages has always been part and parcel of who you are.

P. M. It's part and parcel of who I am, and I would say it's a necessary skill for the work I want to do because I'm very interested in communication and community, both of those "C" words. Being able to switch into Spanish, even if the audience is totally monolingual English, is a way of signaling something; it's a way of claiming some linguistic space.

H. T. What percentage of your work is done in code-switching dialect versus English versus Spanish?

P. M. I would say that it's such a large number. It's more like a skill, the way someone might have a skill for singing. And you might say for this audience, if you could sing, it would mean you could reach them in a different way. I would say it's that skill. I love the thought that if I walk into a school, or if I am asked to visit a school and they say, "Many of our students speak only Spanish," I can say, "That's no problem; this presentation will be bilingual."

H. T. That's wonderful.

P. M. It's a kind of little subversion that brings me a zing of pleasure. Here we are in an educational environment, and we can speak Spanish because it's for literary reasons.

H. T. So it's not quantity; it's quality.

P. M. Right.

H. T. That's wonderful. After *Chants*, you have *Borders*, and then?

P. M. *Communion*.

H. T. Another work of poetry?

P. M. Another work of poetry. People who look at it more objectively than I do would say that in *Communion* I move out of the border for some of my interests. My basic interest in the role of women, the repressions they experience in those roles, remains, but because I've had the advantages by then of some international travel, *Communion* might be about Pakistani women; it might be women in Latin America; it is not limited to Mexico and the United States.

H. T. And after *Communion*?

P. M. After *Communion* some children's books begin to come out. After the publication of *Chants* in 1984, *Borders* in '86, and *Communion* in '91, the children's books start coming out in '92. But I had actually sold *Tomás and the Library Lady* years before, though it took eight years to be published. Even though when you look at the list of publications, it looks like the children's books don't start until '92, really by the '80s I had already placed the first one. It was just slow coming out.

H. T. You were writing in all these different areas contemporaneously: children's literature, poetry, and prose.

P. M. *Nepantla* is prose, and it comes out in 1993. A first collection of essays, it really emerged from speeches that I was giving. I had become a university administrator at UTEP in 1981. I felt that if I continued teaching Freshman Composition I would never write. I always speak to teachers of composition with tremendous sympathy and I have tremendous respect for them because I remember the unending stacks of paper. And I remember that the last semester that I taught Freshman Composition I felt myself experiencing great frustration because I would think, "I shouldn't be marking your work; I should be marking mine." I had gone through this divorce in 1981. I knew I was going to have to work full time, and I came up with what seems to some a foolish plan: that if I could go into administration I could work really hard during the day, but I wouldn't have to take any papers home at night. And so then at night, I could be a mom *and* get to my writing. And so that's what happened. I would work intensely during the day as an administrator, but although it didn't always make people happy, I made it clear that at 5 o'clock, I would turn into a mom. I would do that. As I said, my children were wonderful students, but after they would go to sleep, or on weekends when they were with their dad, I began as I've always said, writing out of the edges of my life, which is where I think many women begin—where you can find the time. Poetry particularly lends itself to that; it's very difficult to do prose that way. And indeed, though I started giving speeches as an administrator and doing poetry readings, it's when I leave administration in 1989, and when I leave the Southwest, that I have a little bit more time, allowing me to begin on *Nepantla*. So then I took the drafts that I had from the speeches and began reworking them. But all those genres have always interested me.

H. T. You accomplished your goals, being the self-motivated woman that you are?

P. M. I accomplished some of my goals. I remember that my family always would get *Life* magazine, and that in the back of *Life* there was always a personal essay. One of the writers was a woman, and I used to think, "That would be so grand." That's why I know I loved the essay form, and not just in an academic setting, but out there in popular magazines where people could read your opinion.

H. T. In light of that, does *House of Houses* have a privileged place in your body of work?

P. M. Oh, it has a very privileged place. I've said often that I wondered if I would ever be able to give it up because I wrote it at the School of American Research while living in Santa Fe. I was looking out at this wonderful garden and listening to some of my favorite voices in the world, because I had Lobo and my father and my mother and my aunt and uncle and my sisters on tape. How was I ever going to give this up? It was because of *Aunt Carmen's Book of Practical Saints* that I got so intrigued by playing with the lives of saints and I was able to close *House of*

Houses. I don't think I've ever gone back and reread it, but I've never gone back and read *Nepantla* either. I think it would make me uncomfortable.

H. T. *House of Houses* strikes me as a work of perfection.

P. M. Really? What a wonderful thing to say. I was going to say what I think would make me nervous is seeing all of the places where I probably hadn't succeeded.

H. T. It strikes me that you've fulfilled that conjunction of goals. You saw something in *Life* magazine; you wanted to be public; you wanted to write prose; you wanted to have a more public voice, and it happened through hard work.

P. M. Of course, the question will be whether it gets read. On the one hand, there's part of me that thinks, "Well, it's there and even if it doesn't totally find its audiences for a hundred years, it's there." That's one of the reasons why writers make the time to write; we're investing part in the future.

H. T. Absolutely.

P. M. But of course you always have that sort of nagging doubt whether it will be read. I think that's particularly true for Chicana and Latina writers, and really for all women of color; will the work be sufficiently read? Will it go out into the world and do the work?

H. T. So Chicano literature is inherently political?

P. M. I think it's inherently political, not only because of the topics, but simply by the fact that a Chicana voice needs to be inserted into the definition of American literature. Even if the Chicana writer were writing science fiction and it had nothing to do with being of Mexican background, I still think there's a political element.

H. T. What responsibility does the Chicana writer have to the Chicana community?

P. M. I think the ultimate responsibility is to do your *best* work.

H. T. And that makes it political?

P. M. When you do your best work, that in itself becomes revolutionary. And that's in part because there has been such a pattern of denigration and such a sense at certain times in history, and in certain places in history, that people like us could not do excellent work, so just the doing of it is revolutionary. One of my interests is that the next generation of writers feels a total openness in terms of genre, topic, and style.

H. T.   So you think Chicana literature is changing the American literary canon?

P. M.   It is just by its presence. If you have a room of twelve people and eleven are Euro-Americans, and there's one African American, that presence changes the group, changes the space.

H. T.   That's wonderful. What's in the future for you?

P. M.   The next book to be published is a collection of poems for teens that comes this spring called *My Own True Name*. I try to listen to teachers and librarians; they often have many more ideas for me than I can respond to, but some librarians in California mentioned to me a couple of years ago that they didn't have a lot of Chicana poetry they could hand to their high school students, that is, as a book. And so I asked Nick Kanellos if I could select poems from *Chants, Borders,* and *Communion* that I thought might be particularly relevant for teens, and publish them. Ever the negotiator, Nick said, "Yes, if you write six new poems," and I said, "Okay, but I also want to do a letter to young writers." So that's what we came up with, and that will come out this spring. In the fall, I have a children's book, a Mayan myth called *The Night the Moon Fell* that will come out from a Canadian publisher, a new publisher that I'm delighted to be working with. Her name is Patricia Aldama, and she's one of the few Latina publishers in the profession, and she lives in Canada. She's starting a new line of books called Libros Tigrillos because she's very interested in poems and books that address the need in this country for books by and about Latinos. We're going to do about three books together. The first one, *The Night the Moon Fell*, is already in production. Then I have an anthology, a celebration of Latino moms and grandmoms that I'm editing for Lee and Low Books; we haven't picked a title yet. The poems just came in, so I'm going to be selecting about fourteen poems for that book. I'm going to do two other books with Groundwood Books in Canada. I'm very excited about one I proposed in which we select some famous poems from

Mexico and Latin America that children learn in those countries. I'm interested in poems particularly by such major literary figures as Federico García Lorca and Gabriela Mistral, and them I'm going to translate them into English. It's going to be a great experience for me, and a way of getting the names of those authors a bit more known in public and private schools in this country. I'm a great lover of Sor Juana Inés de la Cruz and I am going to do a children's book about her. Not only do children in this country not know much about her, but teachers and librarians don't either. She was such an amazing woman. Knopf is going to publish that children's book, which I'm actually revising now. In terms of adult books, I brought three projects with me to New Mexico, and all three are going back with me to Kentucky unfinished. One is the next book of poetry, which I'm hoping will be a book of odes. At this time in my life I'm very interested in thinking about the things I love, so the next poetry collection is based on the Neruda idea of writing praise songs. I thought that would be a very salutary thing for me to do. I'm actually playing with a novella about a thirteen-year-old girl and that might be a possibility, though it would be a real departure for me. Then I want to do a sort of a spiritual nonfiction book about the desert. I taught the course here at the University of New Mexico on spirit and space to help prepare for that book. I think there's a reason why we think about hermits and desert fathers going into the desert. Desert spaces can transform us and can give us gifts, and I'm very interested in exploring that.

H. T. Thank you so much for the global scope of your Chicanisma.

P. M. Thank you, Hector.

P. M. You know it's interesting for me, overall, that there is a constant presence of frustration and sadness in how slow change is. It should not have to be this hard. It is always with ambivalent feelings that I encourage Chicano and Chicana writers and illustrators and Latina/Latinos because I know the road is going to be hard for them and I know how many times their hearts will be broken. And they will be.

H. T. Thanks for clearing a large path for us.

Awards

2006 National Hispanic Cultural Center Literary Award
2005 Golden Kite Award from the Society of Children's Book Writers &
       Illustrators
2002 "Literary Lights for Children," Associates of the Boston Public Library
2000 Ohioana Alice Louise Wood Memorial Award for Children's Literature
1999 Pellicer-Frost Bi-national Poetry Award
1997 Premio Aztlán Literature Award, *House of Houses*
1997 Southwest Books Award, Border Regional Library Association
1990 Poetry Award, Conference of Cincinnati Women
1988 Authors of the Pass: El Paso Herald-Post Writers Hall of Fame
1987 Southwest Book Award, Border Regional Library Association, *Borders*
1985 Southwest Book Award, Border Regional Library Association
1984 Harvey L. Johnson Book Award, Southwest Council of Latin American
       Studies, *Chants*
1983 Creative Writing Award, National Association for Chicano Studies
1982 Poetry Award, *New America: Women Artists and Writers of the Southwest*

Primary Works

Agua, Agua, Agua. Glenview, IL.: Goodyear Books, 1994.
A Birthday Basket for Tia. New York: Macmillan, 1992.
Agua Santa/Holy Water. New York: Beacon, 1995.
Aunt Carmen's Book of Practical Saints. Boston: Beacon, 1997.
Borders. Houston: Arte Público Press, 1986.
Chants. Houston: Arte Público Press, 1984.
Communion. Houston: Arte Público Press, 1991.
Confetti: Poems for Children. New York: Lee and Low Books, 1996.
Delicious Hulabaloo/Pachanga Deliciosa. Houston: Pinata, 1998.
The Desert Is My Mother/ El desierto es mi madre. Houston: Pinata, 1994.
Doña Flor: a Tall Tale about a Giant Woman with a Great Big Heart. New York: Knopf,
       2005.
The Gift of the Poinsettia/El regalo de la flor de Nochebuena, by Mora and Charles
       Ramirez-Berg. Houston: Arte Público Press, 1995.
House of Houses. Boston: Beacon, 1997.
A Library for Juana: the World of Sor Juana Ines. New York: Knopf, 2002.
Listen to the Desert/Oye al desierto. New York: Clarion, 1994.
Love to Mama: a Tribute to Mothers. New York: Lee and Low Books, 2001.
Nepantla: Essays from the Land of the Middle. Albuquerque: University of New
       Mexico Press, 1993.
Pablo's Tree. New York: Macmillan, 1994.
The Race of Toad and Deer. New York: Orchard, 1995.
The Rainbow Tulip. New York: Viking, 1999.
This Big Sky. New York: Scholastic, 1998.

Tomás and the Library Lady. New York: Knopf, 1997.
Uno, Dos, Tres/One, Two, Three. New York: Clarion, 1996.

Selected Secondary Sources

Bachelard, Gaston. *The Poetics of Space.* Trans. Maria Jolas. Boston: Beacon, 1969.

Christian, Marie B. "Many Ways to Remember: Layered Time in Mora's *House of Houses.*" *Multi-Ethnic Literature of the United States* 30, no. 1 (2005): 135–48.

Fast, Robin R. "Nature and Creative Power: Pat Mora and Patricia Hampl." *San Jose Studies* 15.2 (1989): 29–40.

Fox, Linda C. "From *Chants* to *Borders* to *Communion*: Pat Mora's Poetic Journey to Nepantla." *Bilingual Review* 21, no. 3 (1996): 219–31.

Hicks, Emily D. *Border Writing: The Multidimensional Text.* Minneapolis: University of Minnesota Press, 1991.

Mermann-Jozwiak, Elizabeth. *Postmodern Vernaculars.* New York: Peter Lang Publishing, Inc., 2005.

Murphy, Patrick D. "Conserving Natural and Cultural Diversity: The Prose and Poetry of Pat Mora." *Multi-Ethnic Literature of the United States* 21 (1996): 59–69.

———. "Grandmother Borderland: Placing Ethnic Identity and Ethnicity." *Interdisciplinary Studies in Literature and Environment* (1993): 35–41.

Rebolledo, Diana Tey. "Tradition and Mythology: Signatures of Landscape in Chicana Literature." In *The Desert Is No Lady: Southwestern Landscapes in Women's Writing and Art*, edited by Vera Norwood and Janice Monk, 96–124. New Haven: Yale University Press, 1987.

Saravia, Leobaldo Quiroz. "Cultural and Literary Writing on the Border: Notes for a Landscape." In *La linea: Ensayos sobre literatura fronteriza mexico-norteamericana. The Line: Essays on Mexican/American Border Literature*, edited by Harry Polkinhorn, Gabriel Trujillo Muñoz, and Rogelio Reyes, 57–67. San Diego and Mexicali: San Diego State University and Universidad Autonoma de Baja California, 1989.

Torres, Hector A. Review of *House of Houses. Aztlán: A Journal of Chicano Studies* 23, no. 2 (1998) 233–38.

Notes to Chapter Seven

1. Linda C. Fox. "From *Chants* to *Borders* to *Communion:* Pat Mora's Poetic Journey to Nepantla," *Bilingual Review* 21, no. 3 (1996): p. 4 of 11. http://web10.epnet.com/ (accessed: June 8, 2006).

2. Ibid., p. 8 of 11.

3. B. Marie Christian. "Many Ways to Remember: Layered Time in Mora's *House of Houses,*" *Multi-Ethnic Literature of the United States* 30, no. 1 (2005): 136.

4. Hector A. Torres. Review of *House of Houses, Aztlán: A Journal of Chicano Studies* 23, no. 2 (1998): 233.

Part Three

Res Publica(e)
HORIZONS

CHAPTER EIGHT

Richard Rodriguez
I Don't Think I Exist ⌒

⌒ Born in 1944, Richard Rodriguez has crafted a literary career filled by the disappearance of the author. This point about the disappearance of the author would make no sense were it not for the fact that the locus where the subject disappears is a contested site of power. Critic Teresa McKenna deploys this model of the speaking and writing subject in modernity to identify the power that Rodriquez seizes with *Hunger of Memory*. McKenna brings an exposition of Michel Foucault's "author-function" to understand Richard Rodriguez, the figure in *Hunger of Memory*, in a more comprehensive way: "Foucault's argument suggests that we have been dealing with a somewhat truncated Richard Rodriguez, whose complexities of author-function have not been sufficiently addressed."[1] McKenna urges other readers of *Hunger of Memory* to appreciate Rodriguez's multiple selves in the text and not just the empirical facts that he owns and uses to market his autobiography. In a similar approach, critic Antonio Márquez ask readers to attend not so much to the "ethnic drama" of *Hunger of Memory* but to the social act of writing itself: "The 'ethnic drama' of *Hunger of Memory* is secondary to the act of writing and to the metaphors that have modified ethnic autobiography."[2] Behind the metaphors modifying American ethnic autobiography stands a fundamental metaphysical question to which Rodriguez's act of writing alerts the reader. "*Hunger of Memory* is an important work because it raises a problematical issue: *What is ethnic literature*."[3] The fact that the metaphors lead to this deeply vexing question probably indicates that the ethnic drama cannot be separated from primary concerns like the social act of writing as an author-function that markets the text as an exponent of power relations that American democracy fosters. It is precisely the ethnic drama that divided the reception of the text in the academy and provoked the social act of writing in the academy.

When critics objected to *Hunger of Memory*, they did so on the ground that the conservative Right in America was appropriating it to buttress arguments about the virtues of assimilation into Anglo-American society. In a reading of *Hunger of Memory* that addresses in a fresh way the hostile reception of the text in the academy, critic Randy Rodriguez proposes that it was not just the politics of the age that Rodriguez bucked but a primordial order of experience—the sexual mores of Chicano/Mexicano/Latino culture: "It was not solely his arguments with affirmative action and bilingual education, nor his so-called individualist aesthetic that incited such heated critical responses to him and his writings. I would argue that it has as much to do with the cumulative effect of the effeminate signposts throughout his narrative."[4] Rodriguez bases his analysis on what he call a "sissy" aesthetic: "A sissy wrote *Hunger of Memory: The Education of Richard Rodriguez*. A (closeted) homosexual: 'Mr. Secrets.'"[5] The sissy in this mapping of homosexual identity, Richard Rodriguez plays the role La Malinche. The critic Rodriguez puts it succinctly: "What I argue is that Rodriguez is critiqued and rejected not merely due to the supposedly inauthentic content of his writing and apparently 'conservative' politics but because he is a *joto* or *puto*, a passive homosexual—a nonman in Mexican/Chicano/a defined cultural terms."[6] He betrays *chicanidad*/Mexican America to Anglo America as Malinali betrayed the Aztec empire to Cortés by sleeping with and translating for him. The Richard Rodriguez controversy, from the standpoint of Randy Rodriguez's analysis, appears as a severe hysterical symptom within chicanidad, something along the order of a cultural pathology that I too participated in.[7] The stylistic choices sissy Rodriguez makes, his metaphors, even his metaphysics, are signs of this pathology. The critical side of this pathology is the intensity of the social act of writing to repress how Rodriguez stages what he says in his drama. The critical repression of Richard Rodriguez is intense because it deals with the fundamental question of representation. Critic Rosaura Sánchez takes issue with both *Hunger of Memory* and *Days of Obligation* presumably because the texts do not represent Mexican/Hispanic America accurately: "For his good services, following the publication of his first book of essays, the author became the darling of right-wing politicians and conservative groups. In time he was tapped by mainstream media as if he were the official representative of the very populations that he views with disdain; his opinions have since been published in the *Los Angeles Times* and he has appeared on the *MacNeil/Lehrer NewsHour* to provide the 'Mexican American' perspective."[8] The call for hard realism that Sánchez issues to Richard Rodriguez does not allow her to see the great generosity of the texts Richard Rodriguez has already produced. Up against the issue of representation and the crises that surround it, the generosity of Rodriguez's text must not be overlooked.

The triptych *Hunger of Memory, Days of Obligation: An Argument with my Mexican Father*, and the recent *Brown: The Last Discovery of America* reverberates with the question: what must Mexico be to Anglo America? Correlatively, what must a Mexican presence signify to Anglo America that the latter must keep the former at bay, invisible, in oblivion? Or, what must the signifier "Mexican" mean to Anglo America that it must repress it with such intensity? Márquez compresses that point with the question: what is ethnic literature? But Rodriguez's texts, through the selection of metaphors and stylistic choices, desire something more from his readers than the postmodern truism that identity is a constantly changing commodity in the marketplace of literary value. In the new American global *ágora*, Rodriguez offers up a rich and generous textuality driven in its metaphor and style to the fundamental question of representation. The drama of losing Spanish to attain the acrolect is a common one from colonial through postcolonial and neocolonial worlds, but Rodriguez gives it such a generous exposition that his readers know that he chose acrolectal English to exercise power over this issue, even if he didn't know it all at once.[9] Rodriguez disrupts Anglo America's fair face in the mirror when he writes: "My face is mournfully long, in the classical Indian manner; my profile suggests one of those beak-nosed Mayan sculptures—the eagle-like face upturned, open-mouthed, against the deserted, primitive sky" (115). Ten years later in *Days of Obligations* he tells us in a mature style:

"I take it as an Indian achievement that I am alive, that I am Catholic, that I speak English, that I am an American. My life began, it did not end, in the sixteenth century" (24). The alterity that he wants to excavate and represent takes still another turn in *Days* when he says, "Success is a terrible dilemma for Mexican Americans, like being denied some soul-sustaining sacrament. Without the myth of victimization—who are we? We are no longer Mexicans. We are professional Mexicans. We hire Mexicans. After so many years spent vainly thinking of ourselves as exempt from some common myth of America, we might as well be Italians" (70). Here, like Sánchez, Rodriguez references the power of the author-function and not just for himself but for the new Mexican *haute bourgeoisie* as well. With equal power he references a common trope in Mexican American culture, which stipulates that as long as one is going to be marked as Latino, Italian is the best kind to Latino to be. This trope is also at work in Ana Castillo's letter number three in *The Mixquiahuala Letters*. Furthermore, when he introduces Alexis de Tocqueville in chapter one of *Brown* to raise the issue of race, he again reminds America not only that he knows Prospero's books, but that he's here to stay. In italics, Rodriguez addresses De Tocqueville: *"But cher Monsieur: You saw the Indian sitting beside the African on a drape of baize. They were easy together. The sight of them together does not lead you wonder about a history in which you are not narrator?"* (3). In the gaps that span these statements, readers can find the generosity of his texts in opening up this issue of representation that is so vexing, Rodriguez must press his face as a sign of alterity against Anglo and Mexican American mirrors.

Richard Rodriguez's work in the field of broadcast journalism also comprises a complex body of work. As an editor for Pacific News Service, Rodriguez scripts broadcasts for the *Jim Lehrer NewsHour*. In 1997 Rodriguez won television's highest honor, the George Foster Peabody Award, for his *NewsHour* "Essays on American Life." His work in broadcast journalism includes "A Dialogue on race with President Clinton," and the recent "Danger and Grace—September 11 and America's Religious Movement." Having among his accolades the Charles Frankel Prize from the National Endowment for the Humanities as well as the International Journalism Award from the World Affairs Council of California, Rodriguez occupies the position of a public intellectual in American life and letters.[10]

Langue(s)

H. T. Richard, can we begin by talking about when and where you were born?

R. R. I was born in San Francisco, about a mile from where we are sitting now, in a place called St. Joseph's Hospital. My mother and father lived over on O'Farrell Street, which was only about five blocks from where we are. They were married in a church, which is also about four or five blocks away. But I grew up in Sacramento. I came to San Francisco and live in this neighborhood quite coincidentally, but my sense of hometown is Sacramento, and that's where all my childhood memory resides. I was a child of the 1940s and '50s; my conscious life begins in the 1950s, within working-class Spanish. Both of my parents come from western Mexico. My father is from the state of Colima—a small village within the state of Colima. He was in Mexico during the revolution, and his disgust with Mexico came out of that revolution and the way he saw Mexican kill Mexican. *Viva México!* My mother, on the other hand, is a great Mexican patriot to this day. She grew up in the state of Jalisco and she's always been the patriot in the family, and that side of my conscience that always calls me to the past. My father is completely unconcerned with Mexico, has no emotional tie to it, has no interest in it, but in some way his darkness is very Mexican and I grew up within these two polarities: my very Mexican-loving mother, my Mexican-hating father. He was morbid, melancholic, in many ways very, very Mexican; she was optimistic, buoyant, in lots of ways very Californian, very American, very optimistic about the future.

H. T. Brothers and sisters?

R. R. I have an older brother, an older sister, and a younger sister. My older brother and sister share with me a kind of linguistic sense of the transition between Spanish and English. My younger sister grew up really only within the English language and barely has a sense of that drama, which for me was a crucial linguistic adventure in my life: the loss and acquisition of a new language, which entailed for me, psychologically, the loss of the old, of the home language.

H. T. So that moment when the nuns come to visit your home and your parents try to speak in English seems to be a great dividing line in *Hunger of Memory*. And you speak about it very frankly. I want to ask you some questions to fill in the details. For instance, did your parents speak any English at all before the nuns came to your house?

R. R. My sense is that my mother particularly had some bilingualism because she, in fact, worked in San Francisco in various jobs. My father was much more of a laborer and to this day his English is very bad. To this day—he's ninety-seven—very, very bad English.

H. T. Ninety-seven? Your father?

R. R. Ninety-seven years old. My father. He was in his fifties when I was born. But there was some English in the house. I remember knowing some words when I got to the classroom, but I remember it being very vague. Obviously, I was taught by the Irish, literally Irish immigrant women. When I listen to their voices years later I realize that they were enormously accented voices. They were almost foreign when I heard them later in my life. But when I was a child they were so rare to me that they seemed to be American voices. I could make no differentiation between their voices and the voices I might hear over the radio. They were American voices to me when they spoke English.

H. T. That dividing line that I'm speaking of here and that you chronicle in *Hunger of Memory* seems to be quite hard. Was there any time in your household in your growing-up years where both Spanish and English coexisted in some way?

R. R. Yes, in playful ways. I remember there was a time when we began to learn English in which we played with it. I remember my mother, who was much more linguistically playful than my father, making up words, which sort of sounded like they were English words to our Spanish ears. She had that knack for making language up and for stretching it and for reinventing it. That was always an amusement in the house. But we knew that was partly our rebellion against English in some way. Do you know what I mean? We insisted on making our own version of it, our own pidgin. I remember, however, that my relationship to the radio was almost totally without my parents. When I really began to get to English, it was without any familial resource. They just weren't there. I can remember that as a surreptitious adventure, listening late at night to the radio in my bedroom. That was just not done with the family. I can remember my mother's records, her Mexican records, and then I would start buying American records as I got older. These were two different sets of music in our house—profoundly different.

H. T.   The oldies?

R. R.   Well, now they're oldies! But in some way, like Elvis Presley, it remains still quite a rebellion. That sound of Lola Beltrán coming into the house, is a pretty remarkable sound. It doesn't sound like anything preceding it. It brings in black America with it; it brings in the American adulation of adolescence; it brings in the body in a new way. It has a different kind of sensuality to it. This was not music that my parents shared.

H. T.   Are these some of the reasons why you feel you remember your pre-English childhood with such affection?

R. R.   Yes. It's also one of the reasons why the great language of my life that mediated between home and public was the liturgical Latin in the church. Its loss is so enormous to me. I can't speak of it to this day. The Latin was for me the transition between my public and private life—it was *both* my public and private life. It was a language expressed to God, but it was also a language expressed within the community of an Irish Catholic Church. The music of that Latin was an echo of Spanish, but it was also within such a formality that it belonged to the Irish priests who spoke it. It was a kind of quasi-American English. It's so hard to explain. It was literally a language between, and it was like nothing else. There was a man named Anton Dorendorf who was the music director of our very beautiful church. At eleven o'clock Mass there'd be the Mozart masses. It's just extraordinary to me that I grew up with Mozart masses. There's nothing like that now that I am middle-class; there's nothing like that in the church. But in those years to be able to hear something so stately that also borrowed in some way from the Latin world was very interesting to me. And that was the third language, in some sense.

H. T. Did you have any sense that your life would be shaped by a language other than Spanish? Were there any intuitions about that?

R. R. Before I spoke English, you mean?

H. T. Yes.

R. R. I can remember peeing in my pants in first grade and I remember the feel of that cold between my legs after I'd done it and having to go home in shame and so forth. I remember what it was really like to be aloof from the English-speaking classroom. I can remember that boy. I can remember the pants I was wearing that day. I can remember the texture of the urine on my legs, but I cannot remember the sound of the classroom. It's so curious. It's almost as though in those years, before I committed myself to it, I didn't hear it. It had nothing to do with me. Nothing to do with me. I can remember intrusions into my privacy, like when the nun insisted that I pronounce my name, and she would anglicize it rather harshly. Road-ree-guez, she would say. It came with some intensity, but it had nothing to do with me. It wasn't the language that I really expected to have to use. That went on for some months.

H. T. And then?

R. R. And then the Irish rebelled. I love the fact that I was taught by the Irish. There's a Gaelic resurgence now in Ireland, but in those years the Irish knew what the Irish have known for hundreds of years and that is that you learn the language of public life. You learn your oppressor's language; you learn to spit it back at him, to become James Joyce. To make it better than his, to steal it from him as Caliban would insist. But they forced a language on me, and they were enormously impatient with my reticence. It wasn't interesting to them, they weren't sympathetic to it; they weren't careful about it. They were enormously unsentimental women. They were working-class, and they knew that they had come six or seven thousand miles from Ireland. They had left their families to come to California, by way of Mexico, by the way. When they came to the United States the Irish quota was filled and they entered the Americas through Mexico. They became Mexican citizens, entered the United States through Mexicali and had Mexican passports, and there they were my teachers of English. The world is a very complicated little place—the people who had been oppressed by the British would end up impatient with my reticence about that language.

And then something begins in the house. I remember the story I always tell people, and now I'm beginning to think maybe it never happened because I've said it so often and the lines are so smooth now in the telling. I remember walking into the kitchen. I can see my mother and father. I can see in the corner of the kitchen where they were standing, and when they see me—I didn't know that they were speaking in Spanish—they switch to speaking English, a really horrible English, but I got the point and I knew that they were pushing me away. I can't draw for you easy lines, but in time, maybe as short a time as six months, something flops in my heart and I begin to realize that I want that public life. I want to belong to that world that nuns belong to. I want to be on the billboards. I want to belong to that voice on the radio. I want that.

H. T. That's what I'm thinking about when I ask you if you had a sense of your life being lived in more than one language.

R. R. I think I did, but more than one language is a little tricky because there was this psychological malady that I suffered once I began to speak English. I began to feel this enormous embarrassment about Spanish in my own mind. My brother and sister seem not to have felt it. To this day my brother is effortlessly bilingual. From those years he has never lost Spanish. He'd gone back to school and learned it as I did in high school, but by that time it was gone to me.

R. R. What is your brother's name?

H. T. Leo. He's older, more generous, more glamorous, less sentimental than I am and less tortured than I am. He became a lawyer; he deals with language at a very different level than I did. I felt in some way that I had betrayed my family. I've never made any sense of that, except that I read somewhere that D. H. Lawrence, whose father spoke with a broad Derbyshire accent, never—although Mellers in *Lady Chatterley's Lover* speaks English that way and at a moment's wish he will switch into that accent to keep Lady Chatterley at bay once he went to school, never again spoke the language of his father, never spoke that version, never spoke that dialect, never spoke that accent. I understand that. People say to me, "Surely you can, surely you are able to," and I tell people, "No, it's not possible." It is not possible; there *is* some impediment. I cannot explain it. Maybe in my inability is a kind of lesson that I just felt so profoundly that I was switching social allegiances and I felt forever stigmatized. I remained my grandmother's favorite grandchild. She would speak to me and would mock me for not speaking back to her, but we spent many, many hours together and I was her translator in public. To this day I am eared, but not mouthed. I will venture, or I will float through Mexico or through Latin America or through Spain, all ears, and I can understand everything said around me. Or I am all eyes; I can read everything around me, but it is like I am asleep, because I don't speak.

H. T. Richard, what is that experience like of sensing in yourself that you are shifting language loyalty?

R. R. I was a child of so many secrets and so many layers of betrayals. Obviously there was a sexual secret I had pretty early in my childhood. Homoeroticism was beginning to develop, not quite in those years, but soon after. That was a secret. The embarrassment also of my darkness in a white world, and the depth of that embarrassment, in a family that accentuated embarrassment. My parents, like a lot of Mexican families, inclined toward light and spoke well and admiringly of it. My father was very light-skinned, my mother less so, my brother was very light-skinned, very attractive to girls. My sister Sylvia was very dark and tortured by that, beaten one day by a child on the street. I am almost as dark, certainly more Indian-looking, hideously Indian-looking, at a time when I didn't even know how to describe this face as Indian. My parents are so Mexican that my mother for example to this day won't use the word *indio*. She would be horrified if I said into a microphone, *"Soy indio."* She wouldn't know what to do with that; she's really Mexican.

What was it like? I mentioned the psychosexual drama only because I remember feeling, especially with my uncle from Mexico who was my mother's favorite, his disdain for me because I couldn't speak to him when he came to visit.

H. T.   What was his name?

R. R.   Juan Morán. He lived in Juárez and had done pretty well for himself. He had lived briefly in the United States and then went back to Mexico. He's dead now. But I remember feeling this enormous effeminacy—I don't know how else to put it, but there was some masculine quality lost in the boy already in that this man had no place for me. I was not his nephew. I was less, a real withering disdain. I've always heard in that word *pocho* a loss of some virility. It's hard to explain.

H. T.   Coming out of those sensations, those intuitions, can you begin to also reconstruct when the sense that English was no longer foreign to you became part of your identity?

R. R.   Well, yes. There are some moments to this day when I'll have to ask friends for a word. For all I swim within the English language, I feel myself quite a citizen of this language, but there are moments when I don't know it. There are just some foreign aspects to it and it seems to me odd. When I seem to be singing in another rhythm—people have remarked that about my poetry for instance—it doesn't sound like it's structured with an English ear. It sounds structured with some other kind of rhythm. I would guess that linguistically there is some grid or something that is still Spanish-speaking, or Spanish-resistant, or that derives from the Iberian Peninsula. I remember when I could pitch my voice in English. That's when I knew that I was speaking it.

H. T.   Pitch?

R. R.   Yes, I remember because it would always bother the nuns that I wouldn't speak out loud. They could never get me to speak in a loud voice. And then they started never saying anything anymore because I was doing it. I *was* speaking in a loud voice and then I knew that I had it. And it wasn't even that maybe I didn't have it. I remember one day the entire class laughing at me. It's so clear to me, these memories; it's so odd. I remember I had said p-r-e-t-t-y, a word that is still hard for me to pronounce properly to this day, and the entire class laughing. It wasn't so much an embarrassment, but I remember the sense that this really wasn't mine. And so when I began to pitch my voice in a loud tone, something had happened to me psychologically. I was using it. I was confident of it. It was mine. I would take it. I would make it mine.

Writing, Style

H. T. Did any of these experiences with your languages give you any sense that your life was being moved toward the profession of writing?

R. R. No, no.

H. T. Nothing like that? Was the screen a blank screen?

R. R. Well, talking about the '50s, I remember there was a black song called "The Name Game" or something like that. It was this loony song. It was about how you change the first part of a word and make it into a new word, and then this woman starts singing and singing. And I knew American blacks just had something that I didn't have. They had been playing with this language for three hundred years. They were doing what the Irish did, what James Joyce had done to English. They were just taking it and turning it on its head. I knew that I would never have that confidence; that I would never be playful with the language the way that blacks were. When I started to hear American black rock and roll, I knew something was up.

I remember years later reading Alexis de Tocqueville's *Democracy in America* and he's riding a horse through a clearing in either Arkansas or Alabama on a summer morning. He comes upon this Indian and African woman sitting together with this white child, and the moment at which these two women see him, the Indian gives the white European this dirty look and she runs into the forest. The black woman, the black

to these new scholarship students who come speaking to me about the barrio.

I had begun by being interested in Renaissance English literature because I sensed that was the source of the English language. I would know about myself by tracing the thread back to its spool. If I could trace English back to the Renaissance then I would find out something about who I was, then I could find out what it meant to be of the English-speaking world. But toward the end of my academic career I got interested in Victorian literature mainly because a lot of the considerations that were interesting to people like Dickens were considerations that are very much part of the modern debate about whether or not you can have ethnic literatures, for example. Dickens tried to incorporate the voice of the working-class man within his novel and never succeeded within the novel, because when the miner begins to speak, all of his speech is misspelled. So there's a sort of pathos to his speech that maybe you would not feel if you were actually hearing it, but on the written page it becomes misspelled. So with the miner's daughter, or whichever character survives from the working class, there's usually some fiction about the fact that she learned English and can speak it in the conventional middle-class ways, so that there's never that grid or haze over her speech. It is invisible when you read it. I was very interested in that.

And then here's these Chicanos coming to my class, doing their little Chicano dance on my head, and there was Wordsworth saying the same thing: Why can't we use the language of the street, man? Why can't we all sort of talk like the Bloods and the Crips? Then we'd really get to the animate source of the language. And there I was at the other end of the linguistic adventure trying to cut my words as sharply as I could.

Wordsworth was very, very important to me for establishing that Romantic tradition that I still think we're part of in literature. But when I come upon Lawrence, the working-class writer—the working-class boy, I should say, who is the son of a coal miner, whose mother I think is a school teacher, Lawrence has these scenes of his father looking at his books that are really quite extraordinary. There was nothing like it in English literature until Lawrence comes along. His short stories, the passion of them, his own sexual ambiguity, his ambivalence about being between classes, at once not being lower class but not being upper class either, the solution of the bilingualism that Mellers and Lady Chatterley achieve with their private sexual language, is very interesting to this young man in my twenties. I begin to think, "Wow! This *is* something."

By that time I was much more an Americanist, too, and I was leaving Britain. I was moving to the United States intellectually and I was becoming interested in American writers. Some of them are so odd, maybe, to you. Vladimir Nabokov, for example, interests me a great deal because, again, what I always detected was this enormous linguistic adventure and anxiety; he writes within three or four languages in his lifetime: Russian, German, French, American English, each time going into the lair to find out where that language source is. It's very exciting to me as a reader, the way he is never bilingual in the same period of time. He knows more than one language, but language is enormously compulsive as a lover. You can't be promiscuous with language. If he's writing in French, he's not simultaneously writing in English. When he's writing in Russian, he's not writing in French. Each language consumes him during a period of time. That was extraordinary, that you could not be promiscuous with language. I still believe that. I still believe you cannot speak more than one language at a time. There's no such thing. It's like being bisexual; you just can't do it. You can perform architecturally. You can perform, but you can't be truly bisexual; you can't be bilingual. There's no such thing.

H. T. There's only one language?

R. R. Yes. There's only one house, only one cave, one lover's arms.

H. T. Who do you read today? Contemporary writers?

R. R. I read a lot of poets, but they're not contemporary. I read Auden a great deal. He's dead. I read essayists like Joan Didion who grew up in Sacramento. I love Joseph Brodsky, who's also dead now. There are a number of British poets that I read still. I read much more poetry than I ever used to. I'm almost reading no fiction now. I can't read a novel. Very rarely do I read a novel. I love the Indian writers like Rohinton Mistry. I think *A Fine Balance* is an extraordinary novel, maybe the best novel of our generation. An Indian in Toronto writing of India is just extraordinary. The sense of snow you have reading that book. I think Salman Rushdie is extraordinary. I think the early novels especially before they become quite so mannered are just wonderful. I love these writers who are taking the English language now as their tongue who are Brown and Black. I love V. S. Naipaul, who is probably the finest stylist within the English language now. Haughty, aristocratic, caste India— upper-class, but diffident toward the lower orders. It's very thrilling to read his stuff. I'm reading *Of the World* now. I loved Octavio Paz when he was alive. I loved everything he wrote. I loved his poetry. I loved his prose. He was a great, great teacher. He was an admirer of the second book. He had written to me about *Days of Obligation*. In fact, he was starting a small publishing house called Vuelta, which is the same name as his magazine in those years. They were going to publish the book in Mexico, but for various reasons it didn't happen. Then he died. How shall I say this without overstating it—it was for the son, the ultimate act of pleasure for the father to give him his blessing in that way. It was really astonishing. When Paz blessed me it was the only time Mexico has ever given me anything that I cared about. Nothing else can Mexico give me.

H. T.   And yet, in *Days of Obligation*, it seems like—and here I'm going to use the word "reconciliation" under erasure—there's a fair amount of reconciliation going on in this work with Mexico and with mestizaje.

R. R.   Mestizaje, and also with the Indian, I think. I really do make the feminine principles in that book—which is the Indians' absorbing quality—stronger than the conquistadors' aggressive qualities. I do think that I've come to terms with feminine culture in Mexico, something that maybe had frightened me for a long time. I think that that's right. There's some reconciliation. I love Mexico. I think in some ways Mexico is the stronger of the two countries. As I said to you about Tijuana, I think there's something about that place. It's like India. It's real and it's deep and it's strong. There are times I think it's just going to wither the United States. It's going to withstand it. It's going to overwhelm it. You go to these small towns in South Carolina and there's all these Mexicans, and they're painting their houses Mexican orange and Mexican red. It's like this advancing army, except that they come and pluck chickens or whatever they're doing.

H. T. The browning of America.

R. R. Yes! The real browning of America is that they are Mormons, and they're Evangelical Protestants. It's that they're impure; they're not pure Mexicans. It's that they're already the Indians, already speaking the language of the conquistador, and they're now learning the language of the conquistador's rival in the Spanish Armada: the English. But there is all of this complexity in the world. When I speak of browning, I don't mean it as a literal brown. My skin is not interesting to me. I'm not a nationalist or a racist in that sense. What's interesting about my life is that from the sixteenth century onward, I am impure, I am mixed, and I am both raped and rapist, and I am both aggrieved and sinned, a sinner—that notion of being both parties in history. I remember the actor Eddie Olmos went to a high school in Los Angeles, maybe grammar school, and asked all these Mexican kids to raise their hand if they were proud to be Indian, and so of course they all raised their hands. And he said, "Raise your hand if you're all proud to be Spaniards," and of course nobody raised their hands. These same Mexicanitos, who are in love with whiteness, who watch it on *televisa* until the blonde hair is coming out of their ears, who are enthralled by the European, these same kids couldn't deal with father Spain to this day. To be really brown is to be like Ricky Martin. To be really brown is to be impure. It is to change your name to Ricky Martin. It is to dye your hair. It is to be gay, singing about heterosexual love. That's real brown. And it's the reason why it's taking the world by storm. It's the reason the Japanese, who are racists and nationalists in the extreme, are quite fond of Ricky Martin. Because he's absolutely an impertinence against borders. I love that. That's what I mean by brown.

H. T. How do you define style for yourself?

R. R. There was a great architect called Louis Kahn, a wonderful modernist architect. He had on staff at his architectural firm in Philadelphia a kind of guru or a mystic or something. This guy used to go with him—I think he was Buddhist—to these architectural sites where they were going to build the building, whether it was in Bangladesh or Houston or wherever it was. They would sit there for several days and see the same site from different angles, several shadows, several times of the day, and they would ask the question: What does this space want to become? It seems to me that's all I ask when I write. When I look at the blank page, I'm trying to decipher in it: What does it want to tell me? See, it's almost as though when I write I'm cracking it open, you know what I'm saying?

H. T. Yes, I do.

R. R. I don't want to say I'm passive to it, but I'm attentive to it. I very much believe in all the metaphors that writers use to describe both their dryness and their fluidity: the notion of inspiration or the muses, that notion that you are merely the receptacle of something that comes from some other source. That's very much the way I regard writing. I sit here day after day, but I have to sit here day after day, knowing that when it comes I have to be here. When it comes to the door, I have to be here to open the door. And if the muse doesn't come today, the muse doesn't come today. That's just the way it is. When it comes, that page—there was a page I was working on in that corner today that had resisted and resisted and resisted for three years—came today. How does that happen? I don't know what your erasure theory says about such a thing. It comes as a grace; it comes as a kind of crack on the page; it comes as a sudden rendering of a . . .

H. T. A "crack on the page" is a very nice metaphor for the erasure. It's like saying that you're lifting the erasure mark off what it is you're trying to say when a gap occurs and opens up beyond your control.

R. R. Well, I want to reverse the language. What is it the page wants to say?

H. T. I agree. I think that's a good way of putting it, too, because it's a reciprocity that has to take place.

R. R. Yes, in that sense, when you learn how to meditate and you learn breathing exercises, you realize, of course, that the world is breathing on you and you're responding to the world with your body as you breathe out. It is quite clearly the world pressing in on me. In some sense, what I know about language now is that language creates me; language is coming into me in order for it to go out.

What I mean by style is, it seems to me, that people have different levels of generosity about that. And there are some people whose pitch is so fine to hear and to swallow. They're so generous about that; they become very great writers. I have a friend who wants to be a writer, but he's absolutely unable to and not for reasons of grammar, but he's psychologically too confined. He can't break out of the trap that he's in his life. And I don't know how to help him because whatever is wrong with him has nothing to do with anything except the fact that he cannot breathe the world in. He doesn't know how to release it, to give it up. There's a whole world in there, but he doesn't know how to give them out again. I just think style is a kind of openness to the world. That's all I know how to say. I don't want to be writing these books. I didn't want to write this third book. I swear to you I was sitting here one day and I thought to myself, "I want to write about other things; I want to write about the death of a moth. I want to write about eighteenth-century Madrid. I want to write about anything but this! I don't want to write about Latinismo no more! *No más*. Nothing, nothing, nothing!" And then I looked up in that space, and there were these Mexican Indians all dressed in blue, in little blue jumpers, who were working with this Korean contractor reroofing our house. And one of them begins to sing in this high-fluted Indian voice this song about the lover of his life who doesn't return his love. And I thought, "I can never escape it." And then they would [*stomping sound*] on my ceiling; the whole room would shake, and Caliban's library would go up and down like it was in a frenzy and I realized that all I have to do as a writer is just accept the world as it is given to me. This, the world I have, this is what I know. This is the drama that I deal with, and I can't write about anything else. I have to listen to the way that drama structures itself within my soul. That's all my style is.

H. T. This listening, this waiting for, does this demand a certain practice from you, a daily routine?

R. R. Yes, constantly. It is as close as I come to prayer. In fact, Thomas Aquinas says that writing is a form of prayer, and I hope he's right, because when you're really good at being a writer, you're really good at listening. You're really good at it. And sitting still. And you get humble because you realize it has nothing to do with you.

H. T. So do you write in the mornings, or afternoons?

R. R. Always early in the morning. Even when I speak. I was giving a series of lectures at Berkeley last week at a Methodist seminary, and they prayed for me before I spoke. It's very rare that this ever happens. But this woman got up with this extraordinarily beautiful voice, and she sang this Protestant hymn about the holy ghost ascending, and I really felt when I got up to the microphone—it was in this big, big church and there were maybe a thousand people there—and I felt that if it was going to work, it was not going to be anything that I did. It just wasn't.

I'd gone to the banquet and then I went to the dressing room for this at the church. I was looking over my notes at the church and I thought, "This is all dry. It needs music." It needed music to come off the page. I don't know how to explain this to you. But I'm going to need to be free with this stuff; it's going to have to spring somehow. But until I got to the microphone it was not clear to me what this would be. And then it became a song. It became its own rhythm. It took me to lines that I had not rehearsed, that I didn't know I was going to say. It's extraordinary. It's not automatic writing, but it feels very much like grace.

Love

H. T. Let's turn back to some of the things we've been saying earlier about the Chicano academy or those members of it. They took you to task. They were very harsh on you when *Hunger of Memory* came out.

R. R. You know the deeper loss I feel? Since I don't live in the academy, I don't read any of that stuff. I don't read the criticism. *Hunger of Memory* now is twenty years out of my life. It's not very interesting to me. I barely know how to respond to it. I barely know how to look at that guy on the cover; I mean he looks like Bambi. I've never even read the book since I've written it. So their criticism doesn't hurt me. What does hurt me, in some way, is that they're much sharper and very smart with this, the fact the second book had almost no intelligent criticism that I've seen. It got nothing. And I suddenly realized, of course, that the better way to deal with Richard Rodriguez is just to ignore me. That's hurt me more.

H. T. Some critics were harsh on you because you didn't come out alongside the book with your homosexuality.

R. R. They are? I didn't know that. See, I don't even read them. I didn't know that's the case.

H. T. I presented a paper at an MLA conference and afterward I was chastised for not having dealt with your homosexuality, which in the text I had no clue was there, until in conversation the critic Juan Bruce-Novoa informed me there was this expression "dropping the beads."

R. R. Dropping the beads?

H. T. Yes, that there were . . .

R. R. Clues?

H. T. Yes, clues in the text. One of them, of course, was your eroticisation of the Mexican laborers.

R. R. Oh, yes. Except that when I wrote that material, that I did not want to describe it as purely homoerotic. You can say that there's a deliberate refusal to come to terms with my homosexuality. This was at a time in which I was living quite consciously as a homosexual man. But I thought that it was like Lawrence—there's a very, very strong homoerotic element in Lawrence. Think of the wrestling scene in *Women in Love*. I mean, it's an extraordinarily erotic scene. There's a kind of psychoanalytic reductionism now that when a man expresses admiration for another man's body that must mean he's gay, but I know heterosexual men who do that all the time. I watch them at the Super Bowl hit each other on the ass. For me there was something in that experience, which I do not think is particularly homosexual. I think that ambition of the child, that anxiety about his lack of maleness, that sense of the soft hands. I've talked to too many boys who become men who know that and who are not gay, as far as they're telling me. To render it as a gay experience would have diminished that book. I'm convinced of it. Whereas when I want to write about homosexuality, I'm perfectly willing to.

In *Hunger of Memory* and *Days of Obligation*, the other criticism from the gay left was that I'm too Catholic. There's a whole group of people out there who just want you to be whatever they want you to be, but I don't write that way. I worked one summer with a man named Jan who had this wonderfully ambivalent name, a woman's name. Jan, in fact, is a man's name, but there's something feminine about the name. He was a gardener. I worked as a gardener with him one summer. He was extraordinarily beautiful. We used to talk about things, but he was married, and he had children. There was a kind of erotic energy between the two of us, never consummated, never literal, but clearly charged, as I think can happen between any two human beings. A boy's anxiety about his effeminacy with books was one that Lawrence knew. It's one that I think every scholarship boy knows, especially if he comes out of a very strong working-class culture with men who work with their hands. To say that is specifically homoerotic is just, I think, reductionism at its worst. That's why I don't talk about it, but if you had asked me in those years if I was gay I would never have denied it.

H. T.   I have the same feeling that it was not necessary to talk about the text in that way, but invariably when I have presented work on *Hunger of Memory* that has been the reaction. "How come you're not talking about the fact that he's gay?"

R. R.   Well, there it goes. You see, I think there are people who want to read literature in a way that trivializes literature. I'm not even sure that I'm the author of that book. I really am not. I don't think the gay man who now lives in San Francisco in this apartment wrote it; I don't think I'm the author of that book. That boy was exactly his own author; that voice created itself. Do you know what I'm saying?

H. T.   Yes, I do.

R. R.   I was going to dinner parties with Goldie Hawn when I was writing that book, and I assure you that I was not sounding that voice. That voice comes out from a different part of my soul. It has nothing to do with the life I was leading. Nothing. So invariably friends say, "But I've never heard you sound like that." And I say, "Well, of course," because that's why I had to go into the room to let Richard Rodriguez make that noise, to give him that expression. But I'm not sure that my biography on the outside should lord over his existence. I just don't think so.

H. T.   How do you reconcile gay identity with your Catholic guilt?

R. R.   Well, I reconcile it in very specific ways. I consider it an expression of love. I think love is the most dangerous thing to the world right now. I said this to the Methodists last week, "You know the notion of hate crimes as reprehensible suddenly is okay, and every time a synagogue gets burned or a church gets burned in the South, a group of people get together and sing *Kumbaya*, and they light candles and talk about hate crimes." How terrible. Hate crimes are nothing. Hate is easy. You can hate on a freeway. You can give somebody the bird on the freeway and that's a hate crime. It's really, really dangerous when the world is loving somebody. I knew it when I was a kid and I know it now.

When I started reading books about Southern lynchings of black men who looked—who just looked—too long at a white woman, I began to realize that the most interesting crimes in America have nothing to do with hate; they have to do with love. Fifty years ago when I was a boy in this country, the majority of states had laws against miscegenation. Not simply black and white, but lots of times Asian. My uncle was from India. At the time, there was a restriction on the immigration of Asian women so that these men would all go back. The Chinese would all go back; the Filipinos would all go back. My uncle married my Mexican aunt precisely because brown married brown. They lived in California. I knew that there were prohibitions in white America against love—that was always the case. And when it begins to throb in my heart, when I begin to get attracted to men, or to other boys, or when there is that adolescent desire in me, I know to keep it secret. Because there is nothing more dangerous than the love that dares not speak its name.

I have sat in so many Catholic churches and I've heard homosexuality referred to as a lifestyle because that's what heterosexuals want to describe it as. But I assure you it's not a lifestyle. The man downstairs has made love with this man over here for over fifty years. It's love. While the man over here has been unfaithful to him and now lives with this person over here, he still lives within proximal range because of something that is so irrational and so durable. Anybody who wants to call it a lifestyle is just insane. And my church, which has for years tolerated slavery, why would it not be within the capacity of this church, as indeed within the capacity of most Christian churches, to tolerate hate, which is what it did for a long time? It always seems to me that the Messianic tradition comes at the advance of the church. The church is by instinct and by necessity conservative. But I don't consider myself conservative or institutional. I consider myself at the edge. I have lots of friends who are priests. I'm a dinner guest at the archbishop's house. He knows what I write. It's like we're within a large family. I live very comfortably within this. Here I am Hispanic, or at least I am Mexican—they talk about gringo family, what the Southern Baptists call family values, by which they mean only having children exactly like yourself. In the Mexican tradition there's no way you can sin yourself out of the family. No matter what I did. I could murder you today and my mother would still come to the trial every day and would insist that I was innocent. Or if I were not innocent, I was still a good person. I'm always part of her family. Do you understand? There's no way.

The person that I have been with now for fifteen years takes my father to church when I am out of town on Sunday Mass. And the little Italian nun wanted to know whether Jim was yet another son, and my father says, without skipping a beat, "He is a member of our family." That's the tradition I come out of. For all of this, it has nothing to do with what the pope says. It has nothing to do with any of it; it's the instinct of family. It's something much older. I remind you that within the Americas, the Indian tribes we come out of were much more flexible sexually than the Europeans. And maybe we are moving toward that Indian civilization again.

Deconstruction

H. T.   So where does Richard Rodriguez fit?

R. R.   That's very interesting—I don't know where I fit. I don't see myself fitting anywhere. I don't think I exist. I really don't. I know this is not true—I'm speaking rationally now. I know that *Hunger of Memory*, for example, is assigned in a lot of schools. I know that to be true. And at term-paper time, I get a lot of e-mails from kids all over the country who are assigned this book and want me to answer some question for them. But I don't think of myself as existing. I don't know how to tell you that. I don't have any relationship to that artifact anymore. If there was something in that, like the homosexual omission, which I need to defend, I will defend it. I will defend Richard Rodriguez's decisions about that book. But I am not the author of that book. The person who is talking to you now is not the author of that book. I don't know whether I want to meet this guy, this Richard Rodriguez. He seems kind of creepy to me. And he doesn't sound like a very good son, if you ask me. But he's interesting. He's an interesting man.

H. T.   That was twenty years ago.

R. R.   Yep. And because he wrote that book, I am not that person because he released me from being that. I was no longer angry after that book. Sometimes I will be speaking to teachers and they want me to be sort of like an old singer. They want you to sing the old song you sang in 1942 during the war. And the old jazz singer gets up and tries her best. Sometimes I try to approximate Richard Rodriguez, but I'm so different now from that man. I don't know how to sound his voice. I don't know how to do that. But sometimes it happens, and it happened as recently as two years ago in Denver, Colorado, and they just asked me to do the same thing in Anaheim because it was so good. But it wasn't me that was doing it. It was Richard Rodriguez that was doing it. He just took me over. He took my voice over. He came out of my throat and then began to sound that voice that I hadn't sounded in all those years. And he just took them to the edge of some sorrow—these were all teachers, grammar school teachers. They were holding their breath at the end of it. They couldn't stand it. And then when it was over, it was gone. He was gone. It's really strange; it really has nothing to do with me. It's just giving yourself to that moment.

H. T.   One more broad question. I want to ask you about the intellectual's responsibility to his/her community. We live in a world right now in which America can wage war anytime she wants. We can go to the Middle East and wage war. We live in the world of NAFTA. We live in a world in which we have a formula that can trace the origin of AIDS. Is the anonymity of a city enough? Can this anonymity protect the intellectual from those things? What is the intellectual's responsibility?

R. R.   Well, I hold myself accountable, in a moral sense, of being a public intellectual. This is probably why I don't, for example, publish my poetry, which is much more private, much more close to a kind of emotional core that is idiosyncratic and not at all concerned with NAFTA. You know I lecture on NAFTA. I talk to business groups. I talk to universities. I go to international conferences to talk about migrant labor. These are not issues in which I was trained. As far as I know, I'm the only defender of illegal immigration. I don't even want to say defender. I see this as a given in the world right now and I think it's extraordinary that the poor are in movement all over the world. I have faced shit because of it, but I say what I say. I don't think I can afford, as an intellectual, to be privatistic. I don't think I can afford not to talk about gangs in L.A., or NAFTA in Toronto, or Roman

Catholicism and the rise of Evangelical Protestantism. These are public issues in my life.

My criticism of the intellectual right now is that most of us have given up our role in the world. We seem to be either at the university engaged in such privatistic conversations within methodologies that are indecipherable to anybody outside the discipline, or we seem too engaged in such propagandistic self-advancement. I am a lesbian, literary critic of Emily Dickinson, and this is all I want to talk about. This is all I am. I'm only lesbian; that's all I am in my life, and fuck men, and I'm just going to talk about that. And I can't imagine being a man, because I'm lesbian. I can't imagine being anybody else except me. I can't imagine talking about anything except my little thing.

It interests me that I had Indian uncles. I had Indian relatives. I remember we used to begin Christmas dinner with a Hindu hymn. And Ramesh would come to dinner and he would stand on his head after dinner and we all thought turkey was going to come down his throat, that he was going to throw it up on the floor. I'm Indian. I don't think of myself as belonging to any one thing. I see myself shaped by the world. I was once being interviewed by a kid from a high school newspaper who said to me the most interesting thing about gays. Not being gay, he said he once saw a black man and a white man walking down the street in very animate conversation, and he assumed they were gay. And I said, "Gee, that's the most extraordinary thing I've ever heard" because I am illegal in this country, because I am a secret, because I am offensive to people, because even to this day I have to decide whether I'm going to say who I am at a Baptist college, or at a Catholic college, or before this audience, because I don't want someone to faint in the front row. I have to guard that way, because I learned how to do that all my life, because I learned how to do that with aunts and my uncle and my family. I learned to introduce friends of mine: "This is my *friend*." There was always this sense that I had to be agile at borders, that I had to be able to play several roles. I had to be able to impersonate. I've loved that as a gift, and finally that served me very well.

One of the chapters in this book [*Brown*] is on impersonations. I remember as a young boy I went to watch Malcolm X when he came to Sacramento. I was very adventuresome. I was sexually completely repressed, but I had a black suit like a Puritan. I used to go to lectures all the time with my little pad. This was in high school. No one in my high school would go to these things. This was just a weird thing that I did. I saw Eleanor Roosevelt. I saw Malcolm X. I went to this auditorium where only blacks were allowed and they let me in. I was impersonating a black that day. I went in and there was this guy who was whiter than I was. I mean he was very, very light-skinned in this severe black suit, warning against skin lighteners and hair straighteners and so forth. But I was impersonating all the time.

One of the things I wanted to impersonate was a preppy. By the time I got to Stanford I started wearing preppy clothes. I used to drape sweaters around my neck and I was a brown Indian preppy, but I loved that. And I remember the great controversy at Stanford in those years. Stanford was just beginning to be embarrassed by the fact that our mascot was the Indian. Woe is us. Native Americans on campus who lived in the Native American Theme House, whatever that was, said we could not have Indians anymore. We've had Indians from the Boston Tea Party. You know, the gringos got dressed up as Indians to prove to the British they were not Europeans. It's been one of the great impersonations Americans have always tried. There was an Indian on the football field who lived in San José who would come every weekend on his own and with the permission of the university would dress up as an Indian. He was an Indian, but he dressed up as an Indian, and he was a problem at Stanford. He called himself Prince Lightfoot. I was watching him, this Indian preppy in my blue shirt with my red sweater around my neck and my loafers. I was watching this Indian impersonate an Indian, and then as the season progressed the crowd started booing him, and it became a big deal at Stanford. Could an Indian impersonate an Indian? We decided, liberal Stanford, leftist Stanford—all of us there—we were all in our little camps: Chicana, Native Americans, and Asian Americans, and all the other claptrap of the time—we decided.

About five years later, he came back to Stanford with a group of thugs, five bodyguards, and he forced his way—with the permission of some people in the athletic department—out to the football field during a UCLA/Stanford game and made a triumphal march around the football field. He got some boos, some cheering, but it was a remarkable moment. He died shortly after in an automobile accident. I write about him in this new book because it interests me very much whether the Indian can impersonate the European. In this case, whether the Indian has the capacity to impersonate anybody but himself. Whether I have the capacity to read any books except my own. Whether I have the capacity to be Chinese, whether I have the capacity to be Irish, whether I have the capacity to be anybody but myself. Well, at the same time, that same year that Prince Lightfoot ran around causing everybody such grief at Stanford, I went to a movie in Palo Alto called *Lawrence of Arabia* starring Peter O'Toole, which was based on T. E. Lawrence's autobiography. T. E. Lawrence, this homosexual man in Oxfordshire, England, decides that he wants to be Arab and there he is. To this Mexican kid dressed as a preppy, watching this screen open with the first scene in that movie—seeing this tiny figure in a desert on a camel these white desert, Bedouin robes—was extraordinary to me. A white man could be an Arab. And not only that, but he could for the next three hours enchant us with that idea. We could find him heroic for taking on the role of the Arab, for being Lawrence of Arabia, for being a black man in the white desert. He could impersonate someone other than himself. But if we were to read a novel in those years, say about a Nigerian who comes to England and wants to impersonate an English banker in tweeds—who wants to assume a British accent, who wants to give up Nigeria in favor of England, who rides around England in his little Rolls Royce—we would find him comic. But Lawrence of Arabia, the white man who does the reverse, we find wonderful.

H. T. What do you think is happening there?

R. R. I think to the victor goes the masquerade. I think the winner always gets to decide what the game is, in some way, and those of us who are the losers in history have to be content with our role. I'm seeing now this meltdown of identities. I'm seeing the UPS man, this African American, and I'm thinking this is forty years after Malcolm X said, "Don't dye or straighten your hair." This guy has dyed his hair a kind of orange, the color of his skin. It looks wonderful on him. I don't say anything. I don't do anything, but I think to myself, that kind of playfulness in the world, that kind of element of play is loose in the world now. And the Puritans—the people who want to say you belong here; you can only use this word to describe who you are; this is your language; this is your literature; you should be interested in these issues and not in those issues—those people are death. The kids who are going to survive are those who can be two things at once. It's just really exciting.

The compartmentalization that academics have allowed themselves to fall victim to is a catastrophe. That's why I really don't want to be a Chicano. I mean, I don't want to be a Chicano writer. I don't know what that is. I don't know what that means. "Hispanic writer" is okay because it's so complicated that it's a joke. I deconstruct that word "Hispanic" in this new book, beginning with Richard Nixon and it's hilarious. I mean, it's a comic chapter. It's an absurdity. "Hispanic" is an absurdity. That why I claim it as mine, in the same way I find the word "gay." Someone asked me on TV whether I was gay and I said, "I'm morose." I can't imagine being gay. I've never been gay in my life; I've never been happy. I don't know what that means. I'd have to be brain-dead to be happy in this world. I've lost forty friends of mine in the last twenty years. How can I be gay?

H. T. You lost your friends to AIDS?

R. R. To AIDS, to cancer. I'm like a veteran of the First World War; it's like I've come back and you ask how I am, and I say, "I'm fine." But I'm not fine.

H. T. So the Puritans are not dead?

R. R. Oh, no. The Puritans want to close the playhouses. They did in the seventeenth century. They managed it. They closed the playhouses. They are against mascara, lipstick, and rouge.

They're against any playing. You are what you are. No, it's too complicated. The world is too complicated.

On Marx

H. T. You say the Puritans are not dead. I'm wondering, do you think that Marx is dead?

R. R. Are you talking about Marx the ideologist or Marx the economist?

H. T. Both.

R. R. No, I don't think Marx is dead. I think that Marx understood that we are economic people. We are people driven by and shaped by economics. I think that notion is very much in the world right now. I live in a yuppie community here. The great energy of this society, this technocratic society around me, is completely economic, and authority, stature, prestige, and failure are all defined economically, in the most radical and brutish ways. I think these are the great Marxists, these yuppies that I live among. They're a cruel race, and they see reality as economic triumph or failure. In that sense, is Marx alive? Yes, I sure think he is. He's not exactly practiced as most Marxists would have him.

I find Marx interesting. I love one of his essays where he talks about how it was better that the Americans took California than the Mexicans. I love his speculations, and I love his brutality. He said the Americans will make more of it. And it's true. This would be Tijuana right now. We'd be sitting in Tijuana if this were Mexico, you know? The calamity of Mexico is an enormous, enormous thing, and the failure of Spain to give us anything like an eighteenth-century pronoun, the "I"—and its terrible, terrible hold on Mexico for so long—is still something we're only now beginning to clear our way of. Are you asking me if Marx is still alive in the sense of "does the left throb?" Is that what you're asking? Is there still a left in the world?

H. T. A lot of the critics that have been harsh on you claim a Marxist premise. And they critique you on the basis of a Marxist premise.

R. R. Well, I critique them on a Marxist premise. Anybody who is a defender of affirmative action is anti-Marxist, as far as I'm concerned. I've never heard in anything I've read in Marx—please quote me the passage, dear critic—where Marx says that it's okay for the middle class to advance in the name of the poor, because the middle class will somehow seek the benefit of the poor when they have achieved their PhD. I've never read anything like that in Marx. I've read just the reverse in Marx. I've read that, in fact, the middle class is after its own good and the middle class is quite prepared to use the poor to get there. The logic of affirmative action makes me the beneficiary of my numerical relationship to those people who are excluded. That's how I become a minority in the university. The linguistic structure of affirmative action makes me the beneficiary of the oppression of other people. If you can argue that it is Marxist for me to take a position in the university because I will therefore, as a middle-class man, seek the benefit of those who are excluded, I think that's an anti-Marxist position. I don't understand what the left has done. I work in prisons, and I work with kids.

At Pacific News Service, we publish a newspaper called *The Beat Within*, which is published for and by kids behind bars, and I remember some years ago when affirmative action was being overthrown in California, there was a group of middle-class kids—Chicanos, blacks, whites—walking to the trustees' meeting, which was being held not far from here. And I had in this room about twelve kids, mainly black, but some Chicanos, very poor. A lot of them were street kids all their lives. Crack mothers. The most dysfunctional families you can imagine, so I thought I would ask them what they thought of affirmative action. You could almost hear the demonstration going on a few blocks away. Here were all these middle-class brown and black bourgeoisie claiming that affirmative action was unfair because it wasn't coming to them; their little gravy train was coming to an end. And I said to these twelve kids, "What do you think of affirmative action? What is your reaction to any of this controversy?" There was this enormous silence. And then

I realized—it took me about forty-five seconds to realize—they didn't know what I was talking about. They didn't know what affirmative action meant. And I thought to myself, Any political, governmental policy that is institutionalized for the benefit of the excluded, which is unknown by the excluded, and is in fact benefiting the middle class, those least disadvantaged, is a parody of Marxism. It's a parody on the left. We will advance those people least disadvantaged.

It is so absurd the way language is now controlling, manipulating the fantasies of the left and the ethnic left. It is the reason why the ethnic left has no footing anymore. All of its treasured positions, affirmative action, bilingual education, they're gone. They're gone from California. *They* are illegal now. Bilingual education ended. You know how it ended in California? Five Latina mothers in Los Angeles wanted to get their kids out of that mess. They wanted their kids to have Irish nuns. They wanted their kids to be able to speak the language I'm speaking now. They wanted their kids to survive the way the Irish survived against the British. So they go to this Anglican nun—who better to go to than a good nun?—and she began to organize what later became this movement against bilingual ed. That's how it ended. Affirmative action—you know how it ends? It ends because what we have is a white underclass who by virtue of not being able to say they're Hispanic is deemed not to be a minority, whereas a white Hispanic, by virtue of being able to say that I'm Hispanic, is therefore judged to be a minority. It is the most ludicrous linguistic puzzle that we have proposed as leftist politics. I refuse to acknowledge this. It isn't left at all. I don't know who these critics are that you refer to, but they better go back to Marx if they're assuming a Marxist position on any of this.

H. T. Richard, thank you very much.

R. R. You're welcome.

Awards

2002   National Endowment for the Humanities Charles Frankel Prize
2000   Melcher Book Award
1997   George Foster Peabody Award

Primary Works: Books

Brown: The Last Discovery of America. New York: Viking, 2002.
Days of Obligation: An Argument with My Mexican Father. New York: Viking, 1992.
Hunger of Memory: The Education of Richard Rodriguez: An Autobiography. New York: Bantam, 1982.

Primary Works: Selected Essays

"An American Writer." In *The Invention of Ethnicity*, edited by Werner Sollors, 2–13. Oxford: Oxford University Press, 1988.

"Aria: A Memoir of a Bilingual Childhood." In *The Best American Essays of the Century*, edited by Joyce Carol Oates and Robert Atwan, 447–66. Boston: Houghton Mifflin, 2000.

"Closed Doors." In *Arguing Immigration: The Debate Over the Changing Face of America*, edited by Nicolaus Mills and Toni Morrison, 143–50. New York: Simon and Schuster, 1994.

"An Education in Language." In *The State of the Language*, edited by Leonard Michaels and Christopher B. Ricks, (pp 129–39). Berkeley: University of California Press, 1980.

"Going Home Again." In *The Norton Book of Personal Essays*, edited by Joseph Epstein, 408–21. New York: W. W. Norton, 1997.

"Horizontal City." In *From Different Shores: Perspectives on Race and Ethnicity in America*, edited by Ronald T. Takaki, 281–82. Oxford: Oxford University Press, 1994.

"India." In *Goddess of the Americas/La Diosa de las Américas: Writings on the Virgin of Guadalupe*, edited by Ana Castillo, (pp 17–24). New York: Riverhead Books, 1997.

"Mexico's Children." In *Strangers at Our Gate: Immigration in the 1990s*, edited by Linda Chavez and John Miller, (pp 153–65). Washington, DC: Center for the New American Community, 1994.

Selected Secondary Sources

Alarcón, Norma. "Tropology of Hunger: The 'Miseducation' of Richard Rodriguez." In *The Ethnic Canon: Histories, Institutions and Intervention*, edited by David Palumbo-Liu, 140–52. Minneapolis: University of Minnesota Press, 1995.

Aldama, Frederick Luis. "Ethnoqueer Rearchitexturing of Metropolitan Space." *Nepantla: Views from the South* 1, no. 3 (2000): 581–604.

Challener, Daniel D. *Stories of Resilience in Childhood: Maya Angelou, Maxine Hong Kingston, Richard Rodriguez, John Edgar Wideman and Tobias Wolff.* New York: Garland, 1997.

Christopher, Renny. "Rags to Riches to Suicide: Unhappy Narratives of Upward Mobility: *Martin Eden, Bread Givers, Delia's Song* and *Hunger of Memory.*" *College Literature* 29, no. 4. (2002): 79–109.

Couser, Thomas G. *Altered Egos: Authority in American Autobiography.* Oxford: Oxford University Press, 1989.

Crowley, Paul. "An Ancient Catholic: An Interview with Richard Rodriguez." *America* 173, no. 8 (1995): 8–11.

Danahay, Martin A. "Breaking the Silence: Symbolic Violence and the Teaching of Contemporary 'Ethnic' Autobiography." *College Literature* 18, no. 3 (1991): 64–79.

De Castro, Juan E. "Richard Rodriguez in 'Borderland': The Ambiguity of Hybridity." *Aztlán* 26, no. 1 (Spring 2001): 101–27.

De Hernández, Jennifer Browdy. "Postcolonial Blues: Ambivalence and Alienation in the Autobiographies of Richard Rodriguez and V. S. Naipaul." *Auto/Biography Studies* 12, no. 2 (Fall 1997): 151–65.

Delden, Maarten van. "Crossing the Great Divide: Rewritings of the U.S.–Mexican Encounter in Walter Abish and Richard Rodriguez." *Studies in 20th Century Literature* 25, no. 1 (2001): 118–40.

Fachinger, Petra. "Lost in Nostalgia: the Autobiographies of Eva Hoffman and Richard Rodriguez." *MELUS* 25, no. 2 (Summer 2001): 111–27.

Fine, Laura. "Claiming Personas and Rejecting Other-Imposed Identities: Self-Writing as Self-Righting in the Autobiographies of Richard Rodriguez." *Biography* 19, no. 2 (1996): 119–36.

Guajardo, Paul. *Chicano Controversy: Oscar Acosta and Richard Rodriguez.* New York: Peter Lang Publishing, Inc., 2002.

Kaminsky, Amy. "Gender, Race, Raza." *Feminist Studies* 20, no. 1 (1994): 7–31.

Kaup, Monika. "The Architecture of Ethnicity in Chicano Literature." *American Literature* 69, no. 2 (1997): 361–97.

Limón, José E., ed. "Richard Rodriguez: Public Intellectual." *Texas Studies in Literature and Language* 40, no. 4 (1998): 389–459.

Márquez, Antonio. "Richard Rodriguez's *Hunger of Memory* and New Perspectives on Ethnic Autobiography." In *Teaching American Ethnic Literatures: Nineteen Essays,* edited by John R. Maitino and David R. Peck, 237–54. Albuquerque: University of New Mexico Press, 1996.

McKenna, Teresa. *Migrant Song: Politics and Process in Contemporary Chicano Literature.* Austin: University of Texas Press, 1997.

McNamara, Kevin R. "A Finer Grain: Richard Rodriguez's *Days of Obligation.*" *Arizona Quarterly* 53, no. 1 (1997): 103–22.

Oliver, Lawrence J. "Deconstruction or Affirmative Action: The Literary-Political Debate over the 'Ethnic Question.'" *American Literary History* 3, no. 4 (1991): 792–808.

Pérez-Firmat, Gustavo. "Richard Rodriguez and the Art of Abstraction." *Colby Quarterly* 32, no. 4 (Dec. 1996): 255–66.

Postrel, Virginia I. and Nick Gillespie. "The New, New World." *Reason* 26, no. 4 (1994): 35–41.

Rivera, Tomás. "'Richard Rodriguez' *Hunger of Memory* as Humanistic Antithesis." In *Tomás Rivera: The Complete Works*, edited by Julián Olivares, 406–14. Houston: Arte Público Press, 1991.

Rodriguez, Randy A. *Richard Rodriguez and the Aesthetics of Transgression*. New York: Peter Lang Publishing, Inc., 2002.

Romero, Lora. "When Something Goes Queer: Familiarity, Formalism and Minority Intellectuals in the 1980s." *Yale Journal of Criticism* 6, no. 1 (1993): 121–42.

———. "Richard Rodriguez Reconsidered: Queering the Sissy (Ethnic) Subject." *Texas Studies in Language and Literature* 40, no. 4 (1998): 396–423.

Saldívar, José David. *Border Matters: Remapping American Cultural Studies*. Berkeley: University of California Press, 1997.

Saldívar, Ramon. *Narrative: The Dialectics of Difference*. Madison: University of Wisconsin Press, 1990.

Sánchez, Rosaura. "Calculated Musings: Richard Rodriguez's Metaphysics of Difference." In *The Ethnic Canon: Histories, Institutions and Interventions*, edited by David Palumbo-Liu, 153–73. Minneapolis: University of Minnesota Press, 1995.

Schilt, Paige. "Anti-Pastoral and Guilty Vision in Richard Rodriguez's *Days of Obligation*." *Texas Studies in Literature and Language* 40, no. 4 (1998): 424–41.

Sedore, T. S. "Born at the Destination: An Interview with Richard Rodriguez." *New England Review* 22, no. 3 (2001): 26–37.

———. "Violating the Boundaries: An Interview with Richard Rodriguez." *Michigan Quarterly Review* 38, no. 3 (1999): 425–46.

Soldan, Angelika and Elizabeth Zavaletta. "Richard Rodriguez's Writings: An Account of Cultural Complexity and Search for Identity." *Journal of Hispanic Higher Education* 1, no. 4 (2002): 313–19.

Staten, Henry. "Ethnic Authenticity, Class, and Autobiography: The Case of *Hunger of Memory*." *PMLA* 113, no. 1 (1998): 103–16.

Stavans, Ilan. "The Journey of Richard Rodriguez." *Commonweal* 120, no. 6 (1993): 20.

Tilden, Norma. "Word Made Flesh: Richard Rodriguez's 'Late Victorians' as Nativity Story." *Texas Studies in Literature and Language* 40, no. 4 (1998): 442–59.

Notes to Chapter Eight

1. Teresa McKenna, *Migrant Song: Politics and Process in Contemporary Chicano Literature* (Austin: University of Texas Press, 1997), 53.

2. Antonio C. Márquez, "Richard Rodriguez's *Hunger of Memory* and New Perspectives on Ethnic Autobiography," in *Teaching American Ethnic Literatures: Nineteen Essays*, ed. John R. Maitino and David R. Peck (Albuquerque: University of New Mexico Press, 1996), 240.

3. Ibid., 239.

4. Randy A. Rodriguez, "Richard Rodriguez Reconsidered: Queering the Sissy (Ethnic) Subject," *Texas Studies in Literature and Language* 40, no. 4 (1998): 401.

5. Ibid., 398.

6. Ibid., 403.

7. Hector A. Torres, "Narrative Syntax and Self-Figuration in the Texts of Richard Rodriguez and Gary Soto: A Stylistic Analysis," (paper presentation, Chicano Literature Discussion Group, MLA Convention, New Orleans, LA, December, 1988).

8. Rosaura Sánchez, "Calculated Musings: Richard Rodriguez's Metaphysics of Difference," in *The Ethnic Canon: Histories, Institutions and Interventions*, ed. David Palumbo-Biu (Minneapolis: University of Minnesota Press, 1995), 158.

9. I borrow the term "acrolect" from linguistic studies in creolization. See Ian F. Hancock, ed. *Diversity and Development in English-related Creoles*. (Ann Arbor: Karoma Publishers, 1985), 30. The term acrolect refers to the variety of language closest to the standard language in a creolized-language-speaking community. The basolect is the language variety most closely associated with the home language.

10. José Limón, "Richard Rodriguez: Public Intellectual," *Texas Studies in Literature and Language* 40, no. 4 (1998): 389–459.

CHAPTER NINE

Demetria Martínez

To Speak as Global Citizens ⌒

⌒ On August 3, 1988, Demetria Martínez and Lutheran minister Glen Remer-Thamert were acquitted of charges of breaking U.S. immigration law. The trial was the first in which an American journalist was charged with smuggling human cargo across the U.S.–Mexico border and the first attempt to pin the sanctuary movement with a profit motive.[1] In what could be called a symbolic antifederalist effect—perhaps even a case of States' Rights—the acquittal hinged on Governor Toney Anaya's proclamation on March 28, 1986, that New Mexico would be a sanctuary state, a safe haven for refugees from El Salvador fleeing state repression. The sanctuary movement in the United States emerged in the early 1980s as a response to state-sanctioned terror in El Salvador—repressive practices with undeniable and ominous ties to U.S. foreign policy in Central America. Governor Anaya pointed to the symbolic status of his proclamation, and yet the symbolic status was sufficient and certainly necessary to keep federative power at the door of New Mexico during those critical months of the trial. Not only the symbolic status of the proclamation came into play but the metaphysics of intention too derailed the case of prosecuting attorney William Lutz.[2] U.S. District Court Judge John Conway instructed jurors to take into account records of international treaties signed by the United States as well as Anaya's proclamation. At the conclusion of the trial, Tova Indritz, defense attorney for Martínez, hailed her unanimous acquittal as a victory for the First Amendment's protection of freedom of the press.

Out of this harrowing experience is born Demetria Martínez's *Mother Tongue.*

Ostensibly, this *roman à l'eau de rose* tells of the love affair between Mary, a young Chicana, and José Luis, a Salvadoran refugee. Beyond that popular genre however, the story refuses Harlequinlike consumption since the roman begins by dedicating itself to the memory of the disappeared/*los desaparecidos*. The opening pages set the story in the context of United States foreign policy in Central America, which saw the assassination of Archbishop Oscar Romero at the opening of the 1980s. Other atrocities followed throughout that decade. As one reviewer of the work puts it: "In *Mother Tongue*, Martínez interweaves the charming romance between Mary and José with shocking accounts of the deaths of nuns, priests, ordinary men and women."[3] The opening sentence of *Mother Tongue* is famous for the way Martínez describes its upwelling while listening to Sandra Cisneros speak: "His nation chewed him up and spat him out like a piñon shell, and when he emerged from an airplane one late afternoon, I knew I would one day make love with him." Thereafter, Martínez describes the story's coming to light as effortless. But if the labor was effortless, the need to recover the time of the story is fraught with trauma. Mary tells the story of her love affair with José Luis twenty years hence and she must repeat the trauma of those memories in the narration. Mary's recovery of narrative time brings to light Martínez's brand of mestiza consciousness. To accomplish this task of recovery Mary makes use of every available resource for memory, gaps and all. Of their first conversation in which José Luis compares his air sickness to breathing tear gas, Mary says: "I'm not sure, twenty years later, that he used the words tear gas. I didn't then know its Spanish translation and I don't know it now. But for the sake of the story, tear gas will have to do. You see, I am good at filling in blanks, at seeing meaning where there may have been none at all. In this way I get very close to the truth. Or closer still to illusion" (11). Martínez oversees her protagonist Mary coming to grips with those events not simply as a matter of events coming into full presence through the narrative. Mary must acknowledge the gaps in memory and make them part of her effort to construct a new life for herself and the fruit of her romance with José Luis, their son of the same name. A mix of genres works in tandem with the acknowledgment of the frailties of memory while affirming the political force of Martínez's aesthetic sensibility as performed by her narrator. Reviewing *Mother Tongue*, Lynn Cline observes: "Mary narrates the story from painful memories, twenty years after this meeting, mixing letters from Soledad, poems, newspaper accounts, and journal entries. She slowly pieces events together, moving back and forth in time to reveal the tragic story of one of El Salvador's disappeared, the countless men and women who suffered unimaginable and unknown fates at the hands of their government's military death squads, backed by the U.S. government."[4] The novel's hasty ending brings the reader up to the time of the narration with another voice added to the mix, that José Luis Jr. Mother and son take a flight to San Salvador where José Luis recuperates his father's middle name, Alegría, and both discover José Luis Sr. is not dead. The name Alegría joins Central and North America in the figure of José Luis Jr., a sign of a mestizaje that the name Chicano is topologically equipped to cover. Twenty years after, there is thus a sign that this *familia Chicana* will be reconstructed—an existential hope that will have to contend with the 9/11 datemark. Martínez's awareness of America's imperial sovereignty and executive power over the globe is at the forefront of this interview.

DATE OF INTERVIEW: April 5, 2003
SETTING: Border Book Festival, Mesilla, New Mexico

H. T. We're here at the Border Book Festival and we're celebrating Chicana writers. I'm here in particular to interview Demetria Martínez whose work is very relevant to my conception of the postmodern. So Demetria, it's been how long since you and I talked about literature and postmodern condition?

D. M. I don't know. It was prepostmodern. I think it was in Guadalajara at the *Féria del Libro*.

H. T. Perhaps paleopostmodern times?

D. M. It's been a while.

H. T. What kind of turns has your career been taking since we last talked?

D. M. Well, I came out with a book last year called *The Devil's Workshop*, a book of poetry. And I'm now doing a book of essays, meditations, and columns—a collection of some of my columns from *The National Catholic Reporter*. I'm also writing a long dreamscape on the war, which of course began some time after I had begun the book. I think it's really significant that one of the things that has come out of this time is how Latinos are addressing not just what are traditionally thought of as Latino issues, or that we have been ghettoized by the outside world. It is exciting to see the strong reflection that has come out as a consequence of this war in Iraq and about any number of issues, but particularly about this war. It's all so refreshing that we're not sitting around debating whether we should call ourselves Hispanics or Chicanos, like some of the old debates, which have their place. It seems in some ways we have grown beyond them, or we're freer to feel that we can address a range of issues that are affecting us and so that has been uplifting to hear this.

H. T.   Your work with *The National Catholic Reporter* has always put you in touch with the world at large. And now you say you're going to develop some essays from that work, which you're now compiling.

D. M.   Right. I'm going to be compiling a number of those columns. They're topical, but at the same time, I chose the ones where the writing is strongest. They have a kind of timeless quality to them. And they also deal with spirituality, which to me is very tied up with how one lives in the world in terms of community. Some people use the word politics here. And so that is important to me as well. And I was going to say too, that in terms of my interest in writing about what we would call the world at large, the world impinged on me in a very real way. You know the story. I was charged with conspiracy against the U.S. government in connection with allegedly bringing refugees into the country and of course it turned into a big First Amendment article. That turns you into a citizen of the world really quickly when the fist of the government comes down on you for attempting in any way to bear witness to the plight of people we think of as far away in Central America. And that of course was not the case at all. They are part of our larger Latino history now, right here in New Mexico. Right here in the Southwest.

H. T.   As you move out into the world, and with your creativity you try to encompass the world, what kind of crises will arise with chicanidad if we are no longer unique?

D. M. We are going to find our power by speaking out of our reality as Chicanos, by addressing the world at large; in other words, realizing that we can be Chicanos and citizens of the world at the same time. And that is so because we are a so-called mixed-race raza—because we have never been able to maintain that mainstream illusion of borders. We are so mixed. We carry many borders inside of us. That makes us especially positioned to be able to speak as global citizens. It doesn't mean that we abandon our identity as Chicanos. It means quite the opposite. It means standing firmly in that identity and knowing our own history and knowing what it means within our blood that we are citizens of the world. I mean, listen to the way that we speak. We're always saying, "God willing," or "Only God knows." I was listening to one of the Saudi princes talking the other day and his talk was peppered with that. "God willing— God only knows." And that echoes our own "*Ójala*," which derives from Arabic. And it is all there. We can take so many cultures within us. And that allows us to explode the myth for everyone because no one is pure stock anything. If everyone in the world can recognize that they carry within them stories, the *sangre* of so many groups, then maybe people can get beyond their own understanding of nationality, religion, and race and begin to act as world citizens. That is our only hope.

H. T. The world spirit right now is in a tumultuous state. We have warring gods, warring technologies. How do you address that? How is your creativity taking that in?

D. M. Right now, I think we all have to wear several hats. We have to be journalists. We have to be activists. We have to show up at the protests. We have to write to the editors. But right now, it has been revealing to write what I am calling a dreamscape about the war because my way into that war is—the way it is for many people—television. I wake up in the morning; I turn on the television and the radio; I have a *New York Times* beside me and I write and I write. I do the same thing before I go to bed. And then I tell myself, "Okay, during the day I'm going to get on with the rest of life," and then I find the war has affected the rest of life. I go to the hospital to pick up my medication—it's a program for the uninsured. I'm uninsured. I'm uninsurable like forty, fifty million Americans. Suddenly I realize I have joined the world of long lines. You know, there are long lines of the working poor—people waiting to get their prescriptions. People treated like numbers. We are seeing a mass disintegration of services here in the United States because of our treasure that is being lost and spent in that war and this is the future—the long line. That is the future in the United States in education, in health, in social services, in every arena. But it is also the kind of havoc we are going to see around the world. So again, the process of writing this dreamscape work has been really revealing because I thought I could play reporter, which I love doing. I'm a news junkie. I just watch the war. That is my way in. I am addicted. I'm not even angry. I'm just curious. But then I go out into the rest of life and the rest of life is an outcome increasingly of the waste of money and human treasure in these wars. And yet we live in exciting times because of the antiglobalization movement, which really provided the foundation for the antiwar movement. I think there is a critical mass of people, again, thinking as global citizens, acting out of their particular local identity, but thinking as global citizens and realizing that these issues are connected. Maldistribution of wealth is unacceptable and in fact increases our problems. There is a critical mass of people who are looking for solutions and who are willing to speak out. It is an amazing time for us as Latinos, again, to be drawn into the international future.

H. T.   You speak of this amazing time. You also spoke about an affliction in the long lines. May I ask you what kind of an affliction? Is it an affliction of mind and spirit, mind and body?

D. M.   It's an affliction of the body politic. We have become a society without mercy, without compassion and that shows up in how little we are willing to allot just for people to live with dignity.

H. T.   Can spirit help us in this?

D. M.   Yes. When you say spirit, I cannot even think of it as a separate reality. I think that we have to have tremendous spiritual strength and allow that to emerge in our lives. Gandhi has talked about how we need to become the solution that we seek. So we have to keep our eyes on the prize in that larger sense of borders falling down. We are one people. That person may live in Palestine. That person may live in Juárez, but we are brothers and sisters. It is a parable. We're having to live that parable now. Our neighbor is no longer just the guy in the 'hood or the barrio. It's everyone and that can be overwhelming. It can also be very energizing.

H. T. But spirit has seen more powerful, more potent times. Today, spirit seems fractured, totally ununified. What fragments of spirit can we look to in order to keep our eyes on the prize?

D. M. Spirit is never fractured. We are. I think we just have to turn inward and try to focus on what is most authentic about being a human being. It's about human rights. The right to pursue happiness—you know that radical document—and not allowing them to be hijacked by right-wingers.

H. T. Can we have faith in the American liberal spirit?

D. M. We can have faith in our ability to be a democracy by allowing all of our voices to be heard: to not be afraid to write, to not feel that we have to leave it to the experts to lead or to articulate. This is the time when we can all be telling our stories and telling stories of people who are silent. That is what democracy is. It is not just about the right to vote.

H. T. At some point, affliction, politics, the fragments, the shards of our lives become poetry?

D. M. Right.

H. T. What can you tell us about the poetry that you are working on right now?

D. M. I thought this dreamscape on the war was going to be a traditional essay or a cry of outrage. Instead it is turning into poetry. It also looks so fragmented and so surreal watching it on TV and the only way I could make sense of so much of it was to fall into—almost like an unconscious thing—a poetic voice. I was very influenced by Homero Aridjis's book about the interpretation of the Persephone myth. I think we just have to find new ways to make connections in fragmentation and I think the poetic voice accomplishes that.

H. T. The myth of Persephone is close to your heart.

D. M. [*Laughs*] I have a way of descending into hell periodically.

H. T. Yeah?

D. M. Yeah. Anything else?

H. T. Just one more thing, a note to close on. It concerns an exegetical problem that I have encountered in teaching your novel *Mother Tongue*: the issue of the origin of the work of art. Students always wonder when you say in other interviews that you heard the first sentence in full and out of that came the origin of the work of art. So many years after this novel's birth, how do you feel about this fully grown child?

D. M. I'm really pleased. I look back at times and I still have a sense that it was written by somebody else, by some other entity. And yet at the same I have come to appreciate that I prepared for that moment of inspiration by working very tediously at my craft over the years, learning to write a good line of poetry. In a sense, creating the jar, creating the pot, the piece of pottery so when the spirit came ready to fill it, it did not shatter. And working every day—writing in your journal, reading poetry, writing poetry—prepares you to be a strong enough vessel to receive inspiration. Inspiration is great, but if you are not prepared, it can disappear.

H. T. Demetria, thank you for your generosity of spirit.

Awards

2006 Eighth Annual International Latino Book Award for *Confessions of a Berlitz-tape Chicana*
1994 Western States Book Award for *Mother Tongue*

Primary Works

Breathing Between the Lines: Poems. Tucson: University of Arizona Press, 1997.
Confessions of a Berlitz-tape Chicana. Norman: University of Oklahoma Press, 2005.
The Devil's Workshop. Tucson: University of Arizona Press, 2002.
Mother Tongue. Tempe: Bilingual Press/Editorial Bilingüe, 1994.
Three Times a Woman: Chicana Poetry. With Alicia Gaspar de Alba and Maria Herrera-Sobek. Tempe: Bilingual Press/Editorial Bilingüe, 1989.

Selected Secondary Sources

Cline, Lynn. "On the Power of Love." *Santa Fe New Mexican*, December 1, 1996, sec. E2.
Franco, Dean. "Re-Placing the Border in Ethnic American Literature." *Cultural Critique*, no. 50 (2002): 104–234.
Holmes, Sue M. "Trial to Determine Whether Minister Selling Babies or Aiding Aliens." *Associated Press*, July 11, 1988, http://web.lexis-nexis.com.
Koh, Harold H. "Why the President (Almost) Always Wins in Foreign Affairs: Lessons of the Iran-Contra Affair." *The Yale Law Journal* 97, no. 7 (1988): 1255–1342.
LeoGande, William M. "A Splendid Little War: Drawing the Line in El Salvador." *International Security* 6, no. 1 (1981): 27–52.
Johnson, David. "*Mother Tongue* is Poetic Work of Conscience." Review of *Mother Tongue*. *National Catholic Reporter* 31, no. 7 (1994): 14.
Martinez, Elizabeth. "Of Passion and Politics." Review of *Mother Tongue*. *The Progressive* 59, no. 7 (1995): 39–42.
Mason, T. David and Dale A. Krane. "The Political Economy of Death Squads: Toward a Theory of State-Sanctioned Terror." *International Studies Quarterly* 33, no. 2 (1989): 175–98.
Matthew, Jay. "Sanctuary Workers Acquitted of Smuggling Illegal Aliens: Albuquerque Verdict Gives Movement Big Legal Victory." *Washington Post*, August 2, 1988, sec. A2.
Moore, John Norton. "The Secret War in Central America and the Future of World Order." *The American Journal of International Law* 80, no. 1 (1986): 43–127.
Mossman, Robert C. "Teaching Demetria Martínez' *Mother Tongue*." *The English Journal* 86, no. 8 (1997): 38–41.
Scheffer, David J. "U.S. Law and Iran-Contra Affair." *The American Journal of International Law* 81, no. 3 (1987): 696–723.
Walden, Daniel. "Parallels between Chicano and Jewish-American Writing." *Multi-Ethnic Literature of the United States* 8, no. 2 (1981): 57–60.

Notes to Chapter Nine

1. Jay Matthew, "Reporter, Cleric on Trial in Aliens Case; Pair Accused of Helping to Smuggle Salvadoran Women into U.S.," *The Washington Post*, July 15, 1988, sec. A3. In this article anticipating the trial, Matthews reports these incidents as firsts in the history of the sanctuary movement and First Amendment rights, adding: "The trial is the first major government move against the sanctuary movement, in which several American churches and religious leaders have sought to help Central American refugees, since the 1986 trial in which eight sanctuary workers were convicted in Tucson of conspiracy and smuggling aliens."
2. Sue Major Holmes, "Sanctuary Defense Fundamental to Acquittal," *Associated Press*, August 3, 1988. Anaya was on record concerning the symbolic status of the proclamation, which theoretically should have had no juridical effect. As Holmes states: "Anaya said the defense hinged on whether Remer Thamert believed the proclamation had legal effect." Anaya himself states, "It did not, but the issue was whether he believed it did."
3. David Johnson, review, "*Mother Tongue* is Poetic Work of Conscience," *National Catholic Reporter* 31, no. 7 (1994): 14.
4. Lynn Cline, review of *Mother Tongue*, "On the Power of Love," *Santa Fe New Mexican*, December 1, 1996, sec. E2.

CHAPTER TEN

Kathleen Alcalá
To Tell the Counternarratives ⌒⌒

⌒⌒ *Spirits of the Ordinary*, Kathleen Alcalá's first novel, translates family history into a literary chronotope of considerable historical breadth and great beauty. From this interview, readers of the trilogy beginning with *Spirits of the Ordinary* can map Alcalá's great-grandfather and great-grandmother onto the figures of Estela and Zacarías. Zacarías's gold fever was also her great-grandfather's gold fever. Similarly, Alcalá's grandfather, born in Satillo and a Jewish convert to Protestantism, finds a literary representative in Gabriel, Zacarías's and Estela's studious son, who travels north to Michigan to pursue an education and there finds his new religion. Reviewers of the *Spirits of the Ordinary* quickly take to the transformation of the historical field into a literary chronotope. Critic Charles de Lint states: "The landscape is mostly desert and badlands. At first glance, they seem to be hard and barren places, but as anyone who has spent any time in such landscapes can attest, they brim with secret life. The history is that of Mexico, distilled here to a few specific points of view: Jews trying to keep their faith where their religion is illegal, the treatment of natives by the government and soldiers, the influence of the large mining companies over their employees whose position is no better than that of slaves."[1] Addressing the Crypto-Jewish background of Alcalá's chronotope, Margarita Donnelly adds: "Zacarías's father, a local pharmacist, studies the Cabala and practices alchemy. His library of esoteric books has been secretly guarded by generations of Caravals, who have long been clandestine Jews. Zacarías's mother, Mariana, has been mute since an anti-Semitic attack by her schoolmates during childhood. She is a dreamy, almost ethereal character, who communicates through sign language. Mariana is the true mystic that her husband Julio is striving to become."[2] The substratum of Jewish culture that pervades this family saga is a powerful source for the material mestizajes to which Alcalá gives literary representation.

Deep in the genealogy of Alcalá's family tree, ordinary spirits have been peeling back the layers of history from daily life to discover reservoirs of something that is neither one substance nor another, but still something else. The practice is enveloped in metaphysical language, as in the magical realism of Gabriel García Márquez and Jorge Luis Borges, to whom Alcalá is compared by Ursula Le Guin. The practice has uncanny effects similar to those of deconstruction when this critical practice demonstrates how languages are often no match for the gravity of history. In Chapter 4 of *Spirits of the Ordinary*, titled "The Tree of Knowledge," Alcalá scripts a moment of deconstruction in Zacarías as the son reflects on the father's devotion to the Cabala: "But what was his father? Outwardly Catholic, inwardly Jewish. Did he seek change or only a perpetuation of who he was, like some creature of the desert that has adapted from more bountiful times? And what did he seek through the Cabala?" (54). The Jewish ways of his father Julio have little hold on Zacarías. The mestiza consciousness it takes to hold two grand metaphysical traditions in suspense without annihilating either one or seeking to synthesize them into a unity escapes Zacarías. The destiny of the son is bound up more with reading the book of nature, his long passages through the desert and into the mountains in search of gold, connoting this other space or mode of search. Later, Zacarías experiences a spiritual revelation that comes through the mediations of nature and arrests his gold fever demanding not a linguistic articulation of it in return but a certain ethical practice: "Zacarías was filled with a great sweetness, a great calm. It had been in front of him all the time. It did not matter if he ever made a fortune. Zacarías had found it here, in this city of the ancients. The gold was in the brown skin of the people, the stone, the quality of light upon the cliff face. He would return home and ask Estela for her forgiveness; he would make peace with his father" (182). The fame of his revelation spreads, giving light to layers of cultural and spiritual mestizaje alive in Alcalá's literary chronotope: "Most of all, people brought their faith—in the old ways, the new ways, the Virgin Mary, Christ the King, Father Sun, Mother Moon, healing signs, heavenly bodies and potions. For faith without works is dead, but works were witnessed every day at Casas Grandes" (184). I call this experience of revelation a deconstruction because nothing in the revelation favors a particular path or orthodoxy.

In the figure of Estela, the reader can decipher yet another form of mestiza consciousness with a kinship to deconstruction. In the interview Alcalá talks about her great-grandmother/Estela in a way that sheds some light on what she calls the counternarratives to official history. Zacarías drains the family treasury in pursuit of gold and Estela must kick him out of the house or be left penniless. Alcalá describes her great-grandmother as someone who went against the official mores of Saltillo society and *Spirits of the Ordinary* tells how she did so. From the moment of Zacarías's departure, Estela feels an alterity entering her consciousness that she can't explain: "A sudden flight of birds or movement of wind made Estela stop and gaze out the window. She could not say why, but she felt a lightness she had not felt in many years" (26). The image of birds in flight and the wind coalesce with Estela's interior consciousness, inside and outside reflecting each other metaphorically. The sense of alterity emerges when she meets and begins an affair with one Captain José Luis Carranza. As the interview makes clear, this event in the family saga leads Estela to see her desire beyond the mores of her society and culture. As Estela reckons with her desire, she does not seek to explain it per se with metaphysical pretensions but rather with a pragmatic outlook: "Part of her knew that this was foolhardy, that it could not last, but in these days of uncertainty, of shifting boundaries and loyalties, of families picking up to move north or south or who knows where, of husbands running off to women of ill repute, nothing was predictable; and for once in her life, Estela would enjoy fresh fruit when it was offered to her" (100). The counternarrative in the form of Estela's mestiza consciousness holds out the possibility that some choices are beyond good and evil.

The epilogue to *Spirits of the Ordinary* belongs to Gabriel, Alcalá's grandfather, son of Estela and Zacarías. In first person, Gabriel reminds the reader that history doesn't end but is continually beginning. "The time had come to begin again," concludes the *Spirits of the Ordinary*. In the interview, as Alcalá makes clear, perpetual beginnings mean the endurance of the Mexican and American borderlands. Her discussions of Arab-Palestinian relations give the literary work of art a special function in the current state of global politics. In particular, the tension between history and fiction she addresses in her closing statement disturbs any simple distinction between the two.[3]

DATE OF THE INTERVIEW: May 6, 2003
SETTING: The office of Kathleen Alcalá, Visiting Lecturer in creative writing, Department of English, University of New Mexico

Seizing the Moment to Write

H. T.   Kathleen, I'd like to begin by saying that some of us are late-comers to your work and, obviously, have not had the long-term exposure to it other readers have enjoyed. I want to situate your productivity, so may I begin by asking you to give us a brief historical timeline of your work?

K. A.   I came late to my work, too. I didn't start studying creative writing until I was in my late twenties. My first book was published when I was thirty-seven. That was *Mrs. Vargas and The Dead Naturalist*, a collection of stories. Over the next nine years or so I wrote three novels set in nineteenth-century Mexico, *Spirits of the Ordinary*, *Flower in the Skull*, and *Treasures in Heaven*.

H. T.   So you have how many novels?

K. A.   Four books in print, all [of them] works of fiction.

H. T.   What are the dates of publication for those works?

K. A.   1992, 1997, 1998, and 2000.

H. T.   What prompted or awoke your desire to write?

K. A.   I was always interested in writing. But I went to college from '72 to '76, the postsixties. It was sort of the "morning after," and people were very focused on practical things. Most of my class-mates at Stanford were prelaw or premed. At that time, I knew I was interested in language, and having a relationship with language, especially linguistics. After graduating, I went into the practical application of that. I worked for the Democratic

National Committee in the press office. I worked for NBC in Los Angeles. Then I went to work for the Corporation for Public Broadcasting and did that for some time. When we moved to Washington State in 1983, I was finally in a position to pay for, and think about, graduate school. That's when I decided that if I was going to write fiction as anything other than a hobby, this would be my opportunity to see if I could really deliver.

H. T. So you seized the moment?

K. A. I did seize the moment. And, as I often tell my students, it was really good that there were eight years between my undergraduate and graduate work because I was finally mature enough to absorb what people were going to tell me. I think I was too immature and had too big a chip on my shoulder when I was younger to get anything out of a writing program. So when I went back I had more confidence in myself to get from the professors what I really needed. I was also able to hear what they said, and I started getting my stories published right away.

Storytelling History

H. T. Your graduate work was done where?

K. A. At the University of Washington.

H. T. Are there any salient moments in that experience? You describe it so positively. I wonder what sort of experience you had.

K. A. It was very good. I was lucky in that I went through the MA program just before the university instated an MFA program. [*Laughs*] Sure, it would be nice if I had the MFA, just for the extra letter. But it was also just before graduate creative writing programs became hugely popular, so I was able to get in and study with people like Charles Johnson before he won the National Book Award and became so famous. And Joanna Russ, who is a feminist and science fiction writer now retired from teaching. With Donna Gerstenberger who taught Twentieth-Century English Literature. I studied Chaucer with David Frye, a wonderful professor who is semiretired but still teaches. He first introduced me to the idea of a story in the framed tradition. And I now use that as a way to teach fiction to young writers.

H. T. What is the story in the framed tradition?

K. A. It's the notion that some of the very earliest stories were composed in India, but Arabic traders picked them up and put a frame around them, which was, we think, invented by the Bedouins. It's this notion that a story comes in three parts. The first part describes the teller and his past experiences. The second part is the story itself. The last part can be something completely different, visiting a ruined campsite or the place of a lost love. So it gives the story a frame that is both enclosing and very flexible in which you can place many stories or few stories. And the stories can relate to the frame or be something completely other, but they are placed in the context of the other stories. The article I used to teach this, in the early research, describes this approach to storytelling as being arranged like a mosque, which has many small portions and can be expanded or made smaller depending on the population, versus the cathedral, which is very hierarchical and has a very linear structure, from the most important to the least important thing. So, I think the notion of storytelling in the framed tradition is also closer to oral storytelling. It gives students access to the notion of writing who otherwise would think, "This is something I can't do. I can't put words on paper." So, it allows me to tap into folk stories and urban legends and the sorts of stories people hear when they're growing up, and students discover they do have stories they can tell.

H. T. How did you make the transition from your theoretical understanding of the historical frame to your own practical reworking of it in terms of the issues important to your storytelling?

K. A. I grew up listening to a lot of stories that, I think, gave me a grounding in my background in Mexico much more than many people of my generation—or younger and older, too—who basically had to start from scratch. I think that was part of our notion of history for Mexicanos born in the United States: that we had no history before the Mexican Revolution, that we somehow sprang fully formed from the earth. I think this was perpetuated by the way history was taught to us in the schools: that we had no history, that we were people from somewhere else, and people were tolerating us as a favor to us rather than the notion that this was our land all along, and that there was already this continuity across the political boundaries of Mexico and the United States that preceded and superceded that. Both of my parents are from Mexico and my mother is from a very large family. When she and her brothers and sisters would get together they would tell stories about the family in Saltillo, Mexico, or of the different places that they had lived because they moved all over northern Mexico and the Southwestern United States. So that gave me a very different sense of story and a grounding in history that other people did not have. Once I started to write stories, I drew on these family stories and began to do historical research for the novels, again, to provide a historical grounding and frame for these stories about individuals.

Family History

H. T. Can you tell us more about your family history?

K. A. Yes. My father's family came north during the Mexican Revolution from San Julian, Jalisco, Mexico. And he would sometimes say to me, "Why don't you write more about my family?" And I would say, "Because Victor Villaseñor already wrote those stories. They're called *Rain of Gold* and *Wild Steps of Heaven*." Victor Villaseñor's family also came from the same town in Mexico to the United States to work for the railroad. And that's what my father's family did. And that's an interesting history, but I didn't want to retell it since this famous work had already been done. I do use some stories from his side of the family, but my mother's family lived for three hundred years in Saltillo. They were descended from the Jews who came over during and after the Inquisition, but hid their Jewishness and were outwardly Catholic, moving into and joining the existing communities. I had grown up with these stories and heard them, but I didn't make that connection to the greater history, the Inquisition and the history of all these people until I was an adult. I just thought we were an anomaly, that we were a Mexican family with a Jewish heritage, who were also Protestant because my grandfather converted. [*Laughs*] I thought, "Fine, we're the only Mexican Jewish Protestant family on the planet."

But it turned out that's not true at all. When I started doing the work on *Spirits of the Ordinary*, my first novel, I happened to interview an elder in Seattle from the Turkish Sephardic community, which was one of the places people went at the fall of the Ottoman Empire. His father was the first Sephardic rabbi in Seattle. And he said, "There's a whole history of people like this. We're all over the world." He goes to these conferences and he speaks Ladino. I'd heard Ladino and I knew that I understood it, but I didn't understand what that history was. He said the only place where people didn't come out and talk about their background at Mexico's Centennial of the Inquisition was in northern Mexico, New Mexico, and the Southwestern United States. Because these people were so integrated with their communities, they just said, "We're pretty happy the way we are. Thank you. This is our place in life." That really gave me something to think about, but it also was the first outward affirmation I had of the family stories. Later I did historical research and found there was a lot to back up what he'd told me. Since then I've done a little bit of research on the family name itself and, sure enough, it holds up that it's part of the Crypto-Judaic background.

H. T. This is what Bahktin would call a chronotope. Can we descend from that chronotope to the specifics of family life? What was that like for you and your family? You mentioned Ladino; how about Spanish? How does that relate to Ladino and family language and family dynamics with language?

K. A. It's really interesting because my parents spoke Spanish at home. We have a lot of anomalies in the family. One of my aunts married a runaway Basque Jesuit priest, and they lived with us for two years when I was little. He would talk all the time, and my family claimed that when I was little—and I was the youngest—I had a Basque accent. But, of course, I wouldn't know that. And I think that because I'm youngest I probably spoke more English than most people in the family. I've been translating my whole life. Because I've been talked to in Spanish, I automatically turn it into English.

H. T.   How many siblings?

K. A.   I have two older sisters who are quite a bit older than I am—eight and eleven years older. We didn't have a big family, and because I was so much younger in some ways, I was an only child. My grandfather, from Saltillo, was born in 1876, so we have these very long generations. And he converted to Protestantism when he was maybe seventeen or eighteen, and that was a big deal. He was disinherited and excommunicated by his family. It's one of those things that if his mother hadn't made such a big deal out of it, it probably would've blown over, right? And he would not have necessarily stuck with the conversion, but because it was made into such an issue, he was rejected. All in one night essentially he was thrown out of the house. So he became a minister. And he moved to Arizona, lived with another relative, and married my grandmother, who was half Opata and half Irish. She was the result of a rape of an Indian woman from Sonora, and probably by an Irish miner in, I think, Nogales. She was very beautiful and started coming to church and eventually married my grandfather. She was barely fifteen when she married him and had eleven children.

H. T.   Wow.

K. A.   People had big families in those days. And the thing we need to remember about them, in the late nineteenth century and early twentieth century, which is still true in most of Mexico, is that your family is your treasure. You may not have anything else, but people really value children, both as an extra pair of hands for working, but also people really admire you for that. My mother would say, "People would always say you're dirt poor, but what a nice family you have, what a beautiful family you have." [*Laughing*] When I traveled in Mexico City four years ago when I was doing research, people would say, "How many children do you have?" And I would say I have one son and they would sort of look at me and say "*pobrecita*" because I just had one child. I think that's still very much the case. So we may have some linguistic influence from my great-grandmother because she probably didn't speak that much Spanish. I didn't know my grandmother, but my older cousins and sisters did and told me many interesting stories about her, so we know that some of that heritage came down to us. That was a much harder thing to research than the Crypto-Jews because the Crypto-Jews were from an educated class and there's a lot of documentation and history in Saltillo. The Opata were a group of people that, under the Porfiriato, were essentially kicked off their land because it was seen as something that needed to be developed to produce capital to make Mexico into a country. So the Yaquis, Mayos, and Opata were all people who fought hard. Many of the Yaquis came north and settled in large enough communities in Arizona to eventually receive tribal status. The Opata also came north but didn't stay in those communities and intermarried more with the Mexicanos in Arizona at the time. Since my second book came out, *The Flower in the Skull*, which is based on that, people have written to me from all over the United States, saying, "I'm also about the same percent as you. A grandparent or a great-grandparent was Opata." And they may know just a tiny bit more. Recently, a woman in Vancouver, Washington, started a website just about the Opata. She's trying to gather information and share it with other people. That's bringing it down to the specifics. That's an act I think I helped perpetuate: to continue that heritage, help people talk about it, and bring these things back together.

Languages

H. T. How many languages are represented in your unconscious?

K. A. Let me see if I can count these things. We have Spanish, we have English. Of course, the kind of Spanish those of us speak from northern Mexico has a lot of Nahuatl in it. I studied Mayan at Stanford as my non-Indo-European language.

H. T. You were a linguistics major?

K. A. Yes, and so that was when I discovered that the Spanish I spoke had Indian words in it. I had no idea. And that was why [*laughs*] the Spaniards looked down on us whenever we'd speak Spanish. We have Nahuatl, we have Spanish, and we have Hebrew. I'm studying Arabic now, and know that Spanish has a lot of Arabic roots, but I don't know if you want to count that as a separate language or not. We have the Opata language, and I think that's about it. That's about five languages. I studied French, too, but I don't know if you want to count it, too.

H. T. Of course I want to count it.

K. A. So that would be six. [*Laughing*]

H. T. How did the languages in the household interact?

K. A. As I said, because I'm the youngest, I grew up hearing these different dialects of Spanish but spoke mostly English. We do have words in the family that are only spoken in the family. I haven't traced these down. At this point, I don't know if I can even remember what they are. They tend to be the private things, like the word for bathroom, but they're not Spanish and they're not English. I don't know if any cousins would be willing to try to remember that stuff so that I could write them down phonetically and see what their sources are. But often a private language will keep some of the older forms of language.

H. T. Did your parents address you in Spanish?

K. A. Yes, they did.

H. T. And you responded in Spanish?

K. A. No, I either didn't respond at all or I responded in English. But, surprisingly, when my son was born—and he's fourteen now—I spoke to him in Spanish, and it was very natural. We spoke mainly Spanish until he was three or four. That was, I realized, clearly my infant language. I had always thought of myself as an English-speaker until that happened. That was the way that having a child made me respond, and only when he was older and realized that not everyone understood Spanish did he become self-conscious about it and begin to speak English in public. Only this year, in ninth grade, is he studying Spanish formally. But he's realized that, from his formative years, he does understand a lot of Spanish.

H. T. So that kind of mirrors your own experience growing up.

K. A. It does. And that really surprised me. Maybe that's the kind of thing you find out when you get older, that these cycles repeat themselves through the generations, how we respond to our relationships with our families, and how they're mirrored in the language we speak and we in turn pass that on to our children.

H. T. Where did you grow up?

K. A. I grew up in San Bernardino, California. I was born in Compton in 1954. We moved to the San Bernardino Mountains when I was one because my father became superintendent of the Optimists Boys' Ranch, which was a sort of halfway house for juvenile delinquents. You describe that to people today, and they say "Okay," but in the '50s it was actually sort of a wonderful place to grow up. [*Laughs*] The juvenile delinquent boys were great; they were my playmates until I was maybe five or six, and we moved into San Bernardino proper where my father became a schoolteacher.

Official History: Liberalism

H. T. You seem to be able to bring to bear all your experience on your storytelling. Can you say something more about how all this experience, all this history, reaches into your work?

K. A. What I think I'm really interested in is this notion that when you read histories and when you read official documentations of countries and people, they tend to be very much on the macro level. When I did the research on nineteenth-century Mexico, you can find out where all the railroads ran, you can find out the front lines of all the battles, of all the wars, but you can't find out things like how women actually prepared meals in the home every day. That was much harder to find. The outward history, the official history, is easy to find. But the little things of how families interacted were much more difficult to research and I had to dig a little deeper. What interested me about nineteenth-century Mexico, besides the fact that I'd learned all the history that led up to and caused the Mexican Revolution, was the notion that there were a lot of ideas that came over from Europe at that time that talked about the individual—that there was such a thing as an individual—and the notion of free choice and free will. I think this was very novel in Europe and the New World at that time. It caused these few intellectuals to bring these ideas back and help start revolutions because they said, "Look, we don't have to be just a few rich people and a lot of poor people. People can change their place in the world." And this was a really novel idea after four hundred years of oppression.

H. T.   This makes its way into which work?

K. A.   Into all my work, because what I'm writing about in each of these novels is the notion that these are people who look around at the society they live in or the culture they live in and say, "This isn't necessarily where I belong. I need to change my place in history and I need to change my place in this culture." So *Spirits of the Ordinary* was initially sparked by the relationship between my great-grandmother and my great-grandfather in Saltillo. My great-grandmother kicked my great-grandfather out of the house because he had the gold fever, and he was wasting all their money. And I thought, "How could she do this? And why would she do this in this culture?" I started doing the research on what that culture was like at the time. It was clear that my great-grandfather never fit into the existing structure. He wasn't prepared to just do whatever his father had done before him. He was a very eccentric person and just a free soul and probably not a very happy soul. And so many of the stories I tell in the novel aren't made up. They're fictional, but the stories of the things that he actually did and the things that happened to him are just as unusual and just as interesting as the things that happened in the novel. And my great-grandmother was clearly a very independent person who had a mind of her own and very specific ideas about the world. I think in her way she was trying to preserve the status quo as she understood it, but the world was changing around her. So I was interested in how this affected a specific family. In *The Flower in the Skull*, my great-grandmother didn't have a choice. Their village was destroyed, they had to leave, and she ended up a housemaid to a Mexican family in Arizona. And she did not have a happy life, but one of the things that really struck me after I had done the research on the Opata culture and the people and their relationship to the land was the notion that, in spite of everything, people endure and they pass on whatever they can to their children. And in this case, like the Crypto-Jews, the Opata chose to hide their identity in most cases because they would be killed if people found out who they were. They would not speak their language in public. They would only speak it privately. When people would ask them if they were Opata, they would say, "Nah, it's those other people on the other side of the river. They're Opata. You go talk to them." One of the last studies on the Opata was done around 1950 by Thomas Hinton. He got on a horse and he packed a portable typewriter and these half-sheets of paper. He would ride through the villages of the Sierra Madre and he would just sort of look the population over and make a guesstimate on how many of them were Opata. It's very interesting with the photos. When you look at them, knowing the stories that people tell about each other, and really, when you look at how people were describing Indians among them in these mixed villages, whatever they looked like or however they spoke, they were always the poorest of the poor who were the Indians and these were the Opata. Some of them look just like me. Some of them are very dark. Some are very big. Some are very small. But these were the people who either self-identified or were identified as the Opata. By the mid-1900s, it was as much an economic classification as a cultural or genetic identification.

The Creative Drive and History

H. T. It's very clear that when this history merges with your desire to write, to represent, a creative force is unleashed. What happens to you when you notice this convergence of history and creative drive?

K. A. I get really excited. One of the things I got interested in early on was telling the unofficial histories, to tell the counternarratives to official histories. One of the anthropological terms

I've learned that applies to all of these peoples is this notion of syncretism, that cultures and religions come together and forge new cultures and new religions and new languages. And this is really the sign of a living culture and a living history. People are trying to preserve the past and aren't happy with other people if they aren't doing everything the same way that their parents and grandparents [did them], and they'll say, "Oh, that's wrong. You're not doing it right." But the fact that languages change and people change and adapt to new environments is the sign of a living culture to me. I certainly mourn the loss of the heritage that has fallen by the wayside because it was tied directly to landscape. When people moved from the land, they lost that. I also have to admire the spirit of endurance that made people continue to remember. And the fact that they continue to tell their children that they were Opata is significant to me. And we see that mirror with Jews and even the hidden Jews who, when someone would come of age, would say, "By the way, don't tell anyone, but we're Jewish." You see that insistence of history, that insistence of heritage to pass that to the next generation, even though they are living a very different life and practice a syncretism of religions and cultures.

H. T. You recently delivered a paper at the UNM English Faculty Colloquium. Can you tell us how that creative work came to light?

K. A. That was a very interesting experience for me. About three years ago there was a terrible murder in Texas in which a woman drowned her five children. This was Andrea Yates. The facts about it were so disturbing. Apparently she had postpartum depression that she had sporadically been treated for. She continued to have children, even though she'd been advised not to. As I was reading about it, I was thinking, "This really bothers me, but at the same time there's something really familiar about it." But I couldn't quite put my finger on it. One night I sat down and watched an episode of *American Family* on PBS, and there's a very small retelling in that episode of the La Llorona story. As soon as I heard it, I thought, "That's what it is. Andrea Yates is a re-creation of La Llorona." Just for purposes of the record,

La Llorona is one of the most famous myths in Mexico. It is about a woman who, for one reason or another—the absence of a father, the rejection by the father, or jealousy—takes her children to the river and drowns them and, after that, is forever doomed to wander the river banks calling for her children. It's used in Mexico as a cautionary tale to children to keep them in the house at night or to make them behave. So I started researching the different versions of La Llorona, and I found some very interesting information about the different ways that the story is told. About that time, Andrea Yates's case came to trial, and so there was information about her case on Court TV and other sources. I matched up different aspects of her case with different versions of La Llorona's story, and wrote this article because I'd thought that this is the case where these old stories continue: the case where the ills of modern society continue to be relevant to the old stories, or vice versa, the old stories continue to be relevant to society today.

H. T. Mythological thinking is political thinking?

K. A Yes, or at least societal thinking—in this case, the plight of a woman in the modern United States, who wasn't even of Mexican background, but who continued to be put in this position where she felt she could not care for her children and was being an inadequate mother and so drowned them to save them from further sin, in the reference points of her religious background.

H. T. So this contemporary event vibrated with your own history, your own experience? And out of that came this creative work?

K. A. Yes. I think so. And this was a work of nonfiction called "The Woman Who Loved Water," which will be coming out in *Creative Nonfiction* in spring 2004. But even though I write historical fiction, I see it as very relevant to how we live our lives today. Again, I got very obsessed with documenting nineteenth-century family life and our relationship to history because I meet so many people who feel we have no foundation in history. We had to reinvent history after the Mexican Revolution. We have sort of cobbled together a history out of what we know and our place in the United States, which included, from all of society that surrounded us and brought us up, this notion that you are not worth anything; you are at the bottom of society. And so I think it's important that we see that we have roots that go deep into the earth here, in the United States and Mexico and in Spain, and all of this is something we can claim as our own heritage. That's certainly how I take it. Rather than being confined to being a mall rat in Southern California, I claim all of this as my heritage. I guess I would like other people to see that as well.

On World Politics and the Truth of Fictions

H. T. This historical heritage you carry within, what kind of perspective does it give you on the state of the world, especially as it relates to Israel and Palestine?

K. A. I think that's a very interesting thing that's going on right now. There was a very interesting book called *The Cross and the Pear Tree* by Victor Perera about his own Sephardic Jewish family. Perera is, of course, the "pear" in the pear tree. When he did the research, he found that his roots were just as strong in Hebron and Palestine as they were in Israel, and that of course, we're related to people on both sides of this line. He talked to people in Europe; he talked to a priest in Spain who was of clearly Jewish descent. He made it really clear that our ancestral roots and our cultural roots cross back and forth across all of these cultural boundaries, and that only certain people at certain times have felt that they had to exclude others, and that one side feels it has to practice genocide against the other. One of the things he claimed was that once he started saying these things in public about the place of the Sephardic Jew in Israel and the place of the Jew in general, as he called it, his work was "brown listed" in Israel because the primarily Ashkenazi leadership didn't want to hear about this. They didn't want to have people saying this sort of thing because it blurred the lines between "them" and "us," and so it was not politically appropriate. I think there are a lot of people who would like to see some sort of compromise worked out, people who understand that this notion of practicing genocide against other people isn't any more justifiable than genocide that was practiced against us, and, of course, continues to be practiced against us in other places.

H. T. Your work contests this terror?

K. A. Absolutely. Once you start talking about people as individuals, which I try to do in my fiction, it's impossible to say that any group of people can be excluded from full human rights. And any place we're trying to do that, for whatever reason, always comes down to politics. One of the things I learned in studying the Inquisition and the incidences in which it was brought to bear was that it was always for economic or political reasons. It was not for religious reasons that the Inquisition was started up. So when it was brought to Mexico it was not for religious reasons. It was because some of the Catholics wanted things the people they suspected of practicing Judaism had. For example, the governor of Nuevo León at that time was Luis de Carvajal, and they felt that he had too much power, so they looked into his background for something that they could use against him and this was it. Of course, there was a lot of documentation because his wife and his nephew and a number of members of his family were pretty blatantly practicing Judaism at that time. This was in the 1500s in Mexico.

H. T. Today Bush's War on Terror is on the news daily. Can you comment on that?

K. A. A year and a half ago I was in Italy for a few days and I have to say it was such a relief to get away from the war drums that were beating already in the United States in the media. And I'm sorry to say that I felt the media helped perpetuate and helped soften up the United States population to go into this war a year ago. I realized the media here is as much in the pocket of the administration as anyone else. I came back and, of course, we went into war. Visiting Professor Dieter Schulz from Germany said to me this year that Europeans see us as all being united behind President Bush and behind the administration, which is just infuriating because, of course, so many of us are not. I think it's important that our voices continue to be heard in as many ways as possible, and for us to continue to protest this as publicly as we can. I hope that as many people as possible will speak out. If we have time to get into this notion of how politically relevant or how pertinent historical fiction is to politics today, something that interests me is the fact that we continue to document things even if it's after the fact, even if it's a hundred years after the fact, to show that there were other voices, other points of view. I continue to do my work in historical fiction, but whoever we are and wherever we're living, the events around us continue to influence our view of history and we each continue to rewrite history in our own way. There is no set history. Each of us brings a new history to bear.

H. T. Isn't there a contradiction, or at least a tension, between the words "historical" and "fiction?"

K. A. Yes. I think there is, except I've done so much research with what's considered history that I've decided that it's just as fictional as fiction is. And many of the truths that I'm interested in telling need to be told in a narrative form, which history or anthropology or some other disciplines doesn't necessarily lend themselves to. People need to hear things in a certain way in order to understand them, and so I think that fiction in many ways tells truths that history is unable to tell.

Awards

2001 Washington State Book Award for *Treasures in Heaven*
1999 Washington Governor's Writers Award for *The Flower in the Skull*
1999 Western States Book Award for *The Flower in the Skull*
1998 Pacific Northwest Booksellers Association Award for *Spirits of the Ordinary*

Primary Works

The Flower in the Skull. Eugene, OR: Harvest Books, 1999. First published 1998 by
　　Chronicle Books.
Mrs. Vargas and the Dead Naturalist. Corvallis, OR: CALYX Books, 1992.
Spirits of the Ordinary: A Tale of Casas Grandes. Eugene, OR: Harvest Books, 1998.
　　First published 1997 by Chronicle Books.
Treasures in Heaven. Evanston, IL: Northwestern University Press, 2003. First
　　published 2000 by Chronicle Books.

Secondary Sources

De Lint, Charles. Review of *Spirits of the Ordinary*. *Fantasy and Science Fiction* 93
　　no. 3 (1997): 32–33.
Donnelly, Margarita. "In Search of El Dorado." Review of *Spirits of the Ordinary*.
　　Women's Review of Books 14, nos. 10–11 (1997): 44–45.
Franco, Dean. "Re-Placing the Border in Ethnic American Literature." *Cultural
　　Critique*, no. 50 (2002): 104–234.
Levi-Strauss, Claude. *The Savage Mind*. Chicago: University of Chicago Press,
　　1972.
Orr, Linda. "The Revenge of Literature: A History of History." In *Studies in
　　Historical Change*, edited by Ralph Cohen, 84–108. Charlottesville: University
　　of Virginia, 1992.
Pérez, Emma. *The Decolonial Imaginary: Writing Chicanas into History*.
　　Bloomington: Indiana University Press, 1999.
Walden, Daniel. "Parallels between Chicano and Jewish-American Writing."
　　Multi-Ethnic Literature of the United States 8, no. 2 (1997): 57–60.

Notes to Chapter Ten

1. Charles de Lint, review of *Spirits of the Ordinary*, *Fantasy and Science Fiction*
　　93, no. 3 (1997): 32–33.
2. Margarita Donnelly, "In Search of El Dorado," review of *Spirits of the
　　Ordinary*, *Women's Review of Books* 14, nos. 10–11 (1997): 44–45.
3. Linda Orr, "The Revenge of Literature: A History of History," in *Studies
　　in Historical Change*, ed. Ralph Cohen, (Charlottesville, 1992), 84–108. Orr
　　addresses this troubled terrain between history and fiction in a way close
　　to what Alcalá is saying in her closing remarks. For a similar perspective,
　　see also Emma Pérez, *The Decolonial Imaginary: Writing Chicanas into History*

(Bloomington : Indiana University Press, 1999): "Historians who are more traditional in their approach often claim that history is an objective science. When writing the history of the Southwest, the historian who accepts the notion of objectivity can often ignore the colonial relations that are already in place and write a study replete with a coloniality that has not been disputed, but rather accepted as the norm" (5–6).

Index

Acuña, Rudy: *Occupied America*, 95
Alarcón, Francisco, 134
Alarcón, Norma, 129, 134, 157–58, 230
Alcalá, Kathleen, 4; Andrea Yates and, 339–40; awards, 344; childhood of, 336; Crypto-Jews and, 325, 334, 338, 339; education and, 328, 329; English usage and, 335; family history of, 326, 327, 331–34; family life of, 332–33, 335, 337; history and, 338–41; human rights and, 342; La Llorona and, 339–40; Ladino and, 332; languages and, 334–35; literary works of, 328, 340, 344; magical realism of, 326; mestiza consciousness and, 326–27; Mexico and, 333–34, 336–37, 340, 342; *Mrs. Vargas and The Dead Naturalist*, 328; research and, 336–38; Spanish usage and, 332–33, 334–35; *Spirits of the Ordinary* (see *Spirits of the Ordinary*); storytelling history and, 329–31, 336; *The Flower in the Skull*, 328, 334, 337; the Inquisition and, 342; the Opata and, 334, 335, 338, 339; "The Woman Who Loved Water," 340; *Treasures in Heaven*, 328; world politics and, 341–43; writing and, 328–29

Aldama, Frederick Luis: Islas and, 55–56
Alemán, Jesse, 30n77
Althusser, Louis, 24n12
American literature: 19th century, 29n65; Chicana writers and, 115, 244, 267–68; Chicana/Chicano literary discourse and, 10; Chicano literature and, 48, 50, 66, 122; Chicano Movement and, 21; definition of, 66
American Social History Project, 11
Americanization: Mexican Americans and, 4–5
Anaya, Governor Toney: sanctuary movement and, 315, 324n2
Anaya, Rudolfo: *Bless Me, Última*, 88
Anglo-American feminism, 130, 139; Cisneros and, 192, 216–19; hegemony of, 146–47; women of color and, 155–57
Anzaldúa, Gloria, 236; Anglo-American academy and, 115; autobiography and, 116, 135, 145n1; awards, 143; Barthes and, 132; bilingualism and, 129, 140; *Borderlands/La Frontera* (see

347

150–54; bilingualism and, 151, 168–69; Chicana feminism and, 146–47, 154–57, 183; Chicana identity and, 164–65; Chicana language and, 178–80; Chicana literature and, 157–61; Chicano Movement and, 152, 154, 171–73, 183; Cisneros and, 161, 214; Cortazar and, 181–82; critical theory and, 146–47; critics of, 148, 149; education and, 151, 152–54, 167, 169, 171–75, 179–80; family of, 168–69; father and, 160–62; Feminist Movement and, 154–55; gender, sexuality and, 161–62; Hispanic literature and, 159; "i exist," 158–59, 160; influences on, 181; Latin American writers and, 148, 164–65, 181; life of, 166–67; literary ethnography and, 148–49; literary works of, 167, 188; low theory and, 146, 148; *Massacre of the Dreamers*, 146, 148, 185, 186; *My Father Was a Toltec*, 150, 151, 160–61, 163, 176; narrative style of, 148–49; Northeastern Illinois University and, 152, 172–74; objectification and, 158–59, 162; oppression and, 157–59; *Otro Canto*, 167, 168; patriarchy and, 147, 149, 165, 183; poetry of, 162, 163–64, 167, 168, 174–75, 180, 186; politics and, 163–66, 180–87; prose and, 163, 168, 174–77, 180; racism and, 152–54, 168–75; religion and, 154–56; *Sapogonia* (see *Sapogonia*); short stories and, 168, 175–76; *So Far From God*, 149; Spanish and English usage and, 157, 160–61, 163, 179; storytelling and, 163–64, 175–78, 183; subjective identity and, 148; teaching and, 149, 164, 172, 185–86; "The Ancient Roots of Machismo," 147; "The Anti-Hero," 176; *The Invitation*, 167, 168; *The Mixquiahuala Letters* (see *Mixquiahuala Letters*); *The Third*

Woman and, 186; *This Bridge Called My Back* and, 157–58, 186; Tillion and, 147; "*Un cuento sin ritmo/* Time is Fluid," 181–82; University of New Mexico and, 149; utopian dimension in writing of, 149; visual arts and, 151–54, 163–66, 173–74, 182; voices of, 175–76, 183–84; *Woman Are Not Roses*, 167, 177; women of color and, 146–47, 165; writing and, 152, 154, 163–66, 173–75, 179; Xicanisma and, 146–49

Central America: U.S. policy in, 315, 324n1

Cervantes, Lorna Dee, 134, 138

Chabram, Angie, 106, 129

Chacón, Eusebio, 98–99, 100

Chávez, César, 12

Chávez, Denise, 64

Chicana: Bildungsroman, 191; collective consciousness of, 160; critical consciousness, 79; identity, 134, 164–65, 235; language, 178–80; signifier of, 22; status of, 156

Chicana feminism, 20, 79; Anzaldúa and, 115, 122–24, 130, 134; Castillo and, 146–47, 154–57; Gonzáles-Berry and, 93–94; Xicanisma and, 147

Chicana literary discourse, 23, 28n53; American literature and, 10; Anzaldúa and, 126–29; axis mundi and, 17; chaos and, 14–17; crisis of modernity and, 17–18; global politics and, 22; Hinojosa and, 35

Chicana literature: aesthetics and, 105; Anzaldúa and, 138–42; Castillo and, 157–61; Cisneros and, 212–19, 234–40; Mora and, 267–68; role of, 157

Chicana writers: American literature and, 244, 261; Anzaldúa and, 138–42; Chicano literary canon and, 115, 244, 247; Cisneros and, 234–40; code-switching and,

128–29, 235; ethnography and, 148–49, 190n4, 246, 247; feminist presses and, 141–42; Mora and, 267–68; resistance and, 30n77, 239, 263–64; social act of writing and (*see* writing as a social act) (*see also* individual writers)

Chicanas: Chicano culture and, 220; discourses of, 7; education and, 220; integration of, 21; mestiza consciousness and, 22–23; National Organization of Women and, 78–79

Chicano: critical discourse, 19; displacement of the term, 7; family, 57; identity, 2, 213, 235; patriarchy, 147, 149, 165, 183, 194; poets, 21, 47–48; studies, 10; the signifier of, 6, 10, 14, 22; the term, 2

Chicano Authors, 9–10; Chicana and Chicano critical discourse and, 9–10 (*see also* Bruce–Novoa)

Chicano community: Anzaldúa and, 133–34, 137; writers and, 213–14, 223, 236–37

Chicano culture: aesthetics of, 48; American culture and, 47; Chicanas and, 220; Chicano Movement and, 134; linguistic codes and, 56; oppression and, 147–48; patrimony and, 147–48; sexual mores of, 276; values of, 220

Chicano families: sexual divisions in, 119; women and, 119

Chicano history: the Black Legend and, 25n19; Treaty of Guadalupe Hidalgo and, 19

Chicano literary canon, 9–10; Bruce-Novoa and, 18–21 (see *also* Bruce–Novoa; *Chicano Authors*); Chicana writers and, 244; formation of, 18–21, 57; Hinojosa and, 33–34; identifiable, 18; Islas and, 57; Mexican Revolution and, 20; politics of, 18, 20–21

Chicano literary discourse, 15–16, 23, 28n53; Anzaldúa and, 126–29; axis mundi and, 17; chaos and, 14–17; crisis of modernity and, 17–18; Hinojosa and, 35

Chicano literary production, 14; authenticity of, 14–15; inside and outside of, 14–15; resistance and, 30n77

Chicano literary space: transcendental ego and, 16–17

Chicano literature: aesthetics and, 48, 105; Anzaldúa and, 136; Bruce-Novoa and, 9–10, 12–15, 20; Cisneros and, 212–23; deep structure of, 15–16; gender and, 73–74; Hinojosa and, 46–47, 51; historical production in, 126–27; history of, 65–66; identity and, 66; Islas and, 65–68; Latin American literature and, 67; Spanish and, 51–52; Treaty of Guadalupe Hidalgo and, 65–66; women's voices in, 212–13

Chicano Movement, 2; American liberalism and, 21; American literature and, 21; Anzaldúa and, 133–38; Bruce-Novoa and (*see* Bruce-Novoa); Chicano culture and, 134; essentialist practices of, 14; Gomez Quiñones and, 21; Gonzáles-Berry and, 77, 93; identity and, 134; literary renaissance of, 10, 21, 134; literary value in, 10; political elections and, 21; Post- (*see* Post-Chicano Movement); separatism and, 21; sexism and, 134, 183, 219; the Mexican American generation and, 15; Treaty of Guadalupe Hidalgo and, 29n65; U.S. economy and, 10, 12–13

Chicano poets: cultural nationalism and, 47–48

Chicano students: antimexicano sentiment and, 90–93; experiences of, 84–85, 86

Chicano writers, 139, 239; code-switching and, 128–29; language usage and, 46–47, 287

Chicano/Chicana: cultural studies, 13; history, 12; literature, 212–23, 234–40

Chicanos: discourses of, 7; integration of, 21

Children's Book Press, 140–41

Christian, B. Marie, 246

Cinco Puntos Press, 64

Cisneros, Sandra, 3, 57, 161; antipoems and, 201; autobiographical writing and, 204, 205–7; awards, 224, 231, 241; Catholic Church and, 238; Catholic schools and, 194–95, 196, 226–27; characters of, 206, 222; Chicana aesthetic and, 234–40; Chicana writers and, 234–40; Chicano Movement and, 219; Chicano/Chicana literature and, 212–23, 234–40; critics and, 191, 193–94, 209, 242n3; Cumpián and, 200; "Divine Providence," 231; dominant culture and, 192–93; education and, 194, 202, 213, 215, 226–30; *Emergency Tacos*, 207; family background of, 209–12, 224–26; feminism and, 216–19; gender and, 212, 216, 219, 223; Guzmán and, 231; *House on Mango Street* (see *House on Mango Street*); Iowa Writer's Workshop and, 191–93, 196, 197–203, 207, 228–30; life of, 201, 215–16, 224–27; literary influences on, 201–2, 214, 228, 235–36; literary works of, 208–9, 241; "Little Miracles," 231; *Loose Woman*, 207–8; Loyola University and, 195, 196, 198–99, 228; Mexico and, 239–40; "Milagritos," 238; "My Lucy Friend Who Smells like Corn," 231; *My Wicked, Wicked Ways*, 205, 207, 230; near-death experience of, 237–38; "Never Marry a Mexican," 194, 229; "One Holy Night," 230–31; oral poets and, 213–14; patriarchy and, 194, 238–39; poetry and, 205–9, 228, 230, 232–34; politics and art and, 236–37; race and class and, 196–99, 212, 214–15; racism and, 197, 202–3; research for writing, 230–32; "Salvador, Late or Early," 231; social act of writing and, 192–93, 236–37; Spanish and English usage and, 225–26, 235; spirituality and, 237–38; story content of, 220–22; storytelling and, 192; teaching and, 197–98, 200–202, 206; "The Dog Lady," 228; the Minotaur and, 206; the Other and, 192–93, 199–200, 202–4, 220; *The Rodrigo Poems*, 230, 232; "The Three Sisters," 193; values and, 219–23, 225; voices of, 192, 193–94, 207–8, 232; white women and, 216–17; *Woman Hollering Creek* (see *Woman Hollering Creek*); women writers and, 214–15, 216–18, 235–36; writing as a social act, 192, 236–39; writing technique of, 197–98, 206–7; Zapata and, 221–22

Cline, Lynn, 317

Code-switching: Chicana writers and, 128–29, 235, 264

Cold War: end of, 117; U.S. economy and, 11

Conway, Judge John, 315

Corrido paradigm, the, 30n77; resistance and, 99–100; south Texas and, 19

Cortázar, Julio, 148, 181–82

Cota-Cardenas, Margarita: Hinojosa and, 35

Crossing Press, 141–42

Cultural nationalism, 21; Chicano poets and, 47–48

Culture: production of, 13

Cumpián, Carlos, 200

and, 77–78, 84–85, 93; writing in
Spanish and, 79, 102–3, 107–8
Grand, Judy, 142
Gulf War, 30n77; Castillo and, 149
Gunn Allen, Paula, 142
Gutiérrez, Marina, 167
Guzmán, Fernán Pérez de:
Generaciones y semblanzes, 34
Guzmán, Rubén, 231

Haraway, Donna, 123
Hardt, Michael, and Antonio Negri:
U.S. political sovereignty and,
30n76
Harjo, Joy, 197
Heidegger, Martin, 9; Bruce-Novoa
and, 16 (*see also* Bruce–Novoa);
erasure mark and, 13
Hernández-Chávez, Eduardo, 102
Hinojosa, Rolando, 57, 65, 148;
accuracy and, 43–44; aesthetics
and, 44–45, 47–48; Américo
Paredes and, 43; awards for,
44, 53; *Becky and Her Friends*,
50; bilingualism and, 50–51;
Chicano literary canon and,
33–34; Chicano literary discourse
and, 35; Chicano literature and,
46–47, 51; Chicano renaissance
and, 22, 35; creative writing and,
38–43; critics of, 33, 34, 35; *Dear
Rafe*, 49; education of, 37–38,
39; *Estampas del valle*, 33, 35, 44,
49–50; family background of,
36–37, 42–43; fictional characters
of, 48; *Generaciones y semblanzes*,
34; historiography and, 33–34, 35;
humor of, 35; identity and, 48;
Klail City Death Trip, 33, 34, 35–36,
44, 49–50, 139; *Korean Love Songs*,
36, 44; literary influences on, 35;
literary works of, 33–34, 53; *Los
Amigos de Becky*, 49–50; memory
and, 35, 43–44; *Mi querido Rafa*, 35,
49, 139; microtexts of, 34, 35, 54n2;
Partners in Crime, 33; reading
and, 39–42; religion and, 42–43;

research and, 46; Rio Grande
Valley of south Texas and, 34–35,
43–46; Rivera and, 46; Saldívar
and, 33; sense of place and, 48,
49–52; Spanish and English usage
and, 45–46, 50–51; teaching and,
44–45; *The Valley*, 3, 35, 40, 139;
time and modernity and, 36; *topos*
and, 34–35
Hinton, Thomas, 338
Hispanic literature: Castillo and, 159
History: Foucault and, 28n58;
Hinojosa and, 33–34, 35
Holmes, Sue Major, 324n2
Homophobia, 115
Homosexuality: Rodriguez and (*see*
Rodriguez, Richard)
House on Mango Street: as a
Bildungsroman, 191; Catholic
school and, 226–27; characters
in, 191–92, 209; the barrio and,
239; the Other and, 192–93; voice
in, 192, 232; writing of, 200, 222,
226–28, 231, 233 (*see also* Cisneros,
Sandra)
Hunger of Memory: assimilation and,
276; Chicano academy and,
297–98; critics of, 275–77, 297–99;
English language and, 280; ethnic
autobiography and, 275–76;
homosexuality and, 298–300, 302;
reception of, 275–76; the academy
and, 276, 297–98; the author in,
275; the subject in modernity and,
275 (*see also* Rodriguez, Richard)

Identity: politics of, 6, 16; subjective,
131, 132–33, 148
Immigration: sanctuary movement
and, 315, 324n1
Indritz, Tova, 315
Inquisition, the, 331–32, 342
Iraq: war in, 318–21
Iraqi wars: oil crisis and, 12
Islas, Arturo, 22, 142; American
literature and, 66–67, 68; awards,
75; bilingualism and, 55, 61–65;

characters of, 72, 73, 74; Chicano literature and, 57, 65–68, 73–74; critics of, 55–56; education and, 58–59, 62; El Paso/Juárez and, 55, 60; family of, 55, 58; gender in literature and, 73–74; *La Mollie and the King of Tears*, 72–73; life of, 55–56, 58–60; literary influences on, 57, 71–73; literary value and, 68–71; literary works of, 75; *Migrant Souls*, 56, 63, 70, 72; near-death experience of, 55, 60; poetry of, 73; politics of publishing and, 56–57; racism and, 60–61, 62; readers of, 72; Stanford and, 58–59; teaching and, 66–67; the Church and, 70–71; the Mexican American family and, 55; *The Rain God* (see *Rain God*); writing in Spanish and, 63–64

Jews: Ashkenazi, 341; Crypto, 325–26, 338, 339 (*see also* Alcalá, Kathleen); Sephardic, 332, 341; the Inquisition and, 331–32
Justice, Donald, 228–29

Kahn, Louis, 295
Kanellos, Nicolás, 262, 268
Kennedy, Robert, 12
Kingston, Maxine Hong, 235
Kitchen Table Press, 142
Knowledge: constitution of, 25n12; construction of, 6; power and, 6
Kristeva, Julia, 3

Ladino, 332
Latin American literature: Anzaldúa and, 139; Castillo and, 148, 164–65, 181; Chicano literature and, 67; Cisneros and, 234, 236; Gonzáles-Berry and, 95, 108
Latino(s): antihero, 159; relationship with the United States, 159
Le Guin, Ursula, 326
Lesbian(s): authors, 116; self, 116
Lesbianism: Anzaldúa and, 135

Levi-Strauss, Claude: bricolage and, 190n1
Liberalism: American, 21; free-market, 28n53; Keynesian, 11; laissez-faire, 20, 21
Limón, José, 129, 134, 138
Literary value: politics of determining, 20–21; production of, 68–71
López Tijerina, Reies, 19
Lorca, Federico García, 269
Los desaparecidos: El Salvador and, 316, 317
LULAC (League of United Latin American Citizens), 4–5
Lutz, William, 315

Machismo, 147
Márquez, Antonio, 275, 277
Márquez, Teresa, 105
Martin, Biddy, 116
Martin, Ricky, 294
Martínez, Demetria: awards, 323; Cisneros and, 316; critics of, 317; dreamscape of, 318–21; First Amendment and, 318; global citizens and, 319–20; human rights and, 321; literary influences on, 321; literary works of, 323; memory and, 316; mestiza consciousness and, 316, 319; *Mother Tongue*, 315, 322; 1987 trial and, 315, 318, 324n1; Persephone and, 321–22; poetry and, 317, 321; politics and, 318–21; postmodernism and, 317; race and, 319; sanctuary movement and, 315; spirituality and, 318, 320–21; *The Devil's Workshop*, 317; *The National Catholic Reporter*, 317, 318; war in Iraq and, 318–21; working poor and, 320
Martínez, Elizabeth, 78
Martínez, George A., 24n9
Marx, Karl, 25n17; borders and, 26n20; discourse formation and,

and, 276, 287, 307; childhood of, 279–84; class and, 290, 309–10; conservative politicians and, 277; critical repression of, 276–77; critics of, 275–77, 297–98; cultural acquisition and, 287; D. H. Lawrence and, 290, 291–92, 298–99; *Days of Obligation* (see *Days of Obligation*); deconstruction and, 302–8; disappearance of the author and, 275; education and, 282–83, 291, 305–6, 310; English and Spanish and, 252, 279–85; English usage and, 280–83, 285, 288–89, 291–92; ethnic literature and, 275–76, 291; family of, 279–80, 284–85, 300–301, 304; generosity of texts by, 277–78; homoeroticism and, 298–99; homosexuality and (*see* Rodriguez and homosexuality); *Hunger of Memory* (see *Hunger of Memory*); identity and, 285–87; intellectual responsibility and, 303–4; Irish Catholic Church and, 281–83; issue of representation and, 277; journalistic work of, 278, 309; La Malinche and, 276; literary influences on, 290–93; literary works of, 311; loss and acquisition of language and, 280–85; love and hate and, 300–301; Malcolm X and, 305, 307; Marx and, 308–10; Mexican American culture and, 278, 294, 301–2, 307; Mexico and, 293–94, 308; NAFTA and, 303; poetry of, 303; race and, 278, 283–85, 294, 300–301, 304, 307; racism and, 290; sissy aesthetic and, 276; social act of writing and, 275–76; Spain and, 308; Stanford and, 305–6; stealing English and, 282, 287; T. E. Lawrence and, 306–7; the left and, 309–10; the subject and, 275; voices of, 302–4; writing style of, 286–97

Rodriguez, Richard and homosexuality: Catholicism and, 300–302; family and, 284–85, 301–2, 304; hate crimes and, 300–301; homoeroticism and, 298–99; *Hunger of Memory* and, 297–98, 299, 302; identity and, 306–7; sissy aesthetic and, 276; writing career and, 289–90

Romero, Archbishop Oscar: assassination of, 316

Ross, Dorothy, 28n53

Rulfo, Juan, 202

Saenz, Ben, 64

Saenz, Gustavo, 102, 103–4

Saldíval, José David: Anzaldúa and, 129, 138; Hinojosa and, 33, 35–36; Islas and, 56–57

Saldívar, Ramón, 99

Sánchez, Marta: Islas and, 56–57

Sanchez, Rosaura: Castillo and, 148; Hinojosa and, 34, 54n2; Rodriguez and, 277, 278

Sanctuary movement: Martínez and, 315

Sapogonia, 163; ending of, 184–85; Latin anti-hero and, 159; poetry and, 175; prose and, 180; small letter "i" and, 160; storytelling and, 163; voice in, 176, 184; writing of, 167, 180–81 (*see also* Castillo, Ana)

Schulz, Dieter, 342

Sexism: Anzaldúa, 119–21; Castillo and, 148

Sirias, Silvio, 149

Sledd, James, 130

Sommers, Joseph, 19

Soto, Gary, 142

South Texas: *corrido* paradigm and, 19, 30n77; Hinojosa and, 34–35, 43–46; Mexican American War and, 48; migrant farm laborers in, 45; Texas Mexican experience in, 45 (*see also* Texas)

Spanglish, 127

Spanish: Castilian, 128; Chicanos/
Chicanas and, 128; dialects of,
101–2; identity, 20; language
rights and, 102; literary, 107, 128;
losing, 277; maintenance of, 103;
Mexican, 101, 128; New Mexican,
101–3; 19th century, 102; reading
in, 127; reclaiming, 128; switching
codes and, 128; vernacular, 128;
working-class, 128; writing in (*see*
writing in Spanish)
Spanish and English usage: Anzaldúa
and, 127; code-switching and, 235;
Hinojosa and, 45–46
Spanish language usage: barrio
dialect, 64; Gonzáles-Berry and,
79, 102–3, 107–8; Hinojosa and,
46–47; in New Mexico, 101–2;
Islas and, 63–64; publication
barriers and, 63; U.S. literary
production and, 79
Spinsters/Aunt Lute Press, 141–42
Spirits of the Ordinary: alterity in, 327;
borderlands and, 328; characters
in, 325–28; critics of, 325–26;
Crypto-Jewish background of,
325–26; epilogue to, 327–28;
family and, 337; the Cabala and,
326 (*see also* Alcalá, Kathleen)
Stephanson, Anders, 26n24
Storytelling: Alcalá and, 329–31;
Gonzáles-Berry and, 108–9
Sundquist, Eric J., 29n65

Texas: Rio Grande Valley of, 34–35,
43–46; south (*see* South Texas)
Tillion, Germaine, 147–48
Torres, Rafael O. and Dolores A., 4
Transculturation: identity and, 99–100
Treaty of Guadalupe Hidalgo, 15;
Chicano history and, 19; Chicano
literature and, 65–66; Chicano
Movement and, 29n65; López
Tijerina and, 19; NAFTA and,
24n9
Turner, Frederick Jackson, 8

U.S. economy: American liberalism
and, 12; Chicano Movement and,
10, 12–13; Mexican labor and, 12;
OPEC and, 27nn39, 40; the Cold
War and, 11
United States: foreign policy
in Central America, 315;
globalization and, 30n76;
hegemony of, 115; Hispanic
Mexican America and, 12,
159; literary production in, 79;
Manifest Destiny and, 22; political
boundaries of, 331; political
sovereignty and, 30nn76, 77; War
with Mexico, 26n24
University of New Mexico: Castillo
and, 149; Chicano/Chicana
literature at, 78; Gonzáles-Berry
and, 77–78, 84–85

Vallejo, Mariano, 29n65
Vietnam War: Bretton Woods system
and, 11; oil crisis of 1974 and, 12;
U.S. hegemony and, 12
Villareal, José Antonio: *Pocho*, 9–10, 20
Villaseñor, Victor, 331
Viramonte, Helena, 214
Virgin of Guadalupe, 238, 254–55
Voelcker, Paul, 11

War in Iraq. *See* Iraq
War on Terror, 342
Weber, David J., 25n19
Williams, Raymond, 12–13, 24n1;
canon formation and, 19, 20–21;
Marxism and Literature, 28n59,
29n64; residual and emergent
cultural processes and, 19
Woman Hollering Creek: research for,
230; voice in, 192, 193–94, 204;
women and, 222 (*see also* Cisneros,
Sandra)
Women: indigenous, 245; Mexic-
Amerindian, 147–48; Mexican
American (*see* Mexican American
women); oppression of, 147–48,
245–46, 264, 265